LIFE WITHOUT FATHER

WILLIAM WARTMAN

LIFE WITHOUT FATHER

INFLUENCES OF AN UNKNOWN MAN

Franklin Watts   1988
New York   Toronto

Library of Congress Cataloging-in-Publication Data

Wartman, William.
   Life without father: influences of an unknown
man/William Wartman.
      p.   cm.
   ISBN 0-531-15074-7
   1. Wartman William.   2. Children of single parents—United States—Biography.   3. Journalists—
United States—Biography.   4. Paternal depriva-
tion—Case studies.   I. Title.
HQ777.4.W36 1988   87-31597
306.8'74—dc19   CIP

For the memory of my father, William,
the man who couldn't stay;

For my mother, Helen, the woman
who got us through;

And for my son, Joseph, the child
who taught me love.

Author's note: I have changed the names
and minor identifying details of all persons
quoted in this book, except for the members of
my immediate family, to protect their privacy.

I would like to thank the many people who gave so generously of their time, support and encouragement while this book was being written. Some of the most vital assistance was provided by people who cannot be named, my interview subjects. They were unfailingly gracious and cooperative under my probing questioning, and the insights I gained from our often tender discussions affected my life as well as my work.

My sisters, Helen Marie Durso and Anne Mandell, bravely shared the silence of our father's death with me for many years and, when I unilaterally decided to end it, they never allowed their love or kindness to falter.

Kenneth Certa and Estelle Promislo helped me to understand myself and my material. Margaret Robinson, Ullik Rouk and Peggy Anderson were friends and manuscript critics at vital times. Gary Hayden always listened and Bill Lutz always helped keep me going. Michael Schwager was the most wonderful of friends, the one I could perpetually depend on for more than anyone had a right to ask. David Bradley taught me what I needed to know about sentences in spite of myself, and Joan Mellen provided the enthusiasm, advice, concern and warmth of a dozen people.

Thanks also to my friends and editors, Ed Breslin, who had the wisdom to tell me to just keep writing, and Kent Oswald who shepherded me into print with concern and talent.

LIFE WITHOUT FATHER

PROLOGUE

I knew my mother was lying to me about my father. Every time I asked where my father was, my mother would say in a gentle voice that he had gotten sick and died when I was a baby. I knew that wasn't true.

I lived in a house full of women—my mother, sisters, grandmother and an aunt—and the women couldn't tell me what to do when the neighborhood roughnecks with torn pants and scabs on their arms pushed me to the ground and took my toys. Those kids scared me. So did the man next door who hollered when I walked on his grass, and the black dog that chased me every time I got on my bike. Being scared scared me. I knew that my father, a man I loved but couldn't remember, wouldn't die and leave me frightened like that forever.

My father knew how much I needed him, and he wanted to help me, but he had been put in jail and he couldn't escape. My father had been accused of a serious crime—murder or armed robbery—and he had been convicted and sent to prison.

My father didn't do it—he was framed. He was in the wrong place at the wrong time and the real criminal pushed the gun into his hand just as the police arrived. My father tried to tell the cops the truth, but they told him to shut up and shoved him into their car. The real criminal ran around the corner of the building and collapsed in laughter.

All the way to the police station, and all during his trial, my father kept saying, "I didn't do it. I'm a father. I know that men who commit crimes are sent away. I wouldn't risk having to leave my son. He would be terribly afraid the whole time. I wouldn't take a chance of leaving him frightened like that."

The judge told my father to shut up, just as the police had, and then he said my father was going to jail. My father screamed at the judge, so the police beat him with their sticks and pushed him off to his cell. Then they unlocked the door and threw my father in. The cops said they would come back and kill him if he made a sound.

My father's cell was a tiny room with unpainted cinder block walls on three sides and a row of bars across the front. Every time the guards walked by they would curse at my father and dare him to make noise. My father would ignore them. He spent all of his time sitting, turned on his bed, staring at the back wall. His long body would be hunched forward at the waist, with his elbows digging into his thighs and his hands folded between his knees.

I could picture my father sitting there, looking at the blank wall and thinking. He was thinking about me. He knew I needed for him to be with me. He knew I was afraid and he wanted to come and tell me it was all right, that all kids were scared sometimes and that it would go away. He wanted to come and help me, but they had him locked in. That made him so angry he wanted to shout, "I have to go to my son. Let me out." But he knew that wouldn't do any good, so he just dropped his head and ran his fingers through his hair.

My mother thought my father was guilty. When I asked her about my father she would say he was dead and nothing more. She would have talked about my father more, and she would have put pictures of him around the house instead of keeping them in a box in the top of her closet, if she thought he was innocent. She was angry at my father for getting sent to jail and leaving her with three small children to feed. She was mad because we had to move in with her parents and she had to get a job.

I was angry at my mother for thinking my father was guilty, but I was even angrier because she lied and said that he was dead. My mother thought she was smarter than me, but she was wrong. I had figured out that my father was in jail, and I also knew why my mother was lying. She thought I would be upset if I knew about my father. She thought other kids would make fun of me and call my father a jailbird if they knew the truth. My mother thought she was protecting me. She thought it would be easier if I believed my father was dead. She was wrong. Nothing, nothing in the whole world, could be worse than for my father to be dead and never coming home to me. Dying and leaving a young son to fend for himself was the worst thing a man could do. My father wouldn't do that to me.

My mother must have had a meeting with my aunts and uncles and grandparents on the day my father was sent to prison. She told them she didn't want her children to know their father was a criminal, and she had decided to lie and say he was dead. She said she would tell us the truth when our father was released from prison and came home—if they would agree to support her lie. If anyone told us the truth before she decided it was time, my mother said, she would take us away and our father would never see us again.

I didn't like my mother's plan. I wanted her to tell me about my father right away so he could write and make me feel safe. I wanted a letter from him that said what day, exactly, he was coming home. I wanted to tell my mother I wouldn't be upset if she told me my father was in prison because I already knew—and I could take it. "Tell me mother," I wanted to say, "tell me that my father is in jail but he will come home some day. I won't cry. Look, I haven't cried yet and I've known all along. I won't even tell my friends. Just let me know and then it will be okay."

But my mother didn't tell me and I had no choice but to be like my father and remain silent and wait. I couldn't even tell my sisters our father was alive. If I told them, they would run to our mother and tell her what I said, even if I made them swear they wouldn't, and then everything would collapse into a heap.

If I admit to the children I lied, my mother would think, they would never trust me again. They will spend every day waiting for their father to come home. It would mark them for life. No, that's it. They will always be told that their father is dead. He can never come back here again.

Then I would never get to know my father. I would never grow from his shadow to his shoulder, watching him shrink from a god into a man. I would never sense that his gestures were my gestures, my hands his hands. My mother would tell my father it would be best for the children if he didn't try to contact us. Maybe my mother would lie again and tell my father we had been told of his existence and decided he shouldn't return. "Dad! It's not true. I'm scared. I miss you. Please come home. Soon."

Regardless of the reason my mother gave him, my father would repress his loneliness and disappear. I could see that in his long thin face that looked out at me from the box of photographs my mother kept. My father was a tall, boney, yet sleek man with his hair parted in the center and slicked back in an old-fashioned style. His clothes were baggy and he was slim, but he didn't shrink from the camera. He stood there like a man who did what had to be done.

My only recourse was to do what my father would have done and wait for the time to be right. If I kept my mouth shut the day would come when my mother would announce that my father wasn't really dead—that he was coming home. At that moment I would want to jump with glee and shout: "Hooray! Hooray! My father is alive. He's coming home." But I couldn't even do that.

If I didn't act stunned and confused by my mother's words, she might figure out that I had known all along, and then something would surely go wrong. She would change her mind and say she was just kidding, or that the man who was about to enter our lives was a new father and not our real father, and that wouldn't be the same. I didn't want to have to pretend he wasn't our real father when I knew he was. I wanted to be able to take his hand and walk around to the neighbors' houses and ring their bells and say, "Hey, this is my father. He just got home. Isn't that great?"

I couldn't let something stupid, like acting happy at my mother's announcement when I was supposed to be confused, ruin it for my father's homecoming. I had to be very careful of what I did and said, so I made up some rules to help bring my father home. Rule number one was never let adults know what you know. Rule number two was never let adults know how you feel. Rule number three was a special one that was mostly to help me out. It was never let adults know they can hurt you.

While I was waiting for my father to come home, I watched other kids' fathers and tried to guess what my life was going to be like one day. I didn't see boys doing things with their fathers regularly until I started Catholic school and there was one boy in my class whose parents were divorced. The boy's father lived hundreds of miles away and, when he came to visit his son, he would bring the boy's lunch to school and then play with him in the schoolyard.

The boy's father would be steady pitcher when we played baseball or kickball, but he didn't act like a boss or tell us what to do. If we wanted to play on the blacktop instead of the grass, he didn't tell us we had to play on the grass because we might tear our clothes if we fell on the pavement. The father was like a big kid who played for both teams.

The boy played really hard when his father was there, and he always wanted to win. If he was thrown out in kickball, he would stop the game to argue that the ball hadn't hit him. His father would tell him he was out and to give somebody else a chance, but the boy would keep arguing. When that happened, the father would say he needed a rest and tell someone else to pitch. Then the father would put his arm around his son's shoulder and walk him away from the game.

I would stop playing the game then, too, and watch as the boy and his father headed over to sit down on the grass. The boy would still be saying the ball hadn't hit him, but his father would talk to him quietly for a while, and soon they would be laughing and kidding around. After a couple of minutes, they would come back and join the game. I didn't know what the father had said, but, whatever it was, I wanted my father to say it to me.

Another boy's father took me to buy a baseball glove once. I walked around the store and pounded my fist into the pockets of gloves until I found a mitt I liked. I showed it to the boy's father and said I wanted to buy it. The man took the glove, turned it over to look at the printing on the back, and gave it back to me.

"You can buy that if you want," he said, "but it's Japanese. I fought a war with those people, and I'll be damned if I'd buy any of their products."

I was stunned. I hadn't meant to do anything wrong, so I quickly asked the man which glove I should buy, but he had already walked off to find a new bat for his son.

As I sat in the back of other people's cars and watched boys and their fathers talk and smile in the front seat, I knew that I'd be able to relax and stop being scared when my father came home. It would be okay to have to go to the bathroom ten minutes after we got in the car, and it wouldn't matter if I got lost in a store, because my father would hunt until he found me. Oh, he might get mad for a minute, but I wouldn't have to worry about never being asked along again because I was a nuisance.

When my father came home I would have someone I would always be important to, no matter what. When my father came home I would make him laugh as I made the kids in school laugh. I couldn't make adults laugh now because if they saw I was smart enough to make adults laugh they might figure out I was smart enough to know when adults were lying. But soon my father would be home and I could forget about the lie and about having to fool the adults. When my father came home he would be laughing all the time because I could make the kids in school laugh without even trying, and a father was someone who would laugh at every joke his son cracked.

I was making the kids in third grade laugh one morning when the nun told us to pass our report cards, which we had taken home to have signed the day before, up to her. An alarm went off in my head. I had forgotten to get my mother to sign my report, and I knew the punishment was going to be severe. I had already been hit hard on the hands and arms and back with the pointers and yardsticks and had my hair pulled for little things like talking in class. The punishment for screwing up big, like not getting a report card signed, had to be very harsh.

I didn't have much time to worry because the nun was already standing at the front of the first row of desks, taking the report cards that the kids had passed forward. I knew what I had to do. I had fooled adults before, and there wasn't any reason I couldn't fool this woman. I would forge my mother's signature. But there was a problem. I knew "Mr." and "Mrs." were the words that went before parents' names, but I forgot which was for mothers and which was for fathers.

I quickly looked over at the desk of the boy next to me and saw that his report card was signed "Mrs. Paul Graham." Signing report cards was something that fathers did and Paul, like everyone else in school, had a father, so "Mrs." was the way fathers signed their names. I smiled to myself, quickly wrote "Mr. Helen Wartman" on the report card, and gave it to the girl in front of me.

I became frightened when the nun returned to her desk and began checking the signatures. I put my head on my desk and closed my eyes. I heard my name and looked up to see the nun's eyes glaring at me from deep within the white headpiece that encased her face. She called me to her desk with her finger.

My hands were shaking as I got out of my seat. Being called to the front of the room meant my punishment was going to be public, and therefore especially vicious. I was ready to cry in anticipation, but I fought back the tears with everything I had as I walked up the aisle. I was determined this woman was not going to make me cry in front of the other kids, so matter how hard she hit me.

I was going to treat the nun just as I did the other adults—by the rules. She wasn't going to know I was scared, and she wasn't going to know she could hurt me.

"William," the nun asked when I reached her over-sized desk, "who signed your report card?"

I glanced at the thick yardstick sitting on her desk, just inches from her right hand. I was going to take this like a man: no excuses and no pleas for mercy. "I did, Sister."

The nun looked at me curiously for a moment, and then, when I thought she was going to smash the yard-stick into my arm, her face went soft. "Your father is dead, William, isn't he?"

"Yes," I said automatically.

"Very well," she said. "Go back to your seat."

"Excuse me, Sister?" I asked in disbelief.

"Sit down, William," she said.

I could feel the stare of every kid in the class as I turned to hurry to the safety of my desk. The shock of my escape passed quickly, and I realized I had done it again. I didn't understand how it happened, but I had put another one over on the adults, and I wanted the whole class to know, so I made goofy, happy faces that the nun couldn't see.

I smiled at kids from my desk until they stopped looking over, then I tried to figure out why the nun had let me off. I had avoided punishment for an act that was practically a mortal sin, and it could be useful to me to know how I had managed that.

First my whole body started to tingle, then I was breathing real hard and my eyes and nose started to run. I felt sad and afraid and angry all at the same time. My father *was* dead—that had to be it. There was no other reason that would have prevented that nun from hitting me again and again for forging my mother's signature.

My father really was dead and the nun knew it was the worst thing that could happen to a child. Having your father die had to be even worse than I allowed myself to imagine for the nun to have felt bad enough for me to excuse my forgery. And if having your father die was that bad, then my mother, who went off to work all day to buy us food and clothes, and then came home to sleep in the same room with her three children, would never have lied to me about my father being dead.

Oh, no . . . oh, no . . . oh, no, I kept repeating to myself. I was breathing really fast and tears were pouring down my face and I had to run but I didn't know where to run to. Kids were staring at me and the nun kept looking down and I knew I had to get under control fast or somebody would ask me what was wrong and then I would have to tell them and if I talked about it then I might find out how really awful it was that my father was dead and he was never coming home again and I would never get to see him and then I would always be afraid.

No, no, no, I said to myself and I knew I had to stop. I rubbed my eyes with my fists as hard as I could and held my breath so I couldn't breathe so fast and pushed my toes against the floor and wiggled my legs back and forth really fast and then bit my lip and forced myself to stop.

The nun was telling us to get out our arithmetic books and I knew I had to work on the problems with more concentration than I had ever used before. And I knew I needed another rule and that rule was that I was never going to think about my father ever again because he was dead anyway so what difference did it make because I never knew him and it's stupid to miss somebody that you never ever knew.

When I got home from school that day I went into the bedroom where my mother kept her box of photographs and closed the door. I pulled a chair into the closet and climbed up to get the box, and then slumped down onto the floor to look through the pictures for the last time. I knew I wasn't going to cry—I had promised myself I wasn't going to cry or think about my father anymore—but I wanted to have one final look.

I carefully examined the pictures for clues that showed my father was about to die, but there was no fear in his eyes or horror on his lips. Only two things jumped out at me. The first was that my father always wore coats and ties and he looked like he belonged in them. I decided it must be important for a man to dress nicely. The other thing was that my father seldom smiled in those photographs; I knew that had to mean something too.

Those pictures were all I had of my father and I wanted something of him for my own, so I took his posture before the camera. From that day on, regardless of how much my family begged, pleaded or cajoled, I would not turn up the ends of my lips in front of a camera. I was told constantly that I looked like my father, and if my father did not smile for photographs, I would not smile for photographs. I seldom smiled for a photographer before I was an adult.

CHAPTER
1

On any given Sunday afternoon, my son and I might take a long walk, visit a playground or go to a library and sit reading, side by side. But each Sunday evening at seven o'clock, Joey and I watched my favorite television program, "Sixty Minutes." We stretched out on the floor in front of the set, with Joey half watching TV and half doing something else. When he was young, Joey would push toy trucks up my side and through my hair; as he got older he did school work or read.

I might be distracted from the show by the newspaper or by a game I was playing with my son. Yet no matter how little I regarded the television, one aspect of the program always fixed my attention: the loudly ticking stopwatch that filled the screen at the beginning and end of commercial breaks. The program's producer intended the snapping of the clock as cachet. To me it was a belligerent reminder my weekly visit with my son was ending. Soon I would have to pack Joey's books and toys and drive him to my ex-wife's house in New Jersey, twenty-five miles away.

Joey and I were cut from the same cloth; we were quiet and self-contained. We enjoyed our time together without needing constant conversation, except during those Sunday evening rides to New Jersey. As soon as we were in the car and headed through Philadelphia to the Delaware River, we both remembered questions we wanted to ask of the other or stories we had to tell. When Joey was small and sat on pillows to see out the car windows, he might tell me about a playmate; I might ask about nursery school. But now that he was ten, I would be answering one of the series of questions about the workings of the world he saved for these rides. As my son grew and his sun-bleached blond hair darkened a little earlier each fall, he wanted to know what the gears on a ten-speed bike did and why certain bookstores we passed were called "adult." The nature of our Sunday evening chats changed over the years, but one thing remained constant. The intensity of our conversations always increased in direct proportion to the proximity of his house.

The difficulty was that the talk, regardless of how rapidly it flowed, did nothing to ease the moment when we arrived at Joey's house and he went in and I didn't. I would walk my son to the door, pick him up, remark on how big he was getting, hug him with an exaggerated grunt and then hurry to the car without looking back. I didn't know what the expression was on my son's face as I walked away. I didn't want to know.

I had gotten married too young, and I left the marriage as soon as I realized it wasn't going to work. I had

moved quickly because I was haunted by a single fear—
that of having my son get used to living with me. I knew
I wouldn't have the courage to tell Joey I was leaving once
he was old enough to understand what that meant. I
thought I could avoid a paralyzing goodbye scene by leaving while he was still very young. I hoped a fast divorce
would be the least painful exit. What I hadn't understood
then was that, after the divorce, I was going to have to
say goodbye to my son every week.

I was especially dreading the Sunday night goodbye
that was to come in mid-July of 1978. I had to tell Joey I
was going to Europe for a month, and I was afraid he
was going to beg that I take him with me. That was out
of the question. I was a penniless freelance writer and I
couldn't afford to go myself, let alone pay for him. The
trip was senseless. It was going to put me in debt at a time
when my income was sporadic, but I had become obsessed with going.

I was about to turn thirty, and somehow, for some
unexplainable reason, my ambition and drive had evapo-
rated. I was told that a part-time job I held was going to
be eliminated, but I didn't look for a replacement. Instead, I studied European travel guides. I told my friends
I was going abroad until my money was exhausted. Rather
than worrying about burning my bridges behind me and
returning home broke and unemployed at thirty, I set
fires like a pyromaniac and became abusive with people
who could help me in the future.

I spent four months planning the trip and almost
that long considering what I was going to tell Joey. I
couldn't say that I didn't understand why I was making
the journey, or that I had managed to scrape together the
money for myself but not for him. I decided the solution
was to lie to my son. But each time I thought about doing
that, the idea numbed me more.

I worried my son would recognize my lie moments
after my plane left the runway. First he would be out-

raged, and then he would puzzle over why I hadn't told him the truth. He would conclude that I had gone to Europe not for a month but forever, and he would never get to see me again. He wouldn't believe the postcards I sent saying I would be home soon, and he would get really scared about what was going to happen.

When Joey and I got into the car that July evening, I chastised myself for not talking about the trip earlier in the day, and as we left Pennsylvania on the Walt Whitman bridge, I told myself not to wait until we were parked in front of his house. But I knew that I would—and I did. I pulled over to the curb, shut off the engine and reached over to stroke the hair of the boy who so resembled me that it made the joy more joyful and the pain more painful.

"Joey," I said uneasily, "I'm going on a trip this week and I won't be able to see you for a month."

"Where are you going, Dad?" he asked with surprise and youthful curiosity.

"I'm going to Europe, but I'll only be gone a month."

"Why are you going there?" he asked, his voice darkening.

I avoided his eyes and made a sweeping gesture with my arm. "I have business to take care of, Joey. But I won't be gone that long. Does a month seem like a long time to you?"

"I don't know," he said. "Why do you have to go there now?"

"I told you, Joey," I said insistently, "it's business. But you didn't answer my question. Does a month seem like a long time to you?"

"I don't know," he repeated flatly. Joey turned his head away from me and stared directly forward at the dashboard. The last light of the summer evening was angling into the car, and I could see his jaw drop in dejection.

The stillness of Joey's body and the firm set of his

chin told me the conversation was over. I had touched a nerve—which one I didn't know and that multiplied my anxiety—and he had pulled his shield into place. He wasn't going to give me any indication how he felt or what I could do to soothe it. He was going to leave me hanging, feeling guilty and worried. He cut me off like that whenever something troubled him, and it made me furious.

I had to find out what he was thinking before I got on that plane. I had to know if he had already figured out the lie, and if he was already wondering if he was ever going to see me again. I reached over and touched his arm.

"Joey," I asked patiently, "do you know how far it is to England?"

"No," he said quietly.

"Well, do you know how long it takes to fly there?"

"No."

"Do you know what the weather is like in France?"

"No."

I squeezed the steering wheel with both hands. It was no use. Once that shell was in place, there was no penetrating it. Every time my son did this to me, it made me hate myself for all the times I had done the same thing to other people.

"Okay," I said and reached over to rub Joey's head again, "I better get going."

We got out of the car and I pulled my son against me and walked him the short distance to the front door. We stepped inside and I hugged and kissed him and told him I would be back before he knew it. But Joey would only look at the floor and say "Yeah."

I moaned and pushed open the screen door, remorse and anger tearing at me as I walked back to my car. As the motor caught and I slid the transmission into gear, my ex-wife came running out of the house. "Bill," she said. "what did you tell Joey about your trip? He's up in his room crying."

I shut off the car and ran into the house, taking the stairs to the second floor two at a time. Joey was standing close to his desk. His arms hung limp from his slender shoulders and he was turned away from the door. I knelt down next to my son, expecting his face to be wet with tears. But Joey had heard me coming and had wiped every trace of moisture from his cheeks. I leaned against the edge of his bed and looked into his green eyes with their flecks of gold and white. They were eyes that so exactly duplicated mine that, whenever I looked at them closely, I had a reflex that made me want to check that my own eyes were still in my head. Now Joey's eyes were lined with red.

"Joey," I said, terrified my son was going to accuse me of abandoning him, "what's wrong?"

"I don't know." He shrugged and turned from me.

"Listen," I said and grabbed his arms, "you have to tell me what's going on. What are you afraid of?"

"Afraid of?" my son asked incredulously. "I'm not afraid of anything, Dad. I'm just going to miss you."

A flood of tears rushed down my face. They came so quickly my son and I became aware of them at the same instant. I let them flow. The grimness disappeared from Joey's face as his mouth and eyes grew wide in amazement. His father was crying and he didn't understand why.

"I'm going to miss you too," I said and pulled my son to me for a hug I needed more than he did.

I spent a half hour with my son, showing him on his globe where I was going, marking the expected date of my return on his calendar and reassuring him a hundred times that I would be back before he knew it.

I turned thirty on an overcast and unseasonably cold July day in Paris. I told people I had met during the first ten days of the trip that this birthday wouldn't register on the meter, that I would remain twenty-nine for another year, if I was in Paris on July twenty-third. I had almost managed to convince myself of it. I had heard once that if a man was sent into space at the speed of light, he would remain the same age he was when the rocket was launched. I was hoping that somehow my subsonic flight across the Atlantic would have the same effect.

I had avoided discussion of the date with the two friends from home I was traveling with. It was more a day of mourning than celebration to me, and my mood was as gray as the weather. I wanted to escape despair, so I suggested we spend more than the four or five dollars that was our customary dinner allocation and go to a decent restaurant.

I selected a place on the Right Bank that was described in a travel guide as turn-of-the-century elegant, with tuxedo-clad waiters but reasonable prices. The restaurant was dense with smoke and noise when we arrived. The drawers along the walls where the regulars had once stored their napkins between visits were still there, but now the tables were pushed together to form dozens of long rows and were covered with paper tablecloths. There were few empty seats to be found.

I attempted to order the plat du jour from the waiter in my halting French as he swept down on us between frantic trips to the kitchen. He frowned at me and disappeared. He returned twenty minutes later with a dish of cold food that didn't remotely resemble what I had ordered, and then hurried away as I raised my voice in protest.

My friends urged me to calm down and forget it, and I did until the waiter returned to collect the bill. He quickly scrawled a column of numbers on the tablecloth, added, tacked on fifteen percent for service and stuck out his hand. The menu outside the restaurant had said the service charge was included in the price of the food.

I clenched my fist and shook it at the waiter. *"Service compris,"* I shouted, but he only lowered his brow in Gallic confusion and extended his palm impatiently.

"Service compris," I hollered again and slammed my hand on the table.

People at nearby tables stopped talking and peered over, stretching their necks, but the waiter obstinately waited for his money. "Come on," my friends said, "let's pay the bill and get out of here. It's not enough money to worry about."

I grudgingly threw my francs on the table and started from my chair, when the waiter grabbed for the money and bumped me on the head with his tray.

The waiter jerked back in horror when he felt the contact, and then he tried to touch my forehead gingerly by way of apology. I shoved his hand away and jumped up. I cocked my arm and went after him as he held his tray in front of his face and backed away.

"Come on your dirty bastard," I shouted. People edged their chairs out of the way. I was ready to smash my fist into his face when my friends grabbed me and forced me out into the street.

I ranted about the incident for hours as we went from bistro to café and drank beer after beer. We prowled from one *arrondissement* to another until the alcohol cloaked my rage and I felt the tension slip from my shoulders.

It was midnight when I discovered we were in a dank basement-level disco filled with people in stylish party clothes talking in a language I couldn't speak very well. I was standing by myself, leaning against a pillar in dirty jeans. I knew it would be closing time before we left and, by then, the Metro would be closed too. We would have to walk miles while dead drunk to get to our seven-dollar-a-night hotel, a place so shabby I forced myself not to imagine what breed of creatures emerged from the walls when we switched off the lights at night. And tomorrow I would have a massive hangover.

I surveyed the roomful of strangers grimly. The clock couldn't have caught up with me in a more cheerless hole. I raised my beer in a toast to myself. "Happy Birthday, Wartman," I said.

I arrived home in Philadelphia with twenty dollars in my pocket, not much more than that in the bank, and only enough writing assignments lined up to provide me with a subsistence existence. The rented house I shared with four other people was empty, four weeks of mail was piled up on the floor behind the slot in the front door and the house was musty and reeked of silence. My son would be waiting for me to call. I had to get to the typewriter, and I needed housemates to replace those who had vacated the premises. The first thing I did was go to bed for three days.

When I crawled out of bed on the fourth day, I started to write and then decided to paint my bedroom. I thought changing the color would improve my outlook. I visited half a dozen stores and studied paint chips until I found precisely the hue and intensity of brown I wanted for two of the walls. I carefully cut the dark paint in around the adjoining white walls and ceiling, and then spent half a day admiring the results.

I sold little over the winter and I frequently couldn't pay my bills or, for the first time, my child support. Collection agencies called with threats and I learned to laugh at them and hang up. My diet ran heavily toward soups and cereals, with alcohol thrown in for reassurance when I could afford it. My life was getting covered over with dust and cobwebs, and I didn't care.

People were telling me I had to do something, that I couldn't go on like that, and I figured they must be right, so when a friend offered me work helping to complete the renovation of a house, I said yes. It was mindless work, repairing cracked walls and painting, but I had had so little to occupy my mind for the past six months I found it fascinating.

I had been on the job a week when I leaned over to fill a bucket with patching compound and stood up to find myself lost in time. I knew where I was and what I was doing, but was confused by a subtle sense of being disconnected from the world outside of the room I was in. It was more curious than frightening, and I shook my head to clear it and went back to work.

The same sensation slipped over me twice the next day and more frequently on subsequent days. My consciousness would seem to levitate within my skull, and I would try to look inside myself to get a bearing on what was happening. The friend I was working with would see my motionlessness and ask if anything was wrong, and I would answer no because it seemed too bizarre to discuss.

When the renovations were completed a month later, I resolved to make one more sustained push at securing writing assignments and, if that failed, to forget about writing for a while and get a job. In three weeks I had a magazine assignment and a contract for some technical writing that would keep me busy and pay my bills.

I decided to celebrate with lunch at The Eatery, a quasi-health-food cafeteria on the campus of the University of Pennsylvania, not far from my house in West Philadelphia. Much of the food there was awful—mysterious Middle-Eastern vegetarian dishes or coarsely chopped steamed vegetables with sticky brown rice and pinkish undercooked chicken—but they made delicious whole wheat pizza.

I bought two squares of pizza and a container of iced tea and settled in at one of the card tables that lined an adjacent walkway. The surrounding trees and tall buildings isolated the area from the noise of the city streets, and the idiosyncratic members of the university community created a colorful scene as they strolled by. Summer, my favorite time of year, was only weeks away. I would have some money coming in—I felt happy and optimistic.

I was almost through my meal when, with a mouthful of food and my iced tea in my hand, a familiar but unusually intense sensation struck. My mind leapt away from the present, sounds became exaggerated, my ears rang, my mouth went dry, my breathing became labored and sweat began to trickle down my chest and back.

My only reaction was panic, my only thought was to run as quickly as I could. I fought the impulse to flee. I had beaten weaker spells before, I could wait this one out.

I gulped the iced tea, swallowed the food in my mouth, gripped the edge of the table and sat very still, not wanting to inflame the demons twisting my brain. All around me people were talking and eating and laughing, but they seemed actors in someone else's life.

I had no control over what was happening to me. It was trancelike and terrifying, and it wasn't going away. I wanted to push the table out of the way and scream, "Help me! Someone please help me. Something is terribly wrong," but I didn't. Instead I designed a plan for getting home without anyone detecting that I was in trouble. I fought to appear calm, while every nerve ending in my body was sending out distress signals to my distant brain.

I released my grip from the table, slid back and tried to think the fear out of my mind. What actions did I have to complete to make it appear that everything was okay? My tray and dishes. I had to take them to the collection table. I walked over slowly, taking long deep breaths, and then eased off to find my car—all the while wanting to scream and run, all the while trembling to wonder what might happen next.

I located the car and unlocked it. I had parked in the sun, and baked air poured out as I opened the door. I drove as quickly as I could with one hand on the wheel and rolled down the windows with the other hand. I parked half on the curb in front of the house and hurried in to collapse on the bed. The spell was unrelenting and unchanged.

I closed my eyes and tried to relax, but I couldn't lie still. Oppressive and heavy sunlight poured onto the bed from the nearby windows. I yanked the drapes closed and dove back on the bed.

I paced the room, played soft music on the radio, took my clothes off, drank scotch, tried to distract my thoughts by reading—nothing worked. I resigned myself to the spell and sat up in bed to rest my back against the cool plaster wall and wait for it to be over. Several hours later, my mind stopped being a stranger in my body.

Lying quietly on the bed in aftershock, numb and exhausted from the power of the attack, I wondered if I was going crazy. I dismissed that out of hand. I was too strong and self-reliant a person to be having mental problems. One of the positive things about having my father die when I was a child was that I had learned how to take care of myself. I got my first job when I was twelve. Whenever something I owned broke, I taught myself how to fix it. I was iron willed, tough and determined. People like me didn't go crazy.

If I wasn't having emotional problems, then it had to be physical. But I never got sick. The gravest illness I had ever suffered was a broken wrist. Yet people did develop diseases without warning. What kind of illness could I have? With the symptoms being so psychological there had to be something wrong with my brain . . . my brain . . . my brain.

A string of thoughts played themselves out in my mind: My father had died of a brain tumor when he was thirty-one years old. My thirty-first birthday was two months away. I was about to die of a brain tumor.

A growth the size of a thumbnail had taken root in the stem of my brain and, at that very moment, the tumor was expanding and producing these symptoms. In six months, in exactly six months, for my father had died in November, that growth will have swollen to the size of an orange and I will be dead.

I was destined to die at the same age and of the same disease as my father. Like him, I would leave a son behind. But my son was almost eleven. He knew me. We went to the movies, talked on the telephone, gave each other birthday presents. I never knew my father. It hadn't been so bad for me. It would be unspeakable for my son. He had learned to depend on me, while I had learned not to depend on anyone. How would I tell my son I was dying? How would I say goodbye? Would my son die young? And what of his son? . . . At some point during the evening I drifted into a fitful sleep.

I awoke the next morning knowing where I was, but feeling as if my brain were packed in ice. The room was thinly illuminated by light that pushed in around the edges of the drapes, the top sheet from the bed was in a heap on the floor and the pillows were alongside it. I looked at the clock and judged I had been asleep for twelve hours, but I was as fatigued as if I hadn't slept at all. I climbed out of bed and peered into the mirror on the dresser. My eyes were sunken well back into my head and there were massive dark circles under them. My hair was matted to my head in clumps and my complexion was pale.

I went downstairs to make coffee and find something to eat. I was relieved that my graduate student housemates had dispersed for summer jobs around the country. I didn't want to see anyone. I eased into a chair and tried to formulate a plan for dealing with my illness and impending death. The first thing I should do is get a confirmation of my diagnosis. If I was going to die anyway, it didn't make much sense to spend money, which was still in short supply, going to see a doctor. But I didn't have the energy to go to a medical library and do the research myself.

I called my friend Joyce, a psychologist who was

married to a psychiatrist. I hadn't seen her in some time, but I knew she would help. Between her and her husband's medical knowledge, they had to know the symptoms of and prognosis for a brain tumor.

A brain tumor had killed my father, but I knew little about the disease or my father's illness. I knew that doctors had found my father's tumor shortly after I was born, that there had been operations and radiation treatments, but that my father had died two years later nonetheless. I could vaguely remember being upset about my father's death when I was very young, but it was so long ago that I had only a faint memory of it. I could recall it only as a faded artifact of my childhood. I had thought my father's death was a fact of my life. I never dreamed it would become a heritage.

I described my symptoms to Joyce and asked if she knew if a brain tumor could be inherited. Joyce said she didn't have any answers for me, but she would check and call me back. I passed the time watching television, reading and trying not to worry, but that became impossible when, twice during the afternoon, I had mild attacks of the same nature as the day before.

I pounced on the phone when it rang several hours later. Joyce said that my symptoms didn't match the classic signs of a brain tumor, that tumors usually produced a loss of control of the central nervous system and pronounced physical reactions, but that she wasn't certain of anything and, since there was definitely something wrong with me, I needed to see a doctor.

I discredited everything Joyce said as soon as she confessed she wasn't certain. I knew I had a brain tumor, just as women are said to know when they have conceived, but I took her advice and called a doctor she recommended, an internist. I told the receptionist I was extremely sick, and she gave me an appointment for the following day.

I was two blocks from my house the next morning

when it hit me again forcefully. Streets that I had driven dozens of times became four-lane islands, completely detached from the rest of the city and the world. My shirt turned dark with sweat, my mouth went dry as paper and my stomach knotted and contracted as its contents liquefied. I dared not stop to find a restroom—I knew I would become hopelessly lost if I got out of the car—so I drove on in panic.

I stumbled into the waiting room and sat on a low white vinyl couch to await my death sentence from the doctor. It seemed an unlikely place to receive such a prognosis. The doctor specialized in preventive medicine and his office was a testament to all that was vogue in nontraditional medicine. A sign announced the air I was breathing was ionized, and the reading material ran toward magazines on nutrition and diet.

The doctor, a tall, gentle-looking man in his midforties with prematurely gray hair, came into the waiting room and asked for his next patient. He led me into a prissily clean and orderly office, where he sat behind an antique desk, took my medical history and asked who had referred me. I said that my friend Joyce, the psychologist, had recommended him to me and then gave a long and anxiety-filled description of the spells. I told him I was quite concerned about what had been happening to me, but I didn't mention the tumor. I wanted to test the doctor's diagnostic skills to be sure I could trust him.

The doctor placed his pen on his desk blotter, joined his hands and told me with great conviction that he could alleviate my problems quickly with his special brand of medicine. The doctor said he did not use pharmaceuticals in his practice, but healthy doses of vitamins that would cure me in a more natural fashion. I wondered if vitamins could eradicate a tumor.

The doctor led me into his examining room where he took my pulse, poked and probed me, drew blood for tests and then told me to make an appointment for a week

hence when the results would be back from the lab. The
doctor also instructed me to give the receptionist a urine
sample and a snippet of my hair.

I had been desperate for someone to turn my illness
over to when I had arrived at the doctor's office a half
hour earlier. I had had trouble depending on people or
asking for help since I was a child, but now, facing certain
death, I was ready to trust someone. But the doctor's
quirkiness was destroying my resolve. I asked why he
wanted my hair.

He said that he would send my hair off to have it
analyzed for trace minerals and would use the results to
prescribe vitamins and minerals to enact my recovery. I
told him what I really wanted to do was find out what
was wrong with me, that I was poor and that, all things
considered, I thought I would pass on the hair analysis.
The doctor glowered at me.

I returned a week later and told the doctor my
symptoms were occurring more frequently, but the spells
weren't as severe. The doctor mumbled "Humm" and
pulled a long computer printout from my file.

"Your liver is fine, your kidneys are fine," he said,
beginning in a well-rehearsed manner that told me I was
getting the good news first. Soon he was going to tell me
something wasn't fine. He was going to pause for a beat
and say you seem to have a growth in the stem of your
brain, and we—he wouldn't say I, because he would want
to start detatching himself from me—believe it is malignant.

"Your blood sugar is low," he said easily, looking up
from the report for the first time, "and that probably
means that you have hypoglycemia."

The doctor went on to explain that my pancreas was
slow in releasing insulin when I ate sugar, and when it
finally did release insulin, it released too much, causing
my blood sugar to plummet. He told me I could prevent

this cycling by avoiding sugar and by eating frequent small meals.

I was ready to believe the doctor's diagnosis and its implications that I wasn't dying of a brain tumor, but the faddishness that permeated his office caused me to reserve judgment. I went home and followed the doctor's diet with the zeal of someone who has been snatched from the door of death and waited to see what would happen. The symptoms continued unabated for the next two weeks, and the panic of a lost child arose in me.

I returned to the doctor's office and told him with an uneven voice that his plan wasn't working, that the recovery he had promised had not occurred and that he had to do something fast. The intensity of my presentation caused the doctor to frown in concern as he dug in my file for an explanation. He found it on my case history, just where I expected he would—where it said that my father had died of a brain tumor.

He held the history form in his hand, leaned back in his chair, thought for a moment and then said, "Maybe you ought to speak to Joyce about this."

"Joyce?" I asked with outrage. "What does she have to do with this?"

"She is your therapist, isn't she?" he asked. "She's the one who referred you to me."

"No," I said with indignation, "she *isn't*. Joyce is my friend. I'm not in therapy with her."

"Oh," he said. "Maybe you ought to ask her to refer you to a therapist. There isn't anything wrong with you physically."

CHAPTER 2

I avoided thinking about my brain tumor for months. I couldn't think about it. I could only be embarrassed or bewildered. The preposterousness of the fantasy dissuaded me from determining whether it had been produced by foolishness or by self-indulgence or by stupidity. I especially wasn't inclined to talk about it.

Hypoglycemia was a trendy malady at the time, and printed testimonials correlated low blood sugar with everything from hallucinations to impotence. When people who knew I had been ill asked about my health, I told them about blood sugar. When I wondered about the nature of my spells, I told myself about blood sugar.

I wanted to be free of the synthetic tumor, to label it bad theater and go on. Yet at every attempt to dismiss the affair I would remember that my father had been lurking in the back of my mind for three decades, waiting to reappear as my birthday drew near, and I would be unnerved. I knew if my father's death had convinced me I was going to die at the same age and from the same pathology, and if it had sent me off on a compulsive farewell tour of Europe, then it had influenced my life in countless other ways. I didn't like the idea that part of me was a puppet being directed by strings that ran to my father's grave. I knew dismissal wasn't going to work. I desperately needed an explanation.

I began my search in the library where, in one computer database alone, I found summaries of over three hundred publications on the effects absent fathers have on children. Other indexes were equally plentiful with the results of studies. I wasn't the only person interested in this topic. But the more research I read, the less I learned.

The studies all had a similar bent. The researchers put their father-absent subjects under statistical microscopes and concluded variously that the absence of a father might be linked to problems with castration anxiety, juvenile delinquency, achievement motivation or cognitive development in children. Nowhere amidst all of this scientific method was there an article or report that began to explain how, twenty-nine years after the fact, my father's death could be orchestrating my life.

The only words that struck a chord in me were written by literary critic Anatole Broyard. "Without a father," he said, "a son is too lonely, too loud, too hard-edged. He glares, he has no chiaroscuro, no darkness. Half his dialectic has been lost."

As I examined the reports and reflected on my own childhood, I remembered, not manifestations of castration anxiety, but occasions like the day I was playing catch with my next-door neighbor. Our game probably didn't last more than ten minutes, but on one throw the man tossed me a fly ball that I captured squarely in the pocket of my glove.

"Good catch," my neighbor said, "you looked like Duke Snider on that one."

No one had ever told me I looked like anyone other than my father before, and Duke Snider sounded like he was alive, so I leapt on that throwaway remark as if it were a bag of Halloween candy.

"Who's Duke Snider?" I asked.

"He's an outfielder for the Brooklyn Dodgers," the man replied.

At that moment I developed a fixation on Duke Snider that lasted until he retired when I was sixteen. I learned everything I could about Snider and the Dodgers and, despite living in Philadelphia Phillies territory, I became a rabid Dodger fan. The instant the afternoon paper with the large sports section arrived, I devoured the stories about the exploits of Duke and the Dodgers on the previous day.

My friends, Phillies fans all, couldn't understand my attachment to a team headquartered ninety miles north, and I never did explain it to them. All that mattered was that when I caught the ball one day I looked like Duke Snider, and that was good enough for me.

Even though I had only seen them play once when they came to Philadelphia, I was distraught when the Dodgers moved to Los Angeles at the end of the 1957 season. The man who could make me feel wonderful by hitting a home run was going to be three thousand miles away. Yet my reaction to their move was minor in comparison with what happened the day I picked up the newspaper and saw the headline: "Dodgers Cite Snider." I wasn't sure what cite meant, but I knew it had to be bad. I ran for the dictionary with tears in my eyes. I read

the entry three times before it sank in that Snider hadn't
been fired, as I instantly feared when I saw the headline,
but that he had been honored.

When I saw that research wasn't going to give me
the answers I was looking for, I couldn't envision any other
option than going to my mother. She was the one who
knew about my father and my childhood, but she was also
the one who had established the prohibition against talking about him. My family hadn't mentioned my father in
years, and I was skeptical that time could have decreased
my mother's reticence.

It was ironic that I began the hunt for my father's
ghost in a place he never lived: my childhood home. My
mother had moved us to her parents' house in suburban
Philadelphia after my father died. My sisters and I grew
up in that house and then left. Our mother stayed on
alone. My son and I visited her there now, and one Sunday night after dinner I attempted to reach into the vac-
uum that had swallowed my father.

"Mom," I said as my son did his homework on the
kitchen table, "I've been thinking about Dad lately. What
was it like when he was sick?"

"Bill," she said in a voice that ranged from requesting understanding to demanding that I quickly change
the topic, "I don't remember that, any of that stuff. It
happened too long ago." Then she buried her face in the
thick Sunday newspaper.

On my return visits I would press harder. "Mom,
have you remembered anything about Dad's illness since
the last time I asked?"

"No, I have not," she would say, and the reflexive
pinching of her eyes that this question produced would
come faster each time.

Anger would rush into my mouth and urge me to
say something cutting when my mother continuously
evaded my inquiries. I was beginning to suspect that it
was our inability to talk about my dead father that was

responsible for my terminal fantasy, and, to my mind, that meant my mother held some culpability for what had happened to me once—and could happen to me again. I wanted to lash out at her and say I had a right to know about my father, but I would remember she loved me and stop short. That became increasingly difficult when, after I had patiently broached the subject a dozen times, my mother showed no hint of yielding.

"Mom," I implored one day, "if you can't remember Dad's illness, tell me about the jobs he had. What did he do for a living?"

"I don't remember," she said, and shook her head vigorously. "Now stop pestering me about your father."

"That's a lie," I shouted. "How could you not remember what your husband did for a living? Why won't you talk to me about my father?"

"I can't remember," she insisted. "I can't remember."

My mother was on the verge of tears when my son, who had been playing outside, stuck his head in the door to see what was going on. I pressed my lips shut and resolved to come back the next week, without Joey, to see this through.

I was determined to make my mother talk when I returned. I stormed into the living room, prepared to be as nasty as I had to be, only to find my grandmother sitting on the couch next to my mother.

Seeing my grandmother broke my stride. She had been the person my sisters and I came home to after school while our mother was at work. My grandmother was in her eighties now, but she remained as kind and cheerful and full of life as she had always been. I started to say, "Grandmom, I didn't expect to see you here," but I never got the words out.

My grandmother was looking at me with her head angled to the side and her eyes bunched up in a squint. She turned to my mother and said with a voice full of wonder, "Helen, that boy is the picture image of his father. When he walked through the door just now, I thought for a minute that Billy *was* his father."

My mother's eyes darted for something to focus on. She found a magazine on a table and quickly opened it on her lap. "Yes," she said in a tone I had never heard before, one that seemed to come from another time and place, "sometimes I think that too."

My mother was twenty-nine-years old, two months pregnant, with a two-year-old son and a four-year-old daughter when my father died in 1950. I knew that my father had been sick for several years before he died, that his death had profoundly affected my mother and that we hadn't had very much money when we were growing up, but we children never really felt any of that. Our mother protected us, provided for us and kept us focused forward.

The only ones who spoke of our father at all were our grandmother and some aunts. But they talked about him solely in the hosannas one offers to a plaster saint. "Bill Wartman was too good to live," they would say. "Imagine, he was only thirty-one-years old. But, oh, was he a good man. Only the good die young." And our mother would stand on the periphery in stony silence.

For the first time I was beginning to see there was a large measure of self-protection in our mother's protectiveness of us, and I forced myself to accept that I owed it to her to leave that undisturbed. That became easier when I discovered I had another alternative. I could write a magazine article about people who grew up without knowing their fathers. I would interview others about their feelings and experiences. And, under the protective guise of journalism, I would do an end run around my mother and tell my sisters that, for the first time in our lives, I wanted to have a conversation with them about our father's death.

I informed my friends I was seeking people who had had little or no contact with their fathers during childhood, for whatever reason, but who had been raised by their natural mothers. I said the interviews would be for publication, but that I would guarantee confidentiality and anonymity. I was heartened when I started receiving referrals almost immediately—everyone seemed to know someone who met the criteria. But my enthusiasm dampened quickly as phone call after phone call followed the course of the conversations I had with a woman named Jean.

A friend had mentioned Jean to me as a prospective interviewee, saying that, even though Jean was in her mid-thirties and happily married, she told everyone she met that her father had died when she was a year old. My friend asked Jean if she would be willing to be interviewed. Jean consented and said I should call to arrange a time.

I called Jean on a September afternoon in 1981. I identified myself, mentioned our friend's name and asked if there was a time in the next few weeks when we could talk.

"I guess we can set something up," she said hesitantly, "but I'm very busy with my job and my children. I have a tight schedule."

I told Jean I was flexible and that I would accept any time and place she could be available.

"Well," Jean said, "maybe you better tell me more about why you want to interview me."

I explained the events that had preceded my thirty-first birthday, said how disappointed I was with the research I had found and reassured her that I would disguise her identity in anything I published.

"How long will this take?" she asked.

"Jean," I said, "I'll settle for whatever time you can spare. This is important to me, and I will do anything I can to make it easier for you."

We set a date two weeks hence, and as I was about to leave home that evening, the telephone rang. It was Jean. She said she was tired and couldn't keep our appointment. I said I understood and asked if we could schedule another date.

Jean equivocated as we discussed possible times, and then her voice grew firm. "Look, Bill," she said, "the truth is that I don't want to talk to you. When I first heard about your article, I thought it was a great idea. I still think about my father all of the time, but I've never really talked with anyone about it. I've been so worried about doing the interview with you that I can't concentrate at work, and I haven't slept well for a week. I didn't have these problems before you called me, and I'm not going to risk making them worse by going through with it. I'm sorry, but please don't call me again."

It happened repeatedly, with men as well as with women. People who had told various mutual friends that they would do an interview with me suddenly became unavailable when it was time to talk—they were busy, their kids were sick, they had to go out of town. I made follow-up phone calls in which I would pitch my sincerity, my empathy, my trustworthiness. Nothing worked. The voices on the other end of the line would brim with evasiveness—it wasn't that people didn't want to talk to *me*, they didn't want to talk about *this*. With such a track record, I knew I was going to be in trouble with my sisters. They would have neither the cloak of anonymity nor the detachment of being strangers to encourage them to talk. And with our long history of silence on our father's death, a formidable precedent would have to be broken.

I arrived at the suburban New Jersey home of my older sister, Helen Marie, at two o'clock on Thanksgiving Day, 1981. As usual, I found Helen Marie and my younger sister, Anne, busily moving around the kitchen preparing dinner. My two brothers-in-law were gathered in the family room, playing video games with my nephews. Soon my mother would be shuttling between the two rooms, coming into the kitchen every half hour to ask how she could help, only to be told that the cooking was being taken care of and she should go relax.

My routine would have been to say some quick hellos and head for the video games, anxious to have some fun and to find an easy way to pass the day. My sisters and I had started becoming strangers during adolescence. An uncle of ours had bought a gas station just as I was entering puberty, and the garage became my escape from a house where there was always someone sewing. I spent every evening, weekend and summer there, learning how to smoke unfiltered cigarettes and drink black coffee, until I graduated from high school. My pockets always jingled with my own money, and my home became a place I stopped by when I couldn't find anywhere else to go.

My divergence from my family only increased after that. I studied literature in college, got divorced and left my job to become a writer. My sisters went to work after high school, married an insurance underwriter and a computer engineer and bought progressively bigger houses. Everyone in my family worked for corporations, went to church and paid mortgages. I did none of those. I hadn't had a full-time employer in eight years, and I slept with women I wasn't married to. All of these differences made family small talk difficult for me, and when I walked into a room full of relatives without my son to keep me company, discovering that my nephews had a new game was like taking a deep breath of laughing gas.

This time, however, I resisted the temptation of the games and lingered in the kitchen with my sisters. I asked about the weight of the turkey and the nature of the stuffing, while wondering if I would have the wherewithall to follow through with what I had planned. My pulse was steadily quickening as I stood by the oven, fidgeting and getting in the way. My sisters worked around me and didn't seem to find my continued presence in the kitchen odd, but they were preoccupied. The entire family was together only three or four times a year, and there were people to feed and dishes to be washed and children to be put to bed before the day was over. My timing stank, but my experiences with my mother and with the people I had attempted to interview had made me desperate. I felt as if I were undertaking an assault, battling for my peace of mind against a formidable enemy: silence. I had planned accordingly. I reached into a sack I had brought with me and pulled out my first weapon.

"How do you like my new tape recorder?" I asked my sisters, and set the machine on the counter between them.

They said it was nice and turned from their scrubbing and peeling to have a closer look. I moved away and behind them, giving them room and time to take the bait. Ask me why I bought it, I repeated silently to myself, but they didn't. They returned to their tasks and left me standing at the far end of the room, feeling alone and distant.

"Actually," I said, "I bought it because I've started a new project."

"That's nice," they said. They showed no interest. This was not how I had planned it.

"The new project is a magazine article," I said, "and it has to do with something that happened to me . . . to all of us."

"Oh?" they asked, slowing their work and looking over their shoulders at me with curiosity.

"Yes," I said nervously, "I'm doing an article about people who grew up without knowing their fathers, and, ah, I've been using the tape recorder to do interviews."

"Oh?" they repeated and straightened their backs in unison. All work had ceased and their shoulders tightened with warning: Don't you do this to us. Don't you dare. Leave us alone.

My eyes stung with tears and my voice was starting to waver. "Yeah," I whispered hoarsely, "I've been doing interviews and I was wondering if maybe we could talk about Dad's death later today?"

Neither of them moved, or even seemed to breathe, for a very long time. They didn't look toward each other nor toward me, and they didn't utter a sound. We were all frozen in place, locked in a tableau entitled Children Hearing of Their Father's Death.

I wanted to end the scene, to move on to the next act, where I would walk over to my sisters, hug them both and cry, "Isn't it a goddamn shame that this had to happen to us. Son of a bitch, it isn't fair. We were just little kids, what did we ever do to deserve this? . . ." But I couldn't do it. I didn't know how. I had been working on this script for two years, since I thought I was going to die, and I still couldn't put it together.

Helen Marie, the oldest, was the first to speak. "Are we going to get royalties?" she asked sarcastically and jerked the hot water on full force.

Anne, who hadn't even been born when our father died, ran me through with my own words. "You can't miss someone you never knew," she said firmly. It was precisely the reply I had given to anyone who had ever asked me how I felt about my father's death.

I had anticipated this—had planned for it in fact—but that did nothing to temper my reaction. I was exasperated and furious. How in the world could everyone be responding the same way? What universal nerve was I pinching that asking to talk about a long-dead father produced such dread or terror? And, more immediately, how was I ever going to untangle what had happened to me?

I packed the tape recorder away and stalked into the family room. My fists were clenching involuntarily in anger—not, I realized, at my sisters, but at our mother. She was the one who was in charge of the silence in our family, and, I could see from my sisters' reaction, she was the one who was going to have to sanction the lifting of it. And it was clear she would do that only under crushing amounts of pressure.

Every filial instinct in me demanded that I leave our mother alone, but I couldn't anymore. I sat down next to her and prepared to pull my second weapon from my bag. I had brought along a selection of childhood pictures I had taken from our mother's house, ones that hadn't been looked at in years. As Helen Marie and Anne came into the room, their duties in the kitchen suspended until the turkey was ready, I pulled out the snapshots and began to pass them around.

I had moved too swiftly in approaching my sisters before. Now I was more calculating than I had ever been in my life. I carefully paced the talk, spending the next hour involving everyone in nostalgic childhood remembrances. It was during that stage of our lives, I believed, that my imagined brain tumor had first taken root.

I mentioned the article I was working on to my brothers-in-law and my nephews, while taking care not to focus the conversation exclusively on my father. I reiterated several times, very softly, that I would like to talk about fatherless childhoods, but I didn't push too hard.

When the last morsel of dessert had been consumed, my brother-in-law placed brandy and liqueurs on the table and the children hurried away. Dinner had been tense and, now that the table was clear, everyone rushed to fill the space with forced conversation. Anne had no sooner finished relating an occurrence from work before Helen Marie darted in with a story about the kids and school. My mother, sitting nervously at my side, hung on each word with fascination.

I ground my teeth with anger and annoyance, but I wasn't certain if it was directed at my family or at my overbearing self. Did I have the right to do this to them? Why couldn't I leave well enough alone? It had been decades, and my mother and my sisters seemed to have successfully built their lives around the gap that my father's death had left. Shouldn't I put the past behind me as well? Yet, I kept reminding myself, people didn't struggle as determinedly as my family had to avoid talking about something if it had been resolved.

I sat up in my chair, cleared my throat and leaned toward my mother. "Mom," I asked, "was Dad in the war?"

"No," she said quietly.

"Why not?" I asked. "Why wasn't he drafted?"

She shook her head tersely from side to side. "I told you before, Bill, I can't remember all of these things you keep asking me. It's been too long. I forget. I think he had a medical deferment, but I don't know why."

I looked over at my sisters—they were watching our mother intently, but not protectively. They wanted to, needed to, hear this as much as I did. "Was Dad sick, even when you first met him?"

My mother's cheeks began to quiver as she stared at her hands and rubbed a thumb over her knuckles. My mother was a handsome woman with a thick head of hair that was now silver gray. I thought that my father probably liked her hair and her broad German face. My mother shook her head from side to side again, but this time memories came spilling out from her lips.

"No," she said without looking up. "You father wasn't sick until just after you were born. He was at work in city hall—your grandfather had gotten him a job there—and he leaned over to pick something up one day and he fell over. He would have spells like that where he would lose his balance, and he started getting headaches, but none of the local doctors could find anything. Then one of the doctors told him he better go to see a neurologist at the

University of Pennsylvania Hospital. They found a tumor and operated right away.

"Your father had to go back for radiation treatments. Sometimes he'd be fine, and then he'd get sick again. There were times when his balance was so bad he had to stay in bed. His speech and vision were fine, but he would get headaches and he couldn't work."

Our mother stopped talking and there was a deafening silence at the table until Helen Marie, the mother of three, spoke for the first time. "Mom," she asked, "did Dad know you were pregnant when he died?"

"Yes," she said in a barely audible tone, "he was the only one who knew."

"Mom," I asked as delicately as I could, "did Dad know that he was dying?"

"Yes," she said, as tears streamed down her cheeks and the rest of us fought back our own.

I wanted to tell my mother how much these things meant to me, how they helped fill the void, but I didn't get a chance. I had pushed her too far, taken her back to feelings she probably once thought would consume her.

My mother wiped the tears from her cheeks, angled her downturned head in my direction and said, "There now. Are you satisfied?"

CHAPTER

3

I finally did get to play video games with my nephews that Thanksgiving. I overenthusiastically helped with the cleanup operation after dinner to assuage my guilt for having made the day so cheerless, and then hurried for the television and issued an equally overboisterous challenge to the boys to show me their stuff.

It was a relief to give myself over to the frivolity of the games—to holler and tease—and to be appreciated by my nephews for that. I eagerly slipped into a frame of mind where there were no cares beyond protecting your space ship from alien invaders, and where errors of judgment vanished with a flick of the reset switch.

I popped my head up momentarily and yelled a distracted goodbye when my mother left with Anne and her husband. Helen Marie and her mate came in and watched me joust with the boys for a while and then told them it was past their bedtime. They grumbled and headed for the stairs. I didn't move for the door, so my brother-in-law offered me another brandy, which I accepted.

The three of us sat at the formica table in the breakfast area off the kitchen. "Well," I said to my big sister, "did you think I was awful for doing that?"

She gave me a half-smile and folded her arms on the table. "It wasn't the kindest thing I have ever seen anyone do to his mother, but I can understand a little of why you felt that you had to do it. Mom made it clear when we were growing up that we weren't supposed to ask about Dad. She has never wanted to talk about him, and I don't think she ever will."

"She's not alone," I said. "Everybody I try to interview has the same reaction. I don't understand it. You wouldn't talk either. Why not?"

"I don't know," she said offhandedly. "It just seems like something that happened to me once. It bothered me a little bit when we were growing up. I felt like I was missing something the other kids had. I know that I'll never get a job while my boys are young. I want them to be able to come home to their mother after school—I missed that. But other than that, I don't know what to say. I don't think about it anymore."

"Am I wrong for stirring up all of this stuff about Dad?"

"No, not if it means that much to you. I think you should go easy on Mom though."

"I've already written off getting any more information from her. She can be very hardheaded when she wants to be."

"Yes," my sister said, giving me a full smile this time, "and her son can be just like her."

I didn't broach the topic again with my mother for many months. I did, however, keep looking for interview subjects. I was determined to gain a better understanding of what happens when people grow up without knowing their fathers. This was partly to learn if the experiences of others could inform my past, and partly, through learning what people missed in not having a father, to discover what children wanted and needed from their fathers. I was trying to be a father without ever having had one to show me how. More and more, though, I was also motivated to find evidence that would refute some initial conclusions I had drawn.

The only explanation I could formulate for people's mass refusal to discuss their father-absent childhoods was that biological fathers were so important that life in their absence had been too catastrophic to retell. As someone who had left his own son, this was not a premise I wanted to accept.

I hadn't probed into my own childhood very deeply, but I didn't recall it as a period of unrelenting misery and I knew my son's life wasn't like that. I had, I thought, simply gotten on with things, as one is supposed to do, and so had my son.

I had drawn the courage to get a divorce—an act everyone in my family admonished—from my own experience. I had survived with no father, I recalled, and if I continued to be a father to Joey then the effects of my absence on him would be scant. Yet there were occurrences that caused my certainty to waver.

In looking through the second-grade school work that my son had brought with him one Sunday, I discovered a crayon drawing of a house. It didn't resemble the dwelling my son shared with his mother, but, when I saw the name Wartman printed over the front door, I knew the teacher had instructed my son to make a picture of his home. The only feature of the house that varied from the skeletal rendition any child would have drawn was the detailed window dressing.

I had won some trophies racing automobiles when I was a teenager. My son would see the prizes in my bedroom when he visited and gaze at them as if they were assembled from more precious materials than their actual cheap chromed metal and garish felt. They seemed to represent some worldly recognition for my son that his father was as important as he thought I was. The awards were little more than kitsch to me, until I realized the only distinguishing particular of my son's drawing was the trophies he had depicted as residing in the window of his home.

Nonetheless, I couldn't believe that a specific man, as a result of impregnating a woman, became that significant to his offspring. Rather, I theorized it was the interaction of two factors, which occurred in the father's complete absence, that produced the problems: the refusal of the family—because of anger or grief or resentment—to discuss the missing father and the lack of a good stepfather to replace the father.

In the weeks after the doctor had eradicated my tumor by announcing that it was a product of my mind rather than a growth on it, my son and I went swimming one Sunday in a relative's backyard pool. It was a brilliantly clear, ninety-degree summer day, and we had the water to ourselves. There was a large inflated raft drifting in one end, and I swam to it and climbed aboard. All I wanted from life at that moment was to float about, while the sun and the undulations of the water leeched the poisons of the recent past from my pores. But that wasn't to be.

My son dove under the water and torpedoed the raft with his head, he flopped into the pool from the diving board and blanketed me with spray and, when neither method gained him my attention, he attempted to crawl onto the raft with me until we both were catapulted over the side. I was too distracted to either laugh or yell, but Joey's persistent need reminded me of my relationship with an uncle when I was my son's age.

My Uncle Bill, in addition to sharing a given name with my father and myself, was my surrogate father of sorts. He was the one of my mother's three brothers she depended on the most when something requiring a man needed to be done. My Uncle Bill ran a small laundry business with my grandfather out of the basement of my childhood home, and he later opened the gas station where I spent much time trying to grow up too fast. My uncle and his wife didn't have any children, and I was more than willing to be his approximate son, but we never worked out who was going to do what for whom.

My uncle's intentions were good, but he was never sure what he was supposed to do with the boy he had inherited. Uncle Bill was a hard-drinking man who drove fast cars that usually had a never-fired pistol in the glove compartment. He was the chief engineer of the local volunteer fire company, and he tore off with blazing headlights and honking horn whenever the fire siren blared. My uncle always acted without hesitation, except when he turned around and found me on his heels. Then he was stymied.

Women were always very friendly to him—they would remark on his good looks when he wasn't in hearing range—and I believe he accommodated them, although I was never quite sure. He would sometimes take me out on the laundry truck when he picked up and delivered people's cleaning, but he always told me to wait in the truck while he went inside.

I'd get restless when he was gone too long, so I would jump into the driver's seat of the green Ford panel truck with the elaborate gold-leaf lettering on the side and play

driver. I'd push the gas pedal to the floor and stroke the
shift lever up and down on the steering column and then
throw on the brakes, pretending there was a stop sign up
ahead. I'd repeat those steps and bounce the steering wheel
from left to right until I saw my uncle emerge from the
house, when I'd scramble back into my seat on the other
side of the cab. My uncle would get in and turn the igni-
tion key, but the truck wouldn't start.

My Uncle Bill would look at me in mild annoyance—
he never actually got angry at me, regardless of what I
did—and ask, "Have you been pushing on the gas pedal
again, Sport?"

"Yeah," I would apologize, "I was just playing driver."

"I've told you before, though, you can't keep pushing on the gas," he would say as he fired up a cigarette
and waited for the spark plugs to dry. "It floods the engine."

"Oh," I'd mumble, "I forgot about that."

My Uncle Bill thought he could best make amends
for my father's death by acting as a role model for me on
select occasions. He was painfully polite when we met
strangers, and he would even alter his diction, pronounc-
ing multisyllabic words fully and distinctly so he sounded
like a man who had attended a good college, rather than
the high school dropout that he was.

The family laundry business farmed out the actual
cleaning of the soiled goods my uncle transported, so each
delivery day concluded at the plant of the wholesale con-
tractor who did the cleaning. As my uncle walked into the
office there one day, with me in pursuit, he was hailed by
the balding middle-aged manager—a man with the most
prominent hooked nose I had ever witnessed—who hollered, "Yo, Bill, how do you like this stuff?" The man
then unfurled a pinup calendar featuring a woman with
tremendous naked breasts.

My uncle glanced down at me uncomfortably and
boosted his pace as if propelled.

"What's the matter Bill," the manager called after him, "don't you like tits anymore?"

I knew, as an observant ten year old, that my uncle—and most men—liked tits, and I personally found the picture captivating, but Uncle Bill decided that this was a role-model situation, one requiring decorum rather than candidness.

He turned to the manger, curled his lips in contempt and said tersely, "The kid."

The manager hurriedly folded the calendar as his eyes lit on me with feigned surprise. "Who are you with?" he asked.

"My Uncle Bill," I said and pointed toward the man who was vanishing into the plant.

While my uncle presented me with false versions of himself to aspire to, I tried to win his attention by emulating his real character. When he sold the laundry business and opened the filling station, I became a permanent fixture there. I understood that it was the kid's job to win the adult's attention and affection; that the onus was on me to make something happen. I recognized my uncle wouldn't let me work the gas pumps right away—I was only twelve—so when motorists pulled in the driveway I would hurry out and wipe their windshields whether they wanted them washed or not, even if they had just come asking for directions.

I soon began volunteering to wait on customers when everyone else was occupied, and when a man arrived one evening to deliver an elaborate new cash register my uncle had purchased, I stood off to the side and memorized the operating instructions as the man recited them. My uncle seemed to have some trouble following the directions, but I picked them up right away, and I was certain my uncle would be pleased.

When I came into the office to enter my first sale on the new machine, there was an audience of relatives waiting to appraise my performance. I punched the keys so rapidly my fingers were a blur, and I sent the cash drawer flying open with a deft flick of the back of my hand. I was showboating, no question about it, but I was playing for the only applause I wanted—my uncle's approval. Instead, I got his fury. "Don't be a wise guy, Sport," he barked. "That machine cost a lot of money. If you screw it up, you're in big trouble."

I didn't work with my Uncle Bill often—he was on days, I was on nights—but he still managed to express what struck me as his free-floating disapproval frequently enough. Everyone said my uncle was a great mechanic, but he wouldn't teach me how to fix cars, and, when I learned anyway, he got angry at me. I passed a lot of slow nights sitting in the garage office, reading repair manuals rather than school books and teaching myself about automobiles. Some of my other relatives who worked there showed me how to replace brakes and do tune-ups, and, by the time I was fifteen, I knew my way around a wrench. But if my Uncle Bill came in and caught me doing anything other than pumping gas or changing oil, he'd grab the back of my uniform shirt, pull me from under the hood and ask me what the hell I thought I was doing—I was just a kid, I couldn't fix cars.

When my mother judged I needed to feel the wrath of God in my life, she called my Uncle Bill, who would respond as he thought a father was supposed to act and give me a stern talking-to. I was a foot taller than my mother by the time I was thirteen, and, with my earnings rather than her allowance snuggled on my hip, and with a precocious talent for glibness, I could be a tough customer at home. I had managed to break enough rules to get expelled from Catholic high school in the middle of my junior year, and, only two months after that, there was some trouble with the police.

A girl at my new school, one I didn't know but who smiled at me a lot, made sure that I overhead her telling her girlfriends that she was going dancing on Friday at

Chez Vous, a popular teenage nightclub several towns away. I rounded up two of my friends, arranged for the purchase of three quarts of beer and set off for the dance on Friday. My friends decided en route that they would drop me off at the dance and return at midnight, so I guzzled my beer while they reserved theirs for later consumption. Within minutes of leaving me at the dance my friends were stopped by the police, and within seconds of that the officers knew my name and whereabouts.

With visions of backseat necking torturing me with anticipation, I managed to persuade my new girlfriend to ride home from the dance with me rather than with her friends. When we arrived at the designated pickup spot, however, there was a man with a suit and a badge who told her she had better find another means of transportation.

As the detective walked me to the police station, I considered what was going to happen. I wasn't frightened. I knew the worst outcome couldn't be that bad— my mother would sigh in yet more anguish, my Uncle Bill would be obliged by my mother to holler at me and, at most, I would probably have to pay a small fine. There were a number of policemen who frequented the coffee pot at the gas station, and I figured one of them might be convinced to arrange clemency for me.

My two friends, Gary and Mick, looked away as I entered the police station—we all knew they had given me up to salvage their own hides—but their fathers didn't. The men broke off their conversation, one centered, no doubt, on how a common wretch such as myself was corrupting their fine sons, and the men stared at me hatefully as I approached. I struggled not to smile at them and their derision.

Gary's father was an accountant at a local corporation, and, though it was past midnight, he had donned a suit and tie before coming to reclaim his son. Gary's parents considered themselves to be among the first families

of our Catholic parish. The mother led the church choir
and frequently invited the priests over for dinner. Her
son, a strikingly handsome but not overly bright only child,
possessed a wardrobe that was as regal as he considered
himself to be. The area we lived in was rapidly changing
from rural to 1960s suburban, and Gary's family had been
the first to move into a housing development with the
word "Estates" in its name.

Mick's father was an assembly line worker at a car
plant and the quintessential good Catholic father. He had
a fertile wife and seven freckle-faced kids who could have
been models for the characters in the comic strip "Ar-
chie." This man didn't have the same social aspirations as
Gary's old man, but he was equally earnest about playing
a minor role in the community. He insured that his kids
got good grades and helped coach the sports teams, even
when they were teams on which his kids didn't excel.

Mick's family was the first to buy a Volkswagen bug
in a neighborhood where foreign cars, with the rare ex-
ception of some pipe-smoking college boy with a noisy
English sports car, were unheard of. That VW, a beige
one with a matching interior and no options, was the "wife
and kids' car," purchased so Mick's mother and brothers
and sisters could go about the business of being a pro-
gressive suburban family, while the father worked to provide the means.

I wasn't fazed by the venom of Gary's and Mick's
fathers because I was a free agent. I didn't have anyone
to report to save a mother I overwhelmed, with cameo
appearances by my Uncle Bill when he was requested. I
knew these fathers were primarily terrified that their
neighbors were going to discover their sons had been ar-
rested. I didn't have a father who was going to lean on
me to save his stature in the community, or who was going
to have to shake his head in confusion when asked about
his troublemaking son by other fathers. These fathers had

done nothing for me, and I considered my debt to them nil.

I pushed past my reception committee, and the detective told the fathers they could take their errant sons home before leading me to his office for questioning. I evaded his inquiries about my supplier—it was a cousin I worked with whom I wasn't going to involve—until he tired of the game and told me to call my father.

"That's going to be pretty hard," I said. "My father's dead."

"Call your mother then," he retorted.

If I had to stay in jail all night, I wasn't going to call my mother at one o'clock in the morning and tell her that I was at the police station. My much abused mother deserved not to have her sleep interrupted by her intractable son, and the guilt that would have burned in me during the trip home would have been far more painful than anything these small-town police could concoct.

"She won't be home," I said of a woman who was in bed by ten o'clock, and who probably hadn't been in a bar in her life. "She always goes out drinking with men on the weekend, and she doesn't get home until breakfast."

"Try," he said and shoved the phone at me.

I dialed the phone number for the gas station, which had been closed for hours, waited silently through an appropriate number of rings, and then handed the receiver to the detective, who listened and rolled his eyes at me skeptically.

"See," I said, "I told you she wouldn't be home."

After some negotiation, the policeman allowed my Uncle Bob to retrieve me. He was my night-shift partner at the gas station and a former 1950s leather jacket, street corner hanger who was only a dozen years my senior. Uncle Bob illuminated my misguidedness after he had sprung me. "If you want to drink beer, dummy," he said, "you park the car and go drink your beer in a field. You don't drive around with beer in the car that the cops are going to find if they stop you."

In the morning I told my mother. She sighed, "Oh, Billy," and called my Uncle Bill, who summoned me to the gas station.

I knew this was going to be a walk-through. The standing joke at the garage was to wonder whether my Uncle Bill had drunk a greater volume of beer the previous night than the amount of gasoline we would sell that day. He was infamous for his carousing with the boys, and, as part of the gas station crew, I saw this as little more than a fraternity initiation. I presented myself in the office with a sheepish grin on my face that said, "Can you believe the hassles a guy has to put up with from these petty cops?"

"Who the hell do you think you are, Sport?" he barked at me. "A sixteen-year-old kid has no business drinking beer. Do you want to get your ass thrown in jail? Do you want to ruin your health?" He went on for ten minutes as I staggered under the hypocrisy and betrayal.

A detective friend of my uncle interceded and had the charges for the beer dropped, much to the exasperation of Gary's and Mick's fathers, who would have had me sent to a juvenile home, but the unbridgeable gulf between my uncle and me widened after that.

When I started smoking as a teenager, I adopted my uncle's brand, Luckies, but I never had the courage to smoke them in front of him. I smoked with all of my other relatives at the garage, and, after my sisters happened by and saw me smoking and informed our mother of their observation, I took out an ashtray and started smoking at home. But something about my uncle intimidated me.

Lucky Strike began marketing a new brand called Lucky Filters, and my Uncle Bill switched to them while I remained loyal to the originals. When I was seventeen, the last year I worked at the gas station, my uncle received a carton of unfiltered Luckies for Christmas, and when I came into work one evening he had the package sitting on the desk in the office.

"I got these as a present, Sport," he said and edged the carton toward me, "but I don't smoke this kind anymore. Can you use them?"

I considered for a minute whether this was a trap. I didn't even knew that he knew I smoked, much less what brand. My guess was that one of my other relatives had told my Uncle Bill to give the cigarettes to me when he said he didn't want them. His making the offer must signify that it was all right to accept, so I said, "Yeah, sure," and edged over toward my uncle, expecting him to hand them to me. But he didn't. He left the cigarettes sitting on the desk, walked to his car and drove home.

By the summer of 1982, I had located a group of people who pledged that they would sit for interviews, and I began working on the much delayed magazine article. The people I spoke with ranged in age from late teens to early forties, and in social background from lower to upper middle-class. I didn't attempt to assemble a statistically valid cross-section of the population. I knew whatever I wrote would be a subjective look at father-absent childhoods, but I also believed it would have resonance for my readers.

One of my early interviews was with a woman named Janice, a thirty-eight-year-old museum administrator. She lived with her third husband in a historic fieldstone house in a gentleman-farmer suburb of Philadelphia. When I arrived at Janice's home, she introduced me to her husband and led me across the polished-oak foyer floor into a living room appointed with a large Oriental rug and understated furniture.

I knew before I arrived that Janice's father had been

killed in the Second World War, when his wife was five months pregnant with Janice, and that her mother had remarried several years later. I wanted to know how people differentiated stepfathers from natural fathers, so I asked Janice how old she was when she realized that her stepfather wasn't her real father.

"My father's parents told me as soon as I was old enough to hear," she said, "that the man I lived with was not my real father. My father was an only child, and his parents were afraid I wouldn't have a proper respect for and understanding of who my father was after my mother remarried. I heard quite heroic versions of who my father had been from his parents. His death ruined their lives. He was their star and he died at twenty-two. They never really recovered. My grandparents never talked about anything other than my father. His pictures and mementoes were all over their house."

"That makes your experience different from mine and those of the other people I have talked to," I said. "It seems like most families didn't talk about dead or missing fathers at all, and they didn't have pictures of them sitting around—it was as if the fathers never existed. I've been guessing that the disappearance of a father from a child's life without a trace was responsible for some of the bad reactions people have had to the father's absence. At least you knew something about your father."

"Well, yes and no," Janice said. "My grandparents' home was like a shrine to my father and they talked about him in only the most glowing terms—he had been a star athlete and scholar in college and had signed a contract to play professional baseball after the war. But we didn't have a picture of my father at home, and my mother would have been terribly upset if I had brought one home from my grandparents. She would have worried that I was unhappy and that I missed him. She would have said something like, 'But you never knew him, what do you want his picture for?' and she would have worried that my stepfather would be hurt.

"My stepfather was not nearly as accomplished as my father. Both my mother and father came from families with money, and my stepfather was a factory worker when he married my mother. My grandfather constantly made comparisons and belittled my stepfather, and Mother took it as her task to defend my stepfather against my father's memory. My mother acted very bitter and embarrassed whenever I asked about my father.

"When I was eleven or twelve, I asked her how she reacted when she learned that my father had died. I wanted her to recreate the scene. Her answer made it sound like she was expecting my father to die. She said her friends had had husbands who were killed, so she wasn't surprised when it happened to her. She said she knew where he was going and what it was like over there, so she wasn't surprised when it happened, and after all, they had only been married for a short time.

"I felt like I wasn't a wanted child, like my mother and father had had this frivolous college romance and now she was strapped with me. I especially felt this way after my stepbrother and sister were born. I felt like I wasn't a part of the family. I was a little orphan girl standing out on the sidewalk looking in the window at the happy family."

"But," I interrupted, "you were a part of the family. You have said that your stepfather tried hard to be a good parent. Was all of this just because your stepfather wasn't as big a deal as your real father?"

"Yes," Janice said, shifting uncomfortably in her chair while searching for the right words, "but not in the way that you mean it. It was clear that I had my father's genes, that I was his daughter. I have always been a reader. I was reading books when I was four years old. I don't think my stepfather has read a book in his life. I always did well

in school, but my stepbrother and sister never did. I felt
that they were more important to my stepfather because
they were his real children, and that they were more important to my mother because they brought her closer to
her new husband.

"I always felt I didn't have anyone to rely on, that I
couldn't trust anyone to be strong. I had to be utterly
self-reliant. I always had jobs. I started baby-sitting when
I was eleven, I played piano for a dancing teacher, I
worked at a newsstand in the morning. I needed to feel
independent. The government paid over a hundred dollars a month for my care, since my father was killed in
the war, and I knew my parents weren't spending most
of the money. But I couldn't get my hands on it until I
was eighteen, so I always worked as a kid."

"This sounds familiar," I said. "I did the same things—
I always had my own money; I never depended on other
people. But I didn't have a stepfather, so it wasn't because I felt like I wasn't part of a new family. I think I
concluded that people—and especially men—were always
going to disappoint me, and that the only way to avoid
that was not to expect anything from anyone. I tried to
believe I could be totally self-reliant and never need anyone.

"I managed to convince myself I was going to die of
a brain tumor when I was thirty-one because my father
had died from one when he was that age," I said. "Did
anything unusual happen when you approached the age
at which your father died?"

"My father died right after college, and it was in college I realized for the first time there were parts of me
that were very unhappy, and they were related to my father. I went to the same university that my father attended, and when I was about to leave home my mother—
who had always downplayed my father's death—handed
me a package of mementoes. They were really wonderful

things. The purple heart she was sent when he died. A telegram . . ."

Janice stopped talking as tears poured down her cheeks. "It's hard for me to talk about this without crying," she said. "There was a telegram from Belgium, dated about two or three weeks before he died, saying he had gotten my mother's letter that she was pregnant. He said he hoped I was a girl, and if I was to name me Janice. I think that's the biggest connection we have, because at least he knew I was going to be born.

"College was the first time I was ever around people who talked freely about my father as a real person. I had some of the same teachers he did and they spoke movingly, automatically about him—some not even knowing he was dead. They had alumni and their children's pictures in the yearbooks, and I got a long letter of admiration from a man my father had helped out, saying he just wanted me to know. There is a plaque in the gym that is dedicated to my father, and I used to go and stare at it.

"I had never been overweight before and then I gained thirty pounds during my freshman year. During my sophomore year I just kind of sat around the dorm and didn't do anything. I felt that if someone I knew saw me and said Hello, I wouldn't know what to say. This picked up steam during my junior year, and I went home one weekend on the pretext it was my stepbrother's birthday. When my mother was driving me back to school, I burst out in tears and said, 'I hate it. I can't stand it. I don't want to go back.' I ended up dropping out of school for a semester."

"And you believe that all of this was caused by thinking about your father again?" I asked.

"Yeah, I think so. I've noticed tonight, as I have before, that whenever I talk about him and get close to the feelings involved I can't think clearly. When people talked about my father I would feel like a big deal at first, but then I would feel this rage at him for dying. And that would bring back the little orphan girl syndrome, and I would be afraid that my family would forget about me now that I didn't live with them.

"The breakdown may have been an excuse to get home and prevent that. It was really an effort to show my family that I couldn't cope as well as I had convinced them I could when I was a child. The thing I was most afraid of was being left alone to die with no one to take care of me.

"I was very aware when I was growing up that my father had died when he was twenty-two. I got married for the first time when I was twenty-two. I realized after a year that I had made a crazy choice and I got a divorce. My second marriage didn't last long either. It was to a man who was thirteen years older than me, and I know in some ways I married him because he was older."

Janice paused for what seemed like a minute, and a puzzled look came over her face as if she had been stunned by the thoughts that had entered her mind and she wanted to examine them privately before she spoke.

"I have never been left by a man. I have always left before someone had the chance to do that to me. I was always a very independent woman who was the one who ran the show. It was all right for men to get dependent on me, but not for me to get dependent on them. I was never, ever going to put myself in a position where someone was going to leave me or hurt me deeply.

"Both of my previous marriages were like my mother's marriage to my stepfather, rather than her marriage to my father. I married men who were less educated, less ambitious and less successful than myself. In some ways I think I will always be looking for a father-daughter relationship in my dealings with men, and men like my stepfather seemed easier to control and less risky.

"I have a good marriage now, and I am confident enough in it to want to have children. I feel proud that I have achieved the ability to trust men. But things still happen. If my husband leaves me waiting on a street corner too long I panic, and I am filled with rage when he appears. I sometimes have these feelings of anger and sorrow I can't explain, and they always come back to feeling abandoned. Now that we are trying to have children, I am afraid my husband is going to die."

Janice's husband, who had been hovering just out of sight, but not out of hearing range, abruptly entered from the kitchen with a tray of tea and fancy cookies. "I don't want to disturb you," he said of actions that could only be interruptive, "but I thought you might like some refreshments."

I had conducted enough interviews in my life to know this one was over. We would make small talk, and I would stay long enough to be polite, but nothing significant would be discussed. The spell under which one stranger reveals intimacies to another in an attempt to be understood was broken.

CHAPTER

4

My son and I were at the midpoint of one of our Sunday night rides home. We had been at my mother's house for dinner, and now, in the thick darkness of a winter evening, we were caught in the clots of traffic that always formed around Philadelphia International Airport at this time. It was a setting of unrelieved concrete that disposed itself primarily to speculations about the size or speed or destination of the aircraft that flew low in the sky over the car, but that were discernible only in lighted outline.

While caught in the backup on this particular evening, however, my twelve-year-old son startled me by say-

ing without introduction, "You know, Dad, you're shrinking."

I instinctively recognized and laughed at the meaning behind his words. I knew that Joey wasn't talking about
our comparative physical sizes but that, at least subcon-
sciously, he was beginning to see my faults and frailties. I
decided to tease him anyway.

"What do you mean?" I said. "I'm still six-foot-two
and you have a way to go before you catch up with me—
that is, if I decide to let you catch up with me."

"I know," he said, "but when I was little you used to
seem like a giant who was as tall as a building, but now I
think of you as a regular person."

"Let's not forget," I said in a mock-stern voice, "that
this so-called regular person happens to be your father.
What have I done to deserve such a demotion?"

"I don't know," he said. "It's just something I realized one day, and I thought I ought to tell you."

"Well, thanks," I said. "I hope you'll keep me informed of any other developments like this."

I thought about that conversation in the days after I
spoke to Janice. I had asked Janice during our interview
what she thought her life would have been like if her father had lived, and she said that she had spent a lot of
time fantasizing about that as a child. She then con-
structed a detailed verbal picture of an enchanted existence as the daughter of a professional baseball player
who would become a college professor after he retired
from sports. She envisioned that she would have been an
only child of a doting father and would have enjoyed a
childhood of spring-training trips to Florida, followed by
an adolescence of quiet dinners in the faculty club.

Janice's father had seemed full of promise during
his short life, but his daughter had obviously not managed to escape the aggrandizing that she criticized her
grandparents for. Her father was a hero to her, one she
visualized as looking down from the clouds on her with

pride while she graduated from his college in a pretty white dress. Janice had never considered for a moment that her father, in addition to becoming a successful professional athlete as his own father had, might also have become a bully and an alcoholic—as his father had become after his career in sports.

Janice hadn't had the chance to see her father's image slowly check and weather with time—a process my son was experiencing—because her vision was obscured by the grace that we grant to those who have died. She would never feel the devastation of learning of the affair he might have had while he was on the road with his team, or be disappointed on the occasions when he wanted to read the paper instead of playing with her or suffer the injustice of having him punishing her for something that wasn't truly her fault.

Janice's mother played a role in the beatification of her first husband as well, for her continual insistence that Janice shouldn't be concerned about her father could have served no end other than the inflammation of her daughter's curiosity. Too, Janice would be sitting in the fourth grade classroom of the private school that her grandparents were paying for her to attend, when her grandfather would barge in and announce that he was taking his little girl to lunch at an expensive restaurant. Once they got there, the grandfather would fill her ears with tales of the tragedy of her father's unrealized greatness. Meanwhile, Janice was eating meat only three times a week at home because her stepfather, a man who probably hadn't made water boy on his high school team and who never went to college, didn't earn enough money to afford it more frequently.

And then there was the kiss. Janice was taking care of the house when she was thirteen and her mother was in the hospital when, she says, "Something terrible happened. One evening after dinner my stepfather—I think in spite of himself—put his arms around me and kissed me in a sexual way. It terrified both of us. He was extremely ashamed and he begged me not to tell my mother—I never did—but it was a nightmare. We didn't talk about it after that, but for a long time he couldn't look me in the eye."

Janice's claim that her father's death had caused irreparable damage to her life could be dismissed with a multitude of explanations, and people I recounted the interview to were quick to point them out. Yet when people I hadn't interviewed balked at stories like Janice's, and then went on to talk about their own living fathers, there was a stridency to their voices that made me reserve judgment about Janice.

Although I didn't record figures, memory tells me that more than half of those who learned I was writing about people who grew up without knowing their fathers responded unhesitatingly, "My father was alive, and he lived with us, but I certainly grew up without knowing him." Their delivery would be tinged with the resigned bitterness and residual anger of those who have conceded defeat, but not accepted it, after a long and draining struggle.

The contention of the men and women who responded this way was that, living or dead, fathers were frequently a disappointment to their children, so there was no cause for the people I was interviewing to feel they alone had deprived childhoods. They didn't argue against people wanting and needing stronger ties with their fathers. Their point was that, even when they were present, fathers were seldom emotionally available, that most everyone grew up with the sorrow of a lost father.

The people who did insist, sometimes vehemently, that fathers were of little significance to children, were almost exclusively divorced or separated mothers of young children who were angry at their ex-husbands rather than at their fathers. The early 1980s were a difficult time to raise the proposition among single mothers that fathers were important to children, for the traditional acrimony of divorce was being exacerbated by a general enmity toward men that some women created out of the women's movement. "Instead of writing about how children miss their fathers," one woman said to me, "why don't you write about something really important like why men desert their families?"

I didn't really know what to make out of all of this because I didn't know if these women's husbands were as bad as they said they were. I did know there were two sides to every story—that ex-spouses who were vilified as madmen somehow managed to build successful second marriages, and that children from failed marriages forced ongoing contact between people who would prefer not to speak to each other again.

I saw a man I knew only casually at a literary event one night not long after I had spoken to Janice. Frank was in his early thirties and he had been married for several years to a woman who had a six-year-old daughter from a previous marriage. I had told Frank about my project before, so I asked him if he would be willing to talk to me about being a stepfather. He agreed much more readily than I had expected.

As we walked the few blocks to a quiet bar, I told Janice's story to Frank, then asked what he thought about her heroic visions of her father and her disconnectedness from her stepfather, which she had attributed to genetics. Frank shook his head in disgust.

"This is the kind of stuff I have to put up with all of the time," he began, "and it really pisses me off. But what's worse is that I don't know who to be angry at. My wife and I have a terrific marriage, and I really love my stepdaughter. I work hard at being a good father to her. I spend time with her, I help her with her homework, the three of us take trips together and ride our bikes through the park. With all of this, my stepdaughter and I get along fine, and I think she loves me.

"On the other hand, her father is a bum. He is always late with his child support, and he constantly disappoints his daughter. He says that he is going to take her someplace and then he shows up two hours late and they can't go. Or sometimes he doesn't show up at all, and he doesn't even bother to call to say he isn't coming. When that happens she mopes around the house for days. But then, when he finally does show up for once, she goes running over to him and jumps up on him and kisses him and tells him how happy she is to see him.

"I do everything for that child, and her father does nothing, but what she gives me can't even be measured on the same scale with what she gives him. It's like he's her real father, and I'm only her mother's husband. So, yeah, I believe that people are saying these things to you in interviews. Fathers have the greatest deal in the world. They can be the biggest jerks ever and their kids will still think they walk on water."

It was while I was in the midst of these questions about sexual politics that I conducted the interview that had been the most difficult to obtain. A friend who was a political-activist lawyer told me about a neighbor of hers named Clair, a twenty-one-year-old woman whose history seemed to guarantee that her hatred and denunciations of her father would be recited in the superlative.

Clair's father was a successful lawyer who had married and divorced his wife before their daughter was born, and who then moved out of state so his income would not be diminished by child support. When Clair was eight, her mother remarried to a defrocked priest, who began abusing his stepdaughter within months of the wedding ceremony. Clair became extremely promiscuous when she was sixteen—sleeping with dozens of men simultaneously, many of whom were twenty years older than she—and by the time she graduated from high school, she was sleeping with women.

Clair was currently living in a lesbian marriage with

a woman who was ten years her senior and the woman's nine- and eleven-year-old daughters. Clair worked as a freelance musician, was heavily involved in socialist politics and was also active in lesbian causes. In addition, Clair and her lover were in the middle of a bitter custody battle with her lover's former husband, who did not want his daughters being raised in a lesbian household and who seemed committed to spending much of his time and resources to separate the children from their mother.

My initial contacts with Clair followed a by then familiar pattern. Our mutual friend asked Clair if she would talk with me, and Clair responded affirmatively, saying it might be a "kick to talk about her old man." When I tried to arrange an appointment, however, Clair always had a meeting to go to right away, and she didn't have time to talk. After seven or eight telephone calls, Clair began having brief conversations with me, until one night we had a two-hour telephone chat and she finally agreed to see me in person.

Clair lived in a dilapidated tenant-owned apartment building in a section of Philadelphia that might have been called countercultural in the 1960s. She was a short, slightly overweight woman with very dark hair who, on the evening I visited her, was dressed in the uniform of the serious artist: a tailored black shirt that hung loosely over equally baggy black jeans, no makeup or jewelry and wire-frame glasses. The apartment was similarly unadorned. Clair's lover wasn't home when I arrived, but her children were.

I immediately assumed, given there was certain to be some discussion of Clair's sexual history, that the children would be sent off somewhere. To my astonishment, however, Clair informed me that I was to be the children's entertainment for the evening, and they pulled up chairs as I unpacked my tape recorder. The friend who had introduced me to Clair had said that Clair, her lover and her lover's children were being coached by a psychologist for an upcoming custody hearing, and I wondered if the denunciations of fathers that I was expecting to hear from Clair were part of the children's preparation.

As Clair began telling me about her childhood, she affected a wisecracking manner—ostensibly to entertain the girls and to show them this wasn't a troublesome topic—that was too forced to be genuine. I asked her if she had been excited when her mother was about to get married, and she said that she hadn't been. "My mother had this big thing when I was young that she had to get me a father. It was crucial to get me a father. It was ridiculous. Nobody really needs a father."

Yet, other then her general remarks discounting the importance of fathers—-she had said that she planned to have children some day, but the male involved would only be a sperm donor—Clair displayed none of the anger at her father I had expected. When I began probing more deeply into her feelings about her father, and she continued with the same breezy conversational tone, I finally interrupted her.

"Clair," I said, "you haven't once said that you hate your father or that you are angry at him or even called him a bad name. How can that be? He had a great job and he never paid any support for you. He has never called you or attempted to see you. Why don't you hate this man?"

"I think it was a terrible, horrible, rotten thing that he did to my mother," she said. "It may have been different if he had left my mother *and* me, but he didn't. He only left my mother. She told me he left before I was born, so it didn't have anything to do with me. I don't know my father. Anger is very concrete and he is a very abstract man to me. You can't be angry at someone you don't know."

I lost my concentration when I heard Clair speak that last sentence. Here was another incarnation of that universal bromide of the children of absent fathers—you can't miss someone you never knew. The line made sense for someone whose father was dead. It was a formidable defense against eternally longing for a man who was never going to return. But why would the child of a living father not want to feel anger at a man who had abandoned. . . . Suddenly it fell into place. In order for Clair to admit to being angry at her father, she had to acknowledge that her father had left both her and her mother, and it seemed paramount to Clair that she not recognize that her father had left her, and thus she couldn't be angry at him.

"My family always said awful things about my father, but I never thought that he was an ogre and I didn't have bad feelings toward him. And after seeing some of the obnoxious things my mother did to her second husband, I also wondered whether my father was really all terrible. To me, my father was just a man who wasn't there, and he couldn't come to see me because he lived so far away."

"But what about the telephone?" I asked in disbelief. "Why didn't he ever call you?"

"My mother flaunted the fact that my father never called me so much," she said, "that it made me wonder if he didn't call sometimes and she wouldn't let him talk to me. I think she really loved him and that she was badly hurt when he left her. I think my father was the only man my mother ever loved. I don't think she loved her second husband. With all of that stuff going down, she wouldn't have let my father see me even if he wanted to."

"Did you ever think of trying to contact your father yourself?"

"Yeah. He had an aunt who lived near us and we visited her a couple of times. I knew that she knew where he was, and I thought about getting his number from her several times. The first time was when my stepfather started treating me so badly when I was in fifth or sixth grade. He was always giving me a hard time and pushing me around and my mother wouldn't stop him. One day he wouldn't leave me alone, so I bit him. It turned out that he called my father—" Clair stopped in midsentence as she heard what she had said, laughed nervously and then quickly continued. "I mean he called my mother and said I had bit him for no reason.

"The other time I thought about calling him was when I was a teenager. I was with a lot of men who were much older than me and I was being very promiscuous and I . . . " The joking edge had slowly been melting from Clair's voice, and now it took on a pronounced quiver. "I really wanted to be in love with somebody. That's ridiculous at that age, of course. But I was insecure and I wanted that much of somebody's affection."

"I doubt that you're a Freudian," I said, "but you have to know this sounds like a classic case of a little girl looking for her daddy."

"I don't think that is true," Clair insisted. "I was involved with too many different men at the same time for that. Besides, I couldn't go out with guys who were my own age—they were so immature. The guys I was involved with were only ten years older than me on the average, and the only thing wrong with it was that the relationships were just sexual. I was being fucked over and used. What kind of thirty-five-year-old man wants to fuck a seventeen-year-old girl?

"It was during the insanity of having all of those people at the same time and not having strong feelings about any of them that I thought about contacting my father. I had a hard time ending this thing and breaking off with all of those people."

"Have you ever seen a picture of your father?" I asked.

Clair had begun gradually to slouch down in her chair as she talked about her teenage years; now she leaned forward excitedly. "Yeah," she said, "the strangest thing happened about six months ago. A friend and I went to the dental clinic at the university where my father went to law school. While I was waiting for my friend, I decided to walk over to the library and look through their yearbooks.

"It was exciting. It was such a trip. Here I am going to the dentist and I end up having this adventure. The librarian looked up my father in a directory, and it had his current address in Florida and the year he graduated. So I got the yearbook out and there he was."

"Do you look like him?" I asked.

"Not at all. I photocopied the yearbook. Want to see the pictures?" Clair laughed, hurried off to a nearby desk and returned with copies of the four pages from the yearbook that had her father's picture on them.

There was not a strong resemblance between Clair and her father in the more than thirty-year-old photos, save for one feature. "You have his nose," I said.

"Do I?" Clair beamed, obviously pleased.

Clair and I had been talking for over an hour, and during that time her lover's children had sat nearly motionless and had absorbed every word of the conversation. As the interview progressed, Clair seemed not to even notice them—she always spoke directly to me, never making an aside to them and never giving any sign that she was attempting to edit our frank conversation for their benefit. As Clair stood next to my chair and giggled over the pictures of her father in a girlish way, however, she suddenly seemed to become aware of the children for the first time, and she ordered them off to bed in an uncharacteristically harsh way.

I asked Clair how she felt about her father now.

"Pretty neutral," she said. "I feel like this person was my father, and he married my mother, but he wasn't really my father."

"But, he is still your father enough that you got excited when you saw his picture?"

"Yes," she said, "but I don't feel any connection to this person who is supposed to be so intimately tied to your life—which isn't true, of course. I would still like to see him if it wouldn't be such a hassle. I just want to see him. I don't want anything from him, and I don't know that I would want to see him more than once. I wouldn't want to develop any relationship at all. I would just like to be able to gauge what kind of person he is."

"You have his address," I said. "Why don't you go and see him?"

Before Clair could answer, the front door opened and her lover walked into the apartment carrying a set of tools from the construction job she was working. Clair told the woman she had sent the kids to bed and then passed on a few pieces of news, but she didn't introduce me. The woman sat down at a nearby table, and Clair's jocular demeanor resurfaced.

"I've put on some weight over the past couple of years," Clair said with loud and strained laughter, "but when I'm thin my mother and I look very much alike. I always though it would be a trip to go down to Florida and make an appointment to see him about a legal problem under another name and find out if he would recognize me, or tell him who I was at the end of the meeting. I'd do it, but his aunt told me he had a heart attack a number of years ago, and I'd probably give him another one."

"It sounds like you have some affection for your father," I said. "You talk about playing jokes on him and worrying about giving him a heart attack."

"Really? I don't think that's true."

"Would you feel that you were risking some personal hurt if you contacted your father and he said he didn't want to see you?" I asked on a hunch.

Clair forced an impish smile onto her face and said, "I don't know. You have any money? You want to take me to Florida and find out?"

"But you have to admit," I argued, "that the responses that you've had tonight are not the reactions of someone with mere idle curiosity."

"Maybe that's because it's something I don't talk about a lot. But, hey," Clair laughed, "let's find out. Take me to Florida. I need a vacation after this interview."

I left Clair's apartment feeling lost. In my wildest imaginings, I had never thought our conversation would have followed the course it had. Part of it may have been disappointment—an inflammatory diatribe against fathers would have made great copy for my article. What I had come away with instead was not Janice's deifications of a dead father, but what amounted to a blanket pardon of a living but absent and negligent father by a daughter who had clearly suffered in his absence.

Clair's family was working class, and there were no wealthy grandparents just up the hill to provide dancing lessons and prep schools. In fact, Clair had been offered a partial scholarship to a private school, but was forced to refuse it because her mother and stepfather couldn't pay the balance of the tuition. And the man she had lived with in lieu of her father could have been the model for the wicked stepfather in an updated fairy tale.

Clair's stepfather was a sick man, but, in general, all stepfathers were taking a beating in my interviews, and in life as well, according to my friend Frank and the remarried women I spoke with. It made me wonder if the ethereal connections that children maintained with their absent fathers were because of stepfathers or in spite of them. Children seemed to feel that stepfathers were always something less than their natural fathers, which could be written off as fantasy. But, at the same time, it didn't seem impossible to me that women who had lost at love once would be inclined to search for someone who was safer and more reliable for their second marriages. Perhaps children were taking the same tack—deciding there was less risk in remaining attached to their natural fathers in the hopes that their biological links might bring them back some day, rather than hooking onto stepfathers who, should the marriage fail, would have no reason to remain connected with the child.

There also seemed to be an issue of identity involved. Many of the people I spoke to who had stepfathers—and they were split between those whose stepfathers had legally adopted them and those who hadn't—said they had scrutinized their birth certificates at one time or another. Clair had been adopted when she was ten, and she had been happy about it at the time, but she changed her mind when her stepfather turned on her.

"When I was in high school," she said, "I discovered that my name had been changed on my birth certificate and that really upset me. My stepfather was always coming after me, and he wasn't happy unless he made me cry. The only thing that kept me sane through junior high and high school was just letting him hit me and thinking to myself, 'Okay, you can pull this crap, but I'm not your child. I'm going to grow up and move away and you can't stop me. I'm not going to be like you because you're not my father.' When I saw they had changed my name on my original birth certificate, it scared me into thinking that maybe now he really was my father, and my means of preserving my sanity was gone."

Yet when I thought about the chorus of wistful voices emanating from the children whose fathers were present—"our fathers were foreign to us too"—I found myself siding with the remarried women I had dismissed as simply being angry at men. People were giving voice to childhood fantasies in the interviews—wish projections they were draping over themselves like old money gone broke: If only my father hadn't died, or if only my mother hadn't been such a bitch and forced my father to leave, my life would be bliss.

There were all of these fine stepfathers out there—and some exceptions like Clair's—who were willing to support families they hadn't created because of their love for their new wives. These men wanted to be caring fathers to their stepchildren, and the children wouldn't let them because of impossible dreams they had concocted to explain why their lives would always be less than they should have been. Hadn't many of the people I had interviewed said—in fact, hadn't Clair, my left-wing political revolutionary said—that, as children, they had always believed their lives would be just like "Ozzie and Harriet" or "Father Knows Best," if only their fathers would have come home or if only they hadn't died.

And what of the widowed or abandoned wives? The mothers of the people I interviewed had found themselves husbandless in the 1950s or early 1960s, an era when raising a family on women's wages guaranteed ceaseless poverty. It was difficult enough for a woman with children to find a date, and these sons and daughters wanted perfect stepfathers? So what if the men who proposed weren't bemedaled heroes just back from the Pacific theater. The mothers had married such dreamboats, and the dreamboats died on the beaches or found other seas on which to sail. The new husbands were good men who would offer warmth and whom the women would come to love.

What right did dead or long-absent first husbands, or their children for that matter, have interfering with a mother's happiness? It wasn't the mothers' fault that these men had died or drifted out of town. The mothers were building something new, something with a future, to replace constructions that had ceased to exist. Women had families to raise. There was no room nor time for the ghosts of husbands gone.

CHAPTER

5

I stopped at a corner takeout place in downtown Philadelphia and bought two containers of coffee on the way to my interview with Mike. He owned a small record store nearby, and we were going to talk while he watched the place. Mike had attached conditions to the interview—he was willing to see me at the store, but not at his apartment, and only on an evening when no one else was working. The coffee was a minor gesture, but I hoped it would function as a lubricant.

I filed past the racks in the store and found Mike in the stockroom, dressed in a worn flannel shirt and jeans, with his booted feet propped up on a wooden desk. I knew from our preliminary conversations that Mike was a repatriated small-town Texan, one who seemed to have retained a chunk of his good-old-boy demeanor to hide behind when it seemed expeditious to do so. I offered him coffee, and he accepted it with more lilt in his voice than I had remembered from the phone.

Mike was a big man, six-foot-three and over two hundred pounds, with a beard and light-sensitive glasses that darkened in the sun but didn't completely clear indoors. I asked Mike about his family as I pulled a chair into his tiny office, and he said his parents had met at a military installation during the war, married and had him before divorcing when he was two in 1947. Mike's father left town, and the only subsequent contact between father and son had been a few telephone conversations over the years.

I tried to get Mike to talk about his childhood memories of his father's absence, but he was determined to tell me about his maternal grandfather instead.

"My grandfather was the most respected man in my home town," he said, "and I didn't notice much that my father wasn't there. My grandfather was the mayor and a deacon at the Baptist church, and he owned the only grocery store around. He was a very dominant type of figure whom everybody in town, including his partner, called 'mister.' No one ever thought to call him anything other than that.

"I used to spend four hours in my grandfather's church each Sunday listening to hell fire and brimstone. That made a very strong impression on me. My grandfather was bigger than Dallas up there. He was bigger than God. He was the biggest person ever to walk on two legs. My God!

"My mother and I lived with my grandparents, and every night, right after dinner, I would take a bath, get my pajamas on and crawl up into my grandfather's rocking chair. My grandfather would pull me onto his lap and put his arms around me and read me a story. He did that every night, seven nights a week, until he got sick when I was eight. My grandfather died shortly after that, but he was the hero of my childhood."

"Did your grandfather's death make you wish that your father would come back?" I asked.

"No, it wasn't until I entered puberty that I was really aware that my father wasn't around. The high school I went to was several towns away and I didn't know anyone. By coincidence, my best friend in high school turned out to be a boy whose father had died. It wasn't because we didn't have fathers that we were friends, it was just because everyone else was into sports and we weren't."

"Do you think the two of you shying away from physical activities had anything to do with your not having fathers?" I asked.

Mike pursed his lips and examined the tops of his boots on the desk for a moment before answering. "Yeah," he said, "I think you may have something there. One of the most direct things about not having a father was not having anyone to rough and tumble with. Or not being able to go home with an injury and be proud of it rather than ashamed, because you knew your mother was going to cry, whereas your father would tap you on the shoulder and say, 'Way to go, kid.' Mothers tend to be rather confused about physical combat. They expect it from their husbands and can't stand it in their sons."

The phone in the office rang. Mike answered it and had a brief conversation. "Almost everyone I know is missing a father," he continued. "This young boy whose mother just called is that way. He is going through all of this fool stuff now. He's overly aggressive and overly loud, and his mother is wringing her hands because she can't cope with him. I told her to join him up in the service, that way he'll still do the same things, but she won't be able to see him."

"You were talking about high school as being a tough time for you," I said. "What else happened then?"

"That was about the time my mother and my stepfather split up. My mother had remarried after my grandfather died. I can't say my stepfather and I didn't get along. We got along fairly well, but he was a man like Tom Landry, the coach of the Dallas Cowboys. He was very cold and unemotional, and we didn't have a warm relationship."

"So the last man you were close to was your grandfather?"

"Yes, and my relationship with my stepfather was also difficult because my mother and stepfather fought all of the time. To get away from that, I started staying away from home at night—visiting friends and stuff. I was only at home one or two nights a week when they finally got divorced. Then my mother said she was moving to Houston to get a job, and I told her that was fine, but I wasn't going with her.

"I stayed with my grandmother for a couple of months, and then I moved into this deserted army barracks with two or three other boys. The rent was only twenty-five dollars a month, and we lived there with all of these indigents.

"About this time I started to develop a drinking problem, because I wanted to show people how firmly I was on my own. I drank in the morning before I went to school, and sometimes I got so drunk I would pass out in class. And no one ever did anything about it except this one old teacher. She called me to the side one day when I was lying in the sick room with this god-awful hangover, and she said she knew that I was a good Christian boy, and that I was having some problems, but it would be over soon.

"I wasn't able to handle all of the emotional freedom I had bought myself, and trouble was just waiting for me. I discovered how easy some of my mother's friends, and some of my friends' mothers, were to fuck. I began having afternoon liaisons with the married ladies of the community when I wasn't too drunk. Here I was all alone in the world and seventeen, and these ladies would come and put my head on their breasts—and then I was home free."

"How did you manage to pull this off in such a small town?" I asked incredulously.

"Oh, hell, everybody knew." Mike laughed and paused for a beat. "I told them! I almost got caught a couple of times, but the folks in the town figured it was one of those things and let the boy grow out of it, so nobody bothered me."

"Did you ever wonder about your father during this time?" I asked.

"No, I didn't. He was the furthest thing from my mind, but it so happened that this was about when I heard from my father for the first time. I had gotten run down and I was in the hospital."

I wasn't following Mike. "You mean you were run down by a car?"

"No," he said and distractedly recrossed his legs. "I was a little run down physically. I had gotten myself in bad condition, and I was laying up in the hospital gathering strength. I had started out on the ward, but they moved me after me and this other guy got drunk and started a fight."

"You were in the hospital because of your drinking, and then you got drunk right there?"

"Yeah, we got ripped and did battle with these boys from a military school. They put me in a private room after that. About two o'clock in the morning one day a nurse came in and said there was a call for me down at the nurses' station. I got out of bed and went down to answer the phone and, for some reason, I knew it was going to be my father."

"Wait a minute," I interrupted. "How could you have

known it was going to be your father on the phone? You had never heard from him before. How could *he* have known you were in the hospital?"

Mike frowned at my question. He looked at me silently for a moment and then spat out, "I don't rightly know. I always thought my godfather knew where my father was and kept him informed of my doings. But I never inquired about that."

I didn't confront Mike, but, given the systematic way he went about getting in ever-increasing amounts of highly visible trouble—the drinking and carousing and fighting—and his suspicion that his father was monitoring his life, I understood why he wasn't surprised when his father called. Mike had assiduously pursued incapacity for months, searching always for a predicament that was inescapable, until the reports that reached his father became so hysterical the man had to respond.

"Anyway," Mike continued hastily, "I answered the phone and he said 'Who is this?' and I told him. He asked if I knew who he was, and I said yeah. We got through that exchange and those sorts of things. Then he asked how I was and what I was doing in the hospital, and I said I just needed some rest and I would be out soon. Then he told me there were a couple of places in town where you could get good moonshine whisky and that, if I ever got thirsty, I should use his name and he was sure they'd give me a drink."

"It didn't strike you as odd that, when you were in the hospital for a drinking problem, your first conversation with your father was about where to get a drink?" I asked.

Mike erupted with laughter. "No, I don't suppose it did," he drawled. "Everybody always told me I was just like my daddy, even though I never knew him.

"My father told me that he was remarried and he put his wife on the phone for a minute. Then he said he was living in California and that, if I wanted to move out with him, he would send me to college and buy me a new car. I told him, no thanks."

"Why did you do that?" I asked. "You were in a bad way, and your father came along and offered you an out."

"It would have complicated my life. I just wanted to be left alone. I didn't owe anyone anything. Things were moving along fairly well, and my father was an unknown. I had no idea who he was or what living with him would be like. I didn't need a daddy coming out of the woods and trying to buy me off. I knew what I had at the present time and I was willing to accept the burden."

I tried to imagine Mike standing in the deserted hospital corridor at two o'clock in the morning. He'd be leaning over the chest-high counter at the nurses' station to get at the phone, and pressing a finger into his free ear to blot out imagined background noise. His heart would be accelerating—his father was on the line!—but it would be crucial to sound nonchalant. He couldn't let his father know that he had been desperate to hear his voice.

Mike and his father would talk in the clipped and self-conscious sounds of nervous strangers. "Hello. Hello. How are you?"

Mike would want his father to say, "I'm sorry I left you, son. It was all a mistake, and I'm going to make it up to you. I'm going to get you out of the mess you're in, and then we'll make a fresh start. We'll rent a boat and go fishing. We'll take sandwiches and a cooler to ice the fish. I'll show you how to bait a hook. It'll be just like you were a boy again, and your daddy was taking you out to the lake."

But could a ghost of a father make that offer? Could he so absolve himself of his neglect that he wouldn't hear his son shouting, "Why didn't you call me before, you dirty bastard," whenever he considered the telephone? Could he find the self-possession to call a young man he had last seen in diapers and unashamedly announce, regardless of the actual words he used, "I failed you before, but I'm ready to be your father now?"

I didn't think so. I didn't see how a man could spontaneously become a father eighteen years after the fact, and I wondered if Mike was contriving this belated paternal solicitude so that *I* would believe that his father had loved him enough to offer him tuition and a set of wheels.

Yet perhaps the man had found a means to reach for his son, and Mike had turned his father aside because the risk was simply too great. If Mike had moved to California and his father had treated him badly, or threw him out after a month, then Mike would be confronted with what I guessed was the greatest apprehension of the children of living but absent fathers—discovering that the father had left, not because of the mother, but because he couldn't stand his children.

Mike's behavior didn't change once he got out of the hospital, and, after he graduated from high school, he flunked out of college in his third semester. Mike then joined the marines, an experience that, he says, stopped him from being a sissy and changed his life.

"As rebellious as you were, how did you ever handle the marines?" I asked.

"I had to start boot camp over three times," Mike said, "so I had a problem or two with it, but eventually I came to understand we were going to do it the Marine Corps' way."

"What was it that convinced you?"

Mike dropped his feet off the edge of the desk, sat up and pulled a book from a nearby shelf. "Turn that thing off," he ordered and pointed at my tape recorder.

It was the first time during an interview that someone had demanded I shut off my tape recorder. I complied, but I couldn't fathom what Mike might tell me about the marines that would be more intimate than our conversation had been to that point.

Mike placed the book halfway between us on his desk and silently leafed through it. It was a photo essay about marine boot camp that depicted every stereotype the institution was known for. Recruits were shown having their hair buzzed to the scalp, being forced to crawl through slime in full battle gear and being screamed at by hulking drill instructors whose faces, with straining neck veins, were pushed into the fearful eyes of the new soldiers. Mike still hadn't uttered a sound, and I wasn't sure what to say.

"This looks like a bunch of boys being forcefully stripped of their identities and remade into something else," I said. "Did you benefit from that?"

"Absolutely," Mike said. "Without my father around, it took the marines to show me how life was and to make a man out of me. Everything I am today is because of the marines and a man I studied judo with."

Mike and I had been talking for several hours, and I felt that we had just touched on something I needed to know more about. I mentioned it was late and asked if we could talk again the following week. Mike agreed.

I had answered a newspaper advertisement for substitute teachers at a suburban Philadelphia vocational-technical high school in the spring of 1979, and the vice principal asked me to come in for an interview. He was a middle-aged fellow, recently retired after serving twenty years in the military as an enlisted man, and the refrains of his soldier's life were abundant—his shoes glowed like neon, his trousers pulled into creases even while he was seated and, when he told me he would be able to use me occasionally, his words were, "Welcome to my command."

The vice principal led me through the school to show me the equipment-jammed shops and classrooms. He gestured broadly as we walked. "Vocational education has changed dramatically," he said. "Trade students are the new elite. They will always be able to get jobs, and plenty of times it will be at higher salaries than college graduates earn. Do you know what kind of money plumbers make? We have a waiting list to get into this school."

I was skeptical that shop classes could have been transformed from a repository for students who had been labeled "not suitable for further education" into a mecca for the high priests of the new technology in the few years since I had been in high school. I remembered that both the students and the teachers, who segregated themselves from the rest of the school, had been generally regarded as not being very bright. The academic students called them shop animals, and, from their clothes to their behavior around girls, they seemed never to miss an opportunity to epitomize that designation.

I asked the vice principal what kinds of backgrounds his instructors had.

"They're craftsmen," he said with pride. "Most of them have over ten years of experience in their trades, and they've gone to college nights and summers to pick up the courses they needed to be certified. These are men who know how it works in the real world, not people who read about it in a book."

The school called a few weeks later and asked me to fill in for an auto mechanics instructor who was ill. The secretary promised that I wouldn't have any problems with the students, because their regular instructor was an iron-fisted disciplinarian who kept his boys in line. I accepted the assignment but then made the mistake of wearing a sport coat to class. The students in their greasy uniforms looked at me with derision. Fortunately, however, an hour of the morning was going to be taken up with an awards ceremony for the top students in each trade.

Walking to the auditorium for the program was like being in any high school between classes: Kids met up with their friends to joke and make plans, boys flirted with girls and bullies found weaklings to pick on. It was exhilarating to be in the midst of all that raw energy.

The principal started the program, but there was so much noise most of what he said went unheard. When the first teacher took the stage, however, there was spontaneous quiet. The man was an electrician, and he wore the khaki uniform of his trade.

"We had a fair bunch of youngsters in shop this term," he said. "They fooled away a lot of their time like most kids do, but when I finally got them to work they did okay. I had to pick somebody to give an award to, and I picked Jay Scott. He's a long way from being an electrician, and I don't think I'll ever let him wire my house, but some of his projects were a little better than the rest of the boys'. If you want to come up here, Jay, I'll give this to you."

Jay, a thin boy with bad skin and ragged hair, walked to the stage with his chin almost resting on his blue work shirt as if he had done something to be ashamed of. The kids around me started to clap, but then seemed to think better of it and looked up to the stage for direction. The teacher was standing there, hands impatiently on hips, and, when Jay reached him, he awkwardly thrust out a leather belt-pouch for a hammer, mechanically shook the boy's hand and quickly pushed him toward the exit from the stage.

A few of the kids in the audience hooted and booed at Jay as he walked back to his seat. No one, not even the teachers, clapped very much. I assumed this was because of the actions of a single aberrant faculty member. But then every teacher who went to the stage did the same thing—they acted as if what they were doing, giving awards to recognize outstanding individual performance, was painful.

I wondered how the other kids would treat the boys who had been singled out. I was certain the winners would be subjected to that ancient male ritual of ball-busting— the process by which men keep other men safely in place by relentlessly harassing anyone who sticks his head out above the rest. It was the underside of machismo—the battering down of men who attempted to up the ante of attaining manhood by succeeding at anything other than simplistic physical pursuits.

I also wondered how the honored boys would behave when they went home and told their fathers about their awards. Would the students be proud? Would their fathers smile broadly at the news? Or would the fathers mimic the teachers and let their sons know that it was not good for a man to pay too much mind to himself?

One day when I was in eighth grade, the nun distributed the scores from our high school placement tests, which we had taken some weeks before. The nun called each person's name in alphabetical order, and the person went to the front of the room and received a score sheet, while the nun made a public comment on the person's performance. Other students, by urgently whispering, "What'd you get," forced each person to mouth silently his or her score to the rest of the class as the person walked from the front of the room.

I was one of the last to be called, since my family name began with a *W*, and by the time the nun got to me, my score was foretold. The results were stated in percentiles—whatever number you got meant you had scored higher than that percentage of kids in the country who had taken the test.

I belonged to the clique of popular kids in the class— I got invited to all of the parties and hung out with the others who were reasonably attractive, of slightly above average intelligence and didn't have any embarrassing habits—and the popular kids were scoring in the fifty-five to eighty range. Only the brownnosers, a half-dozen plain-looking girls whose lack of sociability was so glaring they could only be friends with each other, and three boys who were known chiefly for their effeminacy and the endless scorn it brought them, were scoring higher. Only the kids from poor families, who were regarded by us with detached pity, were scoring lower.

When my turn came, I went up to get my expected seventy or seventy-five along with a verbal jab. I was a B student but, since I was also the class clown, I knew that my score sheet would be delivered with a caustic comment. The nun handed me the paper and said in a weary and venomous voice, "This doesn't surprise me at all, William. Now if you would only learn to keep your mouth shut."

I snatched the report from her and looked at it. My score was ninety-eight.

My breath caught in my throat and blood seemed to be draining from my head. I felt happy, then scared, but I tried not to let either show. I had placed above all but one of the kids in the class whom my friends hated, and I didn't know where that left me. This could be trouble; I needed to think it through. The score could tip my friends off to the fraud that had already been committed on them. I kept my eyes down and hurried back to my desk.

My best friend, Jim, was the most popular kid in the class. He was a tall good-looking boy who was the star of every sports team. He could hit, catch, throw or dribble every kind of ball that existed, and he was universally liked and admired.

Jim and I played whiffle ball in my yard or shot pool or played ping-pong in his basement, and he always won. The score would be reasonably close, but his victories were assumed. I didn't mind losing. I wasn't an athlete, and I was grateful to be friends with such a popular kid. Yet, since Jim never gloated, I knew he liked me in spite of my lack of talent rather than because of it, and I was never sure why.

When we were in sixth grade, our class had had its first boys-and-girls party and I hadn't been invited. Jim stopped me at recess and said he was going to tell the girl who was giving the party that he couldn't come, but that she should invite me as his replacement. That way, Jim said, I would become part of the crowd and I would be invited to all future parties—and I was.

When I returned to my desk with my score sheet, I looked across the classroom to Jim. He hadn't revealed his score to the class either, and I was praying that his mark was high enough to sanction my score as acceptable. Jim arched his eyes to ask what I got. I told him and then smacked my head and jerked my shoulders to say that I didn't understand this, that perhaps someone had made a mistake.

I pointed at Jim's desk, where his score sheet rested. "Eighty," he mouthed back. My score wasn't that much higher than Jim's. Everything was going to be okay.

The final bell rang and I hurried over to congratulate Jim, but, as I approached, he said to hold up, that he had to talk to the nun. Jim walked away and left his score sheet on the top of his desk. I glanced down and the dizziness returned. Jim's actual score was fifty-two.

I knew that Jim had wanted me to see his results, but I pretended I hadn't seen them. I blathered every thought that entered my mind during our walk home so I wouldn't have to lie that the test wasn't that important or that the scores were probably invalid. I tried to think of a way I could return the favor that Jim had once done me, but I didn't know what I could do. I ricocheted between wanting to be excited about my results and feeling I could only do so at Jim's expense. As soon as we got to the point where our routes diverged, I bolted for the gas station.

I could see my Uncle Bill in the office as I ran past the gas pumps. He was sitting behind the desk making up the invoices for the cars he had repaired that day. My Uncle Bill wasn't an educated man, but he used to brag to people about my good report cards when I rode on the laundry truck with him in second grade. I shoved the door open and pulled the score sheet from my book bag in a single motion.

"Look at this, Uncle Bill," I gasped between breaths. "We had to take this test to get into high school and I scored higher than ninety-eight percent of the kids in the *country*. Not just the other kids in my class, but ninety-eight percent of the kids in the country. What do you think about that!"

My Uncle Bill listened to what I said carefully with an expressionless face. When I gave him the score sheet, he glimpsed at it with a harsh eye, then passed it back to me as quickly as if it had burned his hand. "There's not a test score in the world that will ever buy you a meal, Sport, so don't start thinking you're hot stuff," he said. "Listen, I want to you to come in early tonight. I have a meeting at the firehouse."

I refused to let my Uncle Bill's dismissal crush me. This was the first time in my life I had ever done anything better than most people, and I was going to find a male relative who would tell me it was important and that it was irrelevant if the other kids stopped liking me, because I had accomplished something bigger than what kids thought. I stalked each of my uncles and cousins at the garage until we were alone, then pounced on them with my news. "I heard," they each said, then walked away.

I was late for my second interview with Mike. I hurried into his storeroom and was about to apologize for not bringing coffee, when I saw that wasn't necessary. Mike was again stretched out with his feet on the desk, but this time he had a quart of tequila in his fist, and it was a number of good swigs short of full.

"What kind of things does a boy without a father miss?" I asked.

"The main things he misses are male teachings about

duty, honor and country, and the idea of what it is to be
a man. You miss the male direction toward maleness, because only a father can tell a son what it is to be a man.
It gets distorted when you only have women around, because then male aggression gets subverted by female immorality.

"Men have well-defined rules of conduct for situa-
tions involving conflict, competition and aggression. They
know what is acceptable and what isn't. Women aren't that
way, and they cannot be trusted."

Mike was speaking quickly, his voice getting thick, as
he punctuated his talk with draws on the tequila. I asked
him to give me an example of what he was describing.

"It's like in the family," he said. "Men don't have the
patience to deal with kids. They can only take them in
small doses, and then they have to get away from them.
I've never met a man who wasn't like that, and if I did, I
would be suspicious of him."

"What would you be suspicious of?" I asked.

"That he was a fairy, because he was acting like a
woman. Only women can be mothers, and it's the mother's job to take care of the day-to-day operation of the
family. She is in charge of the routine discipline and such
things. Women are willing to put all of their time and
energy into this, and that's fine. But when something important needs to be taken care of, the mother defers to
the father.

"The father's role is bigger than the mother's. When
she calls him in about the kids, he is either excessively
harsh or excessively good, depending on the situation.
When the father is not there and the mother tries to fill
these roles, or if the mother bothers the father about the
children too much, troubles develop because women don't
understand the rules of how these things are done."

"Is that why you aren't angry at your father for going
away and not being in contact with you?" I asked.

"I don't think my father is a bad man, if that's what

you're asking. And, I would say that my mother was responsible for my father leaving. She is a damn hard woman to live with, and if I found living with her to be that disagreeable, I think my father would have found that also.

"I'm able to understand why my father did what he had to do because it has always been very difficult for me to maintain relationships with women. I got bored with them. I don't see relationships between men and women to be particularly stable things, and that is mostly because of the immorality of women. I have never been with a woman who was trustworthy."

"Ever?"

"Ever. I lost the girl I was going to marry while I was in the marines. She had left her husband to get engaged to me, and then she got married to somebody else while I was away. A funny thing was that her father had died when she was a child, so she didn't have a father around either."

"Did your father ever tell you that your mother drove him away or that she was untrustworthy?"

"No, my father and I have never talked about my mother. He calls me on important occasions and we talk about what is happening with each of us. He called me on the day I got out of the marines and said, 'Well, I guess I don't have to worry about you anymore,' and I said that I guessed he didn't."

I thought of my Uncle Bill and the anger that would course through me when he chimed into my life when he deemed it appropriate, while standing aloof the bulk of the time. I found myself getting angry with Mike's father. "You hadn't seen the man since you were an infant," I said. "Why didn't it strike you as absurd that he would say that? Because he was acting according to male rules?"

"That's right," Mike nodded. "He said he had been moving around a lot. I asked him how my stepmother was, and he said he had to leave her along the way somewhere. I asked him what he was doing then, and he said he had bought a semi-truck and trailer and he and a friend were going out to look over some sunsets, so he might be rolling by my door one of these days. I told him that the latch string was always up and that I was in the book. That was about ten years ago now. It was the last I've heard from him."

"With your father gone, where did you learn about all of these male rules?" I asked.

"Partly from my grandfather. He was quiet, but he had an awesome temper which lent itself to harshness and violence when it was needed. He usually kept himself under rein, but when I did something awful he exploded. Once I walked to the store with a little negro boy, which was an extreme violation of the rules of conduct in my town, and when my grandfather finished with me I bet I was bleeding in a hundred places. But, after that, I understood that rule and I never broke it again.

"My grandmother was also hot tempered, but she flew off the handle in a second, whereas it took a lot to make my grandfather explode. My grandmother would call you every name in the book, throw things, and then, five minutes later, she would wonder why everyone was pissed off at her. That made for a good balance of power between them. He behaved like a man was supposed to behave, and she behaved like a woman was supposed to behave.

"I also learned some things from an uncle who never had a son. After my grandfather died, my uncle and I started writing to each other. My uncle has been deaf since he was twenty, and one of his legs is a good deal shorter than the other. He overcame this to become an engineer, and he married a widow with two children and then they had a daughter of their own.

"My uncle took up boxing and judo, and he became a black belt. I really admired him for all that he had accomplished. My grandfather had been my hero and, when he died, I transferred that over to my uncle. I wrote to him very enthusiastically until there was an incident at my grandmother's funeral.

"My uncle got drunk and started a fight. I told him to calm down, but he didn't, so I had to pick him up and carry him to bed. Well, that is the highest disgrace, when the boy has to take the man home. I was disgusted and I knew right then that I wouldn't be able to have anything else to do with him. And he hasn't attempted to get in contact with me, so I'm sure he understands that our relationship had to end after the way he humiliated himself.

"The other place I learned about the rules was from a man I studied judo with after I got out of the marines. He was about sixty when I started out with him, and he routinely whipped men who were forty years younger than himself. He had been a world champion and he had trained champions. I was a newcomer, so how was I going to get his respect and so forth and so on?"

"What is so forth and so on?" I asked.

"Affection . . . whatever. Those various emotional things that I wanted from him."

"These various emotional things, were they things you had last gotten from your grandfather when he read stories to you in his rocking chair?"

Mike waved his bottle to dismiss my question. "Whatever," he said. "Anyway, I started hanging out around his office in the gym, but he would never talk to anyone. He would sit there and smoke his pipe and play chess by himself. One day I got up the nerve to go into his office and ask how long it would take me to become a black belt. Without looking up, he said to me, 'Go in the corner and practice. Man does not chase rank. Rank follows the man.' That was the most important thing anyone ever said to me, that you don't chase what you want, you prepare for when it will find you."

"Does this apply to your father as well?" I asked. "Will you never attempt to contact him or visit him?"

"No," he said, "it's not up to me to seek him out. It's up to him to seek me out. I'm findable. He never sent me a Christmas or birthday card or present for all of those years. So if he came to town, I'd have dinner with him, but I wouldn't invite him to stay in my house, and I don't know that I'd get on a train to go see him if he was in New York. I'm willing to accept the old rascal, but I'm certainly not going to start loving him. I'll go to the funeral, but that's the only move I'm going to make between now and then."

"How do you think your father feels, knowing he has a son out there and he doesn't even know him?"

"I imagine that he feels the same way about it that I do. He probably thinks that he had all of those birthdays and his son never sent him a card, and all of those Christmases that the bastard never wrote. And he never had a picture of him when he was growing up, and he has no idea what he looked like when he was five or ten or twenty. He probably says to himself, 'That ungrateful son of a bitch, I'm not going to do anything for him.' "

"If your father came to Philadelphia, how would you feel about seeing him?"

"I'd be nervous as a cat. Curious and nervous with anticipation about what I was going to see, but I wouldn't let myself be either optimistic or pessimistic. I wouldn't start expecting anything. I'd probably worry about it and then go get soused."

"In seeing your father, would you be seeing yourself to any extent?"

"Sure. Oh, Christ, yes. Even in his absence I've apparently grown up to be very much like him. Blood will out."

CHAPTER

6

It is impossible for me to see myself as someone a man could love or desire," Abby said as we walked from the dining area of her apartment. "I'm quite self-confident about my other talents and abilities. I have plenty of close male friends and co-workers, and I think I have enough going for me that, when I meet new people, I can make almost anyone like me without being insincere. But when it comes to male-female relationships—boy, then all bets are off."

Abby was a tall, thin and delicately pretty college professor with fine blond hair that touched her shoulders. She had just turned thirty-two and had never been married. "I believe," she said, "that a little girl either learns from her father at a certain time that she is attractive and desirable, or she doesn't. And if she doesn't, then she can never believe it. For God's sake, if your own father couldn't love you, how could any man?

"I sometimes think that, although I'm not attractive, I might be an interesting enough person so that someone could love me. But then I realize it doesn't mean anything for a man to say he loves you. Both my father and my stepfather said they loved me. I don't think they did, but maybe they thought so. Yet even if a man thinks he loves you, it doesn't count for anything. Saying they loved me certainly didn't stop my father and my stepfather from abandoning me.

"I recently went through two brief but very intense relationships in one calendar year. They both barely had a chance to get started—they were still in the white heat stage—before they were over. These men fell in love with me, and they tell our mutual friends they are still in love with me, but that didn't stop them from walking out for artificial reasons—one because he was Jewish and I wasn't, and the other because he was transferred by his employer.

"I went through the worst depression I have ever experienced after that. I started dreaming about my father and my stepfather and about how my mother was always alone. And I realized, especially with my father, that getting loved by a man doesn't mean anything. Even if I could be pretty enough for a man to love me, he still wouldn't want to stay with me. Even if he said he loved me, he could go ten years without calling me and it wouldn't bother him."

The milieu that Abby had created for our interview was the warmest I had spoken to anyone in. She had prepared a preinterview lunch of salad, smoked fish, delicate wheat crackers with jam served from ginger jars and

brewed decaffeinated coffee. We had then moved into the
living room where classical music was playing softly on
the stereo, and neatly framed art posters and prints
brightened the walls.

Abby had fed me and insured my comfort, yet, as
we talked, the mood of the room kept shifting. The hospitality stayed, but it became cloaked with an overlay of
something far less genteel—need. I had come seeking another component for my story. But during this and other
interviews, my need began to appear trivial in relation to
that of Abby and the others who sat on the opposite side
of the tape recorder.

People would recall earlier parts of their lives, and
time would fold in on itself. The present moment would
halt and fade for them, and anger would ease into their
conversations—first as a remark: "I was furious when my
stepfather forgot my birthday," and then ire would become the gist of their talk: "My mother didn't love me
enough." Always, though, the outrage would ultimately
give way to yearnings.

For Janice and others the neediness emerged in college; for Clair at sixteen in promiscuity; for Mike and
Abby at puberty. People would have questions at these
times about who they were, and the answer would be that,
whoever they were, it was not enough, as their stepfathers or mothers had not been enough. As nothing had ever
been enough to quench what seemed to be obsessive, but
undefined, need.

It was odd to find myself thinking about Mike and
Abby in the same terms. Other than their missing fathers,
the two appeared to have nothing in common. Abby was
a decidedly sophisticated and refined woman, while Mike
was a purposefully raw man. The demeanors of the interviews reflected the disparities of the subjects—Mike was
quick to take offense and offend, while Abby's need to
please crowded on obsequiousness. The hook that seemed

to catch them, though, was a doomed compulsion to convince themselves they were male or female enough, or
anything enough, really.

"What my distrust of men means," Abby continued,
"is that when I see a friendship with a man starting to get
romantic, I have to defend myself against the man having
an effect on me, so I won't be hurt. My sister, who is two
years older than me, is just the opposite. She has jumped
into bed with every man who has ever looked at her since
she was a teenager. She is in her second marriage and
she continues to have affairs and boyfriends. She has
brought boyfriends to family parties while she was married, and she has given money to men when she didn't
have enough money to live on herself.

"I think the difference in the ways we relate to men
is rooted in how we responded to our father's absence.
My sister has always loved my father, and I have always
hated him. My father was an alcoholic, and, when I was
four and my sister was six, his drinking apparently got so
bad my mother had to take us and leave the state. We
were living in Florida and we moved to Virginia. My
mother planned for us to live off of some money she had
inherited, but, when she went to get the money, she discovered my father had spent it without her knowledge.

"My mother was able to make a go of it for a while,
but then things got bad for her and she . . . she. . . ."
Abby stopped talking and clutched the front of her neck.
"I can really feel my throat tightening up here . . . this
is still hard to talk about. My mother had to, ah, she . . .
things caught up with her and she had to put us in an
orphanage for a year when I was seven.

"I don't remember much of that except an enormous and total sense of anger and isolation and a complete lack of control. There was a feeling that this could
well be it—that . . . that the world could end at any moment.

"I blamed my father for this happening to us, but

my sister blamed my mother—she claimed that my mother drove my father to drink.

"After we had been in the orphanage for a year, my mother married another man and they came and got us. I think she married him as much to get us out of there as anything, because he turned out not to have been a very good choice for her. But in the beginning I felt that there was a new man who might help us fix things, and, because of that, if he could love my mother that would be wonderful. I began to feel there was a chance life was going to start working for us.

"When my stepfather came home from work, we would all stop what we were doing and run out to greet him. I didn't do this because I had gotten to know him and to love him so deeply, because that never happened, but because of hope. He was quite taken with the idea of having a family, so he adopted us. My father never put up any resistance; he gave his permission right away. We changed our last name, which should have been weird, but I didn't mind at all because we were going to be a new family.

"My stepfather had his own business, and we lived in a beautiful split-level house. He bought my mother a Cadillac. He was just crazy about my mother, but I don't think I ever had a personal conversation with the man in my life. He was only interested in my sister and me to the extent that we were part of the package my mother came with.

"After we had been living with him for about a year and a half, my mother came in one morning and woke my sister and me up and told us to pack our clothes. We were back in Florida by nightfall. Apparently my stepfather had slapped my mother once and knocked her out of a chair, and she had told him that if he ever did it again she would leave, and he had hit her the night before.

"My mother was very direct with my sister and me

when she talked about our stepfather, and how their marriage had been a bad one, but she was very careful when she talked about my father. She would tell us that he was a bright and handsome man with a lot of charm. I think she did that because she really had loved him and because she wanted to establish some grounds for a relationship with us in case my father ever tried to pursue one, which he never did.

"I saw some pictures recently that were taken of my sister and me shortly after my mother separated from my father. It was Easter and we had on these dresses that were ridiculously too large. They were hanging off at the neck, and the waists were almost to our knees. I said something to my sister about where did we ever get those dresses, and she said our father had sent them to us. I thought that was so appropriate—he sent his daughters dresses and he didn't have the slightest idea what sizes we wore.

"I didn't even remember that, but it was one of the few things my father ever did for us. Nonetheless, my sister idolized him. But I sure didn't. I can recall just hating him. I don't know how it built or grew, but my attitude toward my father was completely cynical and harsh. After a while people didn't discuss him around me because they knew how vehement my reaction was going to be."

Abby's expressions of hatred for her father were so stark and aggressive they made me uncomfortable. I involuntarily pulled back from her, as animosity poured from her mouth in torrents. She was talking without pause, and her words rang with bitterness that fed on itself.

I didn't tell Abby she was the first person I had spoken with who had expressed outright hate for a missing or dead father. I wanted to see where she would take the conversation of her own volition. I wondered how hating her father had colored Abby's life, and if her paternal bitterness was related to her doubts about her femininity, or if this anger might have allowed her to escape other aftereffects of her father's absence?

By spending so much time propounding her boundless hatred for her father, however, Abby was also avoiding talking directly about him. It seemed plausible to me that she might be bluffing me with a childhood deceit. Maybe Abby thought the best defense was indeed a good offense, and she had discovered that her shrieks of hatred frightened people from discussing a man she missed more than she wanted to concede. I invited Abby's father into the conversation by asking Abby if she had ever met the man.

"When I was eleven years old, I was supposed to go on a school trip to Atlanta. My father was living there at the time. On the morning I was to leave, I woke up with the flu—or maybe it was something I had eaten—and I decided that I was too ill to make the trip. But then I was fine by mid-morning, and I was disappointed that I couldn't go because I had missed the bus. My mother called my father at work and they put me on a plane or a bus or something, and my father picked me up and dropped me off where my group was . . . none of this is clear, because I have absolutely no memory of it."

I thought of my interview with Mike, and how his self-induced illness had produced his first contact with his father. "Had there been some previous arrangements that you were going to see your father while you were in Atlanta?" I asked.

"Oh, no," Abby said. "I was going to be with my schoolmates the whole time."

"But you knew your father was in Atlanta?"

"Yes."

"What do you think about your getting temporarily sick on the morning you were going to visit the city where your father lived, and that this illness produced your first meeting with your father since your parents had separated?" I asked.

Abby flinched and clamped her hand over her mouth. "I've never thought of that," she said. "I also think it's interesting that I can't remember any of this, because by that age you certainly remember things that happen to you. I feel like I must be talking about someone else, that's how blank my memory is. This must have been *very* frightening to me.

"Wait . . . he only picked me up and dropped me off. . . . Oh, I do remember something. I remember being afraid that I wouldn't recognize him and I did. Mom may have shown me a picture of him before I left."

"And he recognized you?"

"Yes. I'm sure that Mom must have sent him pictures. I know that she would have done things over the years to encourage him to be in touch. I can remember . . . I can remember this really pissing me off too . . . I can remember when I was in junior high my sister went up to spend a month with him, and he got out some pictures to show us . . . God, did you hear that? I just said my sister went to visit him, and then he showed *us* some pictures. I went with my sister that time, but it is so strange—it feels like it was another person who was there.

"I remember some of this. My father asked us to come for the summer. I didn't want to go and my sister very much wanted to go, so we compromised and went for a month. I didn't enjoy it. It was extremely hard to deal with both wanting him to be a father and feeling this tremendous hate and anger at him. He had school pictures of us from every grade that my mother had sent him, and it made me furious that she did that and he didn't even respond. It was so phony—him acting like he cared when he really didn't. He didn't know the first thing about us. Nothing went right.

"I read this poem that I really liked and I showed it to my father because I wanted to share it with him. It was about a man who was searching for meaning in his life, and he went to all of these places and couldn't find it.

Finally he was called home to the death bed of his child, and he realized the answer he was looking for was in the child. My father got livid when I showed it to him. He called my mother that night and screamed at her that she shouldn't allow me to read things like that.

"The odd thing is I went through an extended illness the next year. I had real growing pains and these weird headaches that would produce strange thoughts that were like hallucinations. I would get disoriented and lose my sense of where I was. They thought I had rheumatic fever, but I didn't, and they never were able to figure out what was wrong with me. It gradually went away as I got older."

As Abby talked, I could see that her ability to hate her absent father had done nothing to mitigate his influence on her life. She was recounting symptoms much like those I had experienced when I thought I had a brain tumor; she had gone to the trouble of creating an illness so she could meet the man she claimed to despise; she had shown him a poem that was a blatant cry for attention; and our interview seemed to be reaching an impasse, as her memory continued to fail her and she insisted she couldn't recall any other aspects of her two adolescent meetings with her father, one of which lasted for a month.

I had begun these interviews with what I took to be a well-founded belief that biological fathers couldn't be as important to people as my early findings indicated, and that good stepfathers could become true father replacements. My steadfastness on the former point was being battered by the stories I was hearing and the tears I was seeing shed. It had once been easy for me to dismiss the mythological proportions to which people had inflated their absent fathers as childhood fantasy. It was now impossible to overlook so adroitly the outsized shadow Abby's father had cast over her memory.

The interviews were becoming emotionally exhausting contests in which people, under my probing, would approach the hole of fatherlessness within their lives, only to retreat from it, often in terror, as they detected that something was alive within that abyss, and it was looking out at them. I was beginning to question whether I would ever learn what the darkness concealed.

"I didn't even bother to think about my father very often after that," Abby continued, "because he was obviously not worth the trouble. Everything was going along fine, and then one day, when I was in college, my father's second wife called me, all angry, and said that my father had lung cancer and he had just had a heart attack and why hadn't I been in touch with him? I blew my top. I said, 'Why wasn't I in touch with him? Why hasn't he been in touch with me?' I was ready to kill. I told her I would come to see him, but I don't want to hear any shit about why haven't I been in touch with him.

"I talked to my mom about my father, and I told her I realized that he would never be a father to me, but that, as sick as he was, maybe his life had been punishment enough, and if I could bring him any comfort maybe I should. It was no skin off of my teeth. I had nothing left to lose with him by then, so I called and told his wife that I would come that summer."

"So you were going to see him exclusively for his benefit then? There was nothing in it for you?"

"No," Abby said evenly, "there wasn't anything in it for me. I simply felt sorry for him. I had hated my father for so long that I thought it was time for some compassion. I had managed to create a pretty good life for myself. I had certainly survived whatever he had done to us a lot better than my sister had. At least I didn't have that constant hunger for men my father left her with. And my father's own life was so impoverished I knew that I had to find a way to deal with my anger so I could be his friend."

Abby was a bright, determined and resourceful

woman, and I didn't doubt that she had possessed the same attributes during the period, a decade earlier, we were discussing. Yet I was apprehensive about what she said. She was talking about caring for and understanding her father as though she were the parent and he the child. I couldn't reconcile, given the imperial qualities I had heard people attribute to their absent fathers, that someone who hadn't received such care from her father could reflexively put aside her rage at that loss, and then make a gift to her father of precisely what he hadn't given her. The voices I had heard echoing out of the hollows of fatherlessness were too primal to allow for this polite and reasoned generosity.

"I went to visit my father that July. I got to his house on a Tuesday evening, and the following day my mother had a stroke and I had to leave immediately, so we really didn't have a chance to talk. My mother died a day after I got home. With all of the pain and confusion around her death, and knowing all of the sadness my father had caused my mother, I didn't get back to his place that summer.

"I stayed in closer touch with my sister after my mother died. She had always maintained some contact with my father, so I started hearing more about him, and it was all bad. His second wife left him because of his drinking, and then he went to live with my sister and her husband. That was a real eye-opener for my sister. She always idolized my father, but she came to loathe him very quickly, and she threw him out of her place.

"About two years later I realized that I was still haunted by my father, and I decided I needed to make peace with him. I talked about it with a good friend and decided that I was going to visit my father in South Carolina that spring. I don't know how he ended up in South Carolina or anything, but, a month before I was to visit him, I got a call that he had been rushed to the hospital. So many things were wrong with him that I don't even know what happened. I dropped everything and jumped on a plane, but it was no use. My father was dead by the time I got there.

"I was consumed with anger when I got off the plane and my father's second wife told me that he had died. I couldn't feel anything but rage. I was furious at him that he had died and left me with so little to mourn. My life did not change one iota when my father died. Not one thread, not one detail, would be different because of his absence. That is a pathetic thing to be able to say about your father—that he died and left you nothing to mourn.

"I had been planning to see him—to try and fix things between us—and I was infuriated he would die like that. All I kept thinking was, 'You bastard, you went and died on me. I should have guessed you would do that. Anything to make sure it didn't work out.'

"I was going to give him a chance to love me as an adult. It would have been easy then. I didn't dribble green beans anymore. I didn't spit up. I didn't wet my diapers. There was no mess at all. I wouldn't have been any trouble. I was a grown-up little kid who would be easy to love."

Abby's ability to hate her father had come at the price of concluding that her father had left her, something the others I had spoken to couldn't or wouldn't concede as children and weren't going to risk learning by contacting their fathers as adults. Abby seemed to have decided she had been such an oozing, puking mess of a child that she had driven her father away. Once she had grown up and learned to control herself, however, that explanation for her father's estrangement was no longer tenable. Abby knew that, if she was ever going to find out if she was lovable, she was going to have to journey to her father's doorstep and attempt to win back his heart.

Abby had procrastinated and procrastinated—what would she do if he turned her away?—and then the telephone rang. Her father was dying, and fear was displaced by desperation. Abby darted for an airplane, but, by the time the flight landed, she had lost not only her father, but also her last chance to discover whether she was someone a man could love.

"My sister arrived at my father's shortly after I did," Abby said, "and we decided that we were going to drive to Florida to visit our paternal grandfather rather than stay for the funeral. My grandfather was about ninety and too old to travel to the services, but he had never forgotten my sister and me. He never missed a birthday or Christmas. He would always send a card with a dollar in it, even through I had only met him a few times in my life. He was a dear.

"My grandfather was really surprised and happy that we came, and he got out photographs he had taken of us when we were babies. He had a wood-burning stove going, and he had on a heavy wool shirt, and, at one point, he got hot and pushed up his sleeves, and I looked at his arms in the glow of the fire.

"I have almost no body hair at all, except for this one patch of very long, thin hair on my arm. It used to embarrass me when I was a kid and I would trim it. When I looked at my grandfather's arm, I suddenly realized where that hair came from. I pushed my sleeve back, and then I reached over and tugged the hair on his arm and said, 'Grandpa, you're the one who gave me this hair on my arm.' It was the sweetest moment.

"I flew home from Florida in a catatonic state. I was so overwrought I didn't know what to feel. The plane was almost empty, and I stretched out over a couple of seats and pulled my coat over me. I had my eyes half-closed, and a male attendant came down the aisle and, thinking I was asleep, very quietly reached up, got a blanket and covered me with it.

"I hadn't cried once through that whole weekend," Abby said with bitter sadness in her pursed lips and in her voice. "But when that man, in such an anonymous way, did something so caring, it undid me. I just laid there and let the tears run down my face. I must have cried for twenty minutes. All I could think about was that if my father had remained the man my mother said he once was, he would have been a wonderful father."

Abby lowered her eyes and fell silent, suspended in the memory of her confrontation with irrevocable loss. Her repose provoked thoughts about my Uncle Bill. For most of my childhood he had paid some attention to me— he had taken me on his delivery trips and to local high school football games—but, as I grew, either he became indifferent or my destitution flourished. And as a teenager who couldn't recognize the obligations of an uncle to a nephew were finite, I became sullen and embittered.

I didn't cross paths with my uncle frequently after I graduated from high school and quit the gas station. When I did, though, our encounters were more emotionally kaleidoscopic than ever. My future brother-in-law's automobile broke down while he was visiting my sister one weekend, and we towed the car to my uncle's garage and began disassembling it without requesting permission. The fight that ensued upon my uncle's unexpected arrival was nearly as ugly as a subsequent clash over a telephone call.

I had made a fifty-cent long-distance call during a visit to the gas station one evening, and, after an investigation, my uncle identified me as the person responsible for the charge that appeared on his phone bill. Uncle Bill waved me into his office when I stopped to buy gas, presented me with the invoice and asked what gave me the right to use his telephone. I wanted to say—no, holler— "This nonsense is about fifty cents? I worked here for six years. You're my uncle," but I didn't. I stared at him with defiance, pulled two quarters from my pocket, flung them onto the floor and left.

My uncle became ill from a seemingly undiagnosable illness when I was a sophomore in college. He would spend a month in a suburban Philadelphia hospital and be released, only to be readmitted ten weeks later. Each time he came home thinner, grayer, gaunter—as though he were being hollowed out—and his visible infirmity warded me off as if it were contagious. I buried my face in a book or left the room when he arrived at family gatherings, never saying more than hello.

Uncle Bill didn't improve, and the doctors sent him to a university hospital in the city. I hadn't visited him once since the inception of his illness. I knew I should— this was getting serious—and I was going to, but then I left my marriage and Uncle Bill did it to me again. News of the impending divorce reached the hospital, and my mother returned from her visits with word that my uncle was "going to sit me down and give me a good talking-to when he got home. He was going to tell me a few things and set me straight."

Fuck you, Uncle Bill, I said to myself. You're nobody to me. You're not telling me anything.

I decided then I would never go to the hospital. It was time to extricate this failure of a surrogate father from my life. I was a man with a son of my own now, and I wasn't going to let a sick old man in a hospital interfere in my life—or my son's life. We would get along just fine without him. Neither of us needed him.

My uncle's wife spoke to me. "Your Uncle Bill said last week, 'Billy hasn't come to see me since I've been sick.' "

I jerked my shoulders and said silently, Screw your husband, lady.

The next month Uncle Bill died of cancer. He was forty-four.

I didn't cry at the viewing. I had promised myself that I wasn't going to cry or think about my uncle any- more. He was just another dead man, and I was relieved that he wouldn't be a nuisance anymore. The viewing felt as if it were going to last forever—my uncle had a lot of friends—so I stood on the porch of the funeral home and smoked Luckies in my dark blue high school graduation suit.

It was July and the church was hot during the funeral. I hadn't been to mass in a couple of years, and I couldn't wait for this one to be over. The priest said more prayers at the cemetery. I was muttering, "Let's go. Let's go," and it was nearly finished when, unannounced, a navy honor guard, that must have crept into the cemetery after we arrived, fired a twenty-one gun salute.

The sharp report of the weapons tore into the silent air and bounced from tombstone to tombstone. Blam . . . blam . . . blam. Each blast got louder, the mounds of clean dirt around the grave not absorbing the sound. The noise obliterated the surroundings, and I could sense only the echoes of the guns as they assaulted me. Then the barrage stopped and something started burning hotly in my chest and tears gushed from my eyes. I quickly felt along the front of my shirt to find the bullet hole, but it wasn't there. There was no blood, so I cried over a wound I couldn't find.

My interview with Abby had reached its intrinsic conclusion. Abby's father's death had put her in the same position as myself and the people I had spoken to whose fathers had died—that of wanting something from a man who was no longer able to provide it. I felt sad and was suddenly anxious to leave. I had heard enough for one evening. I asked Abby, as a parting question, if she saw any possibility of redeeming her experience through her own children, should she have any.

"I would want my husband to pay a lot of attention to my daughters if I have them, but I think it would also threaten me—especially when the girls were turning into young women, because that was when I felt my father's absence the most. I would want my husband to help my daughters through that period so they came out of it believing in themselves and their femininity. I still don't believe in myself, and I don't think I ever will.

"I would want my husband to do that for my daughters, but it would be murder for me to see him giving them something I still need but am now too old to really hear. The whole business of having children after not having a father is tricky. You want to give them what you didn't have, but you don't want them to get what you didn't get."

The rancor of Abby's last remark caught me off guard and stayed with me. Removed from the context of the interview, the sentiments she expressed reeked of pettiness and small-mindedness, certainly not qualities I would have attributed to the woman before she uttered those words. I probably would have disregarded the statement as being a throwaway phrase at the end of a long and wearing interview, save for one thing—my older sister had once expressed the same strong feelings to me about having a daughter. It was late Thanksgiving evening in 1981, a few hours after my confrontation with my mother, and I was sipping the last of my brandy at the kitchen table while my sister and I quietly reminisced.

I had been a rebellious and difficult adolescent, but Helen Marie had been the quintessential good daughter. She had been elected May Queen by her seventh-grade class—an honor bestowed on the girl who best exemplified the values of the Virgin Mary—and she had never even skirted anything that could have sullied the family name.

My older sister's kindness was such that, after she lent me her car one snowy evening when I was a teenager, and I proceeded to crumple a fender on it, she hadn't gotten angry at me—then or when it took me months to come up with the money to pay for the repairs, while she was forced to drive around in a badly damaged car.

"There is one way that I can think of that Dad's death affected me," Helen Marie said. "Other women have often remarked to me that it was a shame my kids were all boys, or that I must regret not having had a daughter.

"Well, I never felt that way. I'm happy I've never had a daughter," she said. Her voice jumped a pitch and her eyes beamed malice—as if I were one of the women she was referring to, and I had insisted her life was seriously flawed without a daughter.

"I wouldn't ever want to share my husband with another female," she said.

CHAPTER

7

Robert and I traveled in the same professional circles. That may have been why I was hesitant to interview him. He was the first person I had been able to locate who had reunited with his father as an adult, so I knew it was important for me to talk with him. He volunteered whenever I saw him, and I kept insisting I would call, but I never did. Then Robert telephoned one night and said he had taken a job halfway across the country, and he was leaving in a week.

Robert's parents had divorced when he was two, and he hadn't had any contact with his father for the following thirty-four years. On the seven or eight occasions that

Robert and I had casually discussed our absent fathers, I
had never asked him how he came to meet his father or
what the outcome of their reunion was.

I turned the wrong way onto a familiar one-way street
driving to Robert's apartment that night. I was jumpy and
having trouble concentrating. The distraction was my
wondering if, through Robert's description of his first
contact with his father, I was going to meet up with
prey that I had been stalking for months—the sometimes
exalted and always ominous would-be deity—the absent
father.

Robert led me into his apartment, seated himself in
an armchair and plunged his attention into a large cardboard box on the floor in front of him. The carton was
filled with carefully organized documents—letters, legal
briefs and accumulations of official-looking papers—that
Robert had obviously been studying before I arrived. The
orderliness of the piles was in decided contrast with the
disarray that prevailed in the remainder of his living room.
Robert was a writer, and there were books and magazines
and newspaper clippings haphazardly stacked everywhere—material he excused away as important reading
he was going to get to soon.

Robert had been enthusiastic to the point of insistence whenever we had discussed the possibility of doing
an interview, but, now that the time was at hand, he was
fidgeting and eyeing the box of meticulously kept papers.
He gazed at them as if they provoked a perilous sense of
déjà vu. He fingered the documents with wary familiarity
and then eased into the interview by commenting on what
he had amassed.

"I was born in 1943," he said. "Here is the divorce
decree—that went through in 1946. I have letters he sent
her; telegrams she sent him. I sort of remember being in
the courtroom when some of this was going on. They get
married in late '42. She is ten years older than him. He
gets sent overseas and doesn't come back until '45, which

is when he meets me. He is back one month and then he is thrown out when he admits to having lived with a woman while he was stationed in France.

"It is real hard to determine if there is any memory of him. I suspect what happened was that the boy proceeded to fantasize about his father. It is difficult to say if what I remember is fantasy or not. Do I have any conscious memory from that time? No. Maybe this is just stuff I want to pretend isn't there. Yeah, I'm sure that's it, because I can feel myself getting sad. That boy must have wondered who his father was and why he wasn't there."

Robert slipped into the third person when talking about himself as a child as easily as Abby had remembered her childhood visit with her father as having happened to someone else. And Robert only referred to his father as his father when he was using the third person— the rest of the time his father was simply 'him.' It was a curious phenomena, yet I imagined it was as effective as Abby's selective amnesia in separating Robert from memories that could make sleep difficult.

"When I started going to school, my mother told me to tell the other kids my father had died in the war, even though I knew that wasn't true. Privately, I was told that my father was no good; that he refused to pay child support; that he was into wine, women and song; that I had numerous brothers and sisters all over the world; that he didn't love me or care about me; that my mother had no idea where he was or how to contact him; and that he had tried to kill me with a gun he had brought back from the service.

"I was suspicious of what I was being told because I was raised by people who were suspicious of everyone and everything, so I became suspicious by osmosis. My mother and the two unmarried aunts who lived with us wouldn't say much about their own family or parents, but they said bad stuff about my father. A great big chunk of me believed what they said—I was a kid and they were the only family I knew—but another part of me questioned whether it was true or not. That used to give me nightmares.

"I used to have this dream when I was a kid. I was in a train station with my mother and all of these anonymous people were walking around in the background. Suddenly, this man who is a decrepit bum is crawling across the floor toward us, and when he gets close, he reaches up and touches my mother's ankle. I jump off of the bench and stomp on his hand real hard, and then he cries out, 'Robert, I'm your father.' That scares the life out of me, and I take off running down this never-ending flight of stairs, screaming, 'Jesus, I touched my father.'

"I went to a grade school in New York that was a block long and had a thousand students. One day, when I was in first grade, these older kids came up to me and said there was a man in the school yard who said he was my father, and he was looking for me. I started tearing around like crazy looking for him, but I couldn't find him because I didn't know what he looked like. My mother wouldn't show me a picture of my father. If I had had a picture, I would have known what to look for. I used to walk around New York looking at men and wondering if they were my father. I always hoped that I would be able to meet him some day.

"I now know *it was* my father who was looking for me that day. He had come to the school and asked the principal if I was a student there. She wouldn't tell him. She said that she would neither confirm nor deny anything. So my father waited outside the school at lunch time, and waves of kids came pouring out, and he couldn't find me because he didn't know what I looked like. He hadn't seen me since I was two, so he waited there and walked around looking at all of the kids, and then he gave up and left.

"When I was about eight or nine, we were living in this first-floor apartment in New York. It had a louvered door outside of the front door, and my mother would leave the inside door open so air would come in through the louvers in the summer. One night my mother motioned to me to be quiet because there was a person outside the door. She acted as if it were someone of great significance, and he was trying to see in through the door.

"I was scared. All I could see was a pair of men's shoes outside, and there was this sense of menace. We are living in an apartment building in New York City and someone is standing outside and looking in at us. There was silence on both sides of the door, and then I said, 'Is that my father out there?' The man hurried away from the door, and my mother screamed at me and said that it may have been my father coming to kill both of us.

"For a long time the only tack I took with my mother was to keep saying to her: Tell me about my father. There was this little boy and he wasn't going to give up until he met his father. But I was just banging my head on the wall with my mother. She kept saying he didn't care about me and she was the one who was feeding me and providing for me. She said she didn't know where my father was or how to get in contact with him. Sometimes she would tell me that if I tried to find my father he would only attempt to kill me again.

"I didn't see a picture of my father until I got married in 1968. My mother walked up to me at the reception and handed me this picture. It was like, okay, you're married now, I can show you his picture. She had that fucking picture since 1942," Robert said, and slammed his right fist into his left palm, "and she wouldn't show me the goddamn thing."

I had heard many stories, from both men and women, about the often vexatious relationships between children and their mothers, and between ex-wives and husbands, in the aftermath of divorce. But the bile that Robert's mother heaped on the name of her ex-husband was unmatched. I doubted that Robert's father had tried to kill him, and I was appalled that a mother would say something so malicious to her son. At the same time, though, the interminable tales of hateful mothers weren't leading anywhere. I wanted to hear about fathers.

"Robert," I interjected, "suppose your mother had sat you down one day and given you a few pictures of your father, maybe told you a few things about their courtship and marriage and then arranged for your father to come visit you for a couple of hours? Would that have been enough? Would you have been satisfied then?"

Robert looked at me and smirked. "Obviously not," he said.

"Then what is it you wanted from your father that made you so obsessive about him? What did you need so desperately that it caused you to badger your mother long after you knew she wasn't going to oblige you?"

Robert cupped his hands over his face, then drew them back heavily across his cheeks. The stubble of his beard bristled against his palms in the empty silence of the room.

"Why didn't she tell me he was dead? That would have solved everything for her. . . ."

Robert trailed off into an aimless monologue about his mother as though I hadn't just asked him, quite pointedly, what he had wanted from his father as a child. I thought of Abby and her stern insistence that she had gone to visit her father only for his sake; of Mike and his stammering when I had asked what he wanted from his judo instructor; and of Clair and her nervous laughter when I had inquired about why she hadn't contacted her father when she obviously wanted to.

I was once again at the edge of the void—the emotional black hole where the unspoken terrors of childhood were held in abeyance. I suspected the others I had spoken to had, during our interviews, come as close to entering that zone of unconsciousness as they ever would. But Robert was different. He had leapt off the edge and into the shadows. He had faced down his father. I wanted to know what he had found looking back at him.

"With my mothers and my aunts I was surrounded by femaleness," Robert said, still coursing a route away from my question. "They were always giving me things— food, toys, clothes. I felt like I was drowning. I have childhood memories of hating my mother. I can remember making a fist and repeating to myself, 'I hate her. I wish she was dead.' All of these women were smothering me."

"I hung out at my uncle's gas station to escape the femaleness of my house," I said. "Didn't you have any male relatives around? What about teachers or coaches?"

"Coaches?" Robert blurted out. "Are you kidding me? She wouldn't let me play sports. She even went to my school and lied to them that I had a heart condition so I couldn't take gym classes. I was her precious little boy. She wasn't going to take a chance on me getting hurt.

"There was a certain point in my childhood where I just turned. I was a skinny kid and all of a sudden I got pneumonia and blew up like a balloon and I remained a balloon. I was overcome with despair. Thirteen, fourteen, fifteen—those were not good years for me. I hid within the folds of my skin. I hated her. I hated school. They were real downbeat times."

Robert looked away from me and breathed a loud sigh. "I was in therapy once," he said, "and the shrink told me I had been molested as a child. That, even though no one ever laid a hand on me, there were such erotic overtones to the way all of the women in my house treated me as a child that the effect was the same as child abuse."

I surprised myself by not recoiling in horror and disbelief at Robert's remarks. I had been extremely skeptical, many months before, when I saw that a large body of the research on father-absent childhoods had a sexual component. I had resisted that information on the grounds that it was unreconstructed Freudian thinking on childhood Oedipal complexes. This theory had been widely questioned as stemming more from Freud's Victorian era than from anything that actually occurs in childhood. I couldn't grant that there was enough sexuality in childhood for a child to be sexually attracted to the parent of the opposite sex, even if the same sex parent was missing. I still didn't believe that, but I had heard enough about lifelong doubts about femininity and masculinity, overly warm embraces from stepparents and homosexual activity to intuit that, in father-absent households, and especially those with only one child, something at least pseudosexual was often at work.

"Did you go out with girls when you were a teen-ager?" I asked.

"Not much. I didn't start going out until I was sixteen or seventeen. I was fat and I didn't think that girls would find me attractive. Most of the dates I had were ones that my mother or aunts arranged for me with these nice safe girls.

"I went out with this older girl who was real hot to trot when I was home from college once. I asked my mother not to be home that night, but of course she was. We went into the dining room and closed the door, and this girl starts putting the make on me. Then the door flies open and it's my mother asking, do we want any soda? The girl starts giggling and I'm trying to shrivel under the chair. The door closes and the girl takes up where she left off. The door opens again, and my mother asks if we would like some ice cream. I was dying."

"Robert," I asked, "why would you ever take a girl home to sleep with when you certainly knew that any mother of that era, let alone one like yours, would act exactly as your mother did?"

Robert shrugged and fell quiet. I let the pressure of the silence build in the hope that it would force him to continue, but it didn't. "When did you start thinking about your father again?" I asked.

"In college," he said. "I went away to school in Kansas, and I began running around after all of the male teachers like a puppy dog who was trying to find his owner. There was a priest who was a father figure to me. He was like Santa Claus—big, heavy, white hair, gentle, but he drank and drew watercolors. He was old enough to be my grandfather. I would look up to him and listen to what he said. Then he pulled this sexual thing on me and that was the end of that.

"During this time I wrote to my mother and said that she wasn't going to hear from me again until she told me where my father was. I didn't take her calls; I didn't respond to her letters. Finally, I get this letter saying, okay, I'll talk to you about your father. I wrote back to her and said here are my terms: You fly me in from Kansas, you fly my friend in from Kansas and you tell me everything you know about my father. I was like a terrorist.

"She sends us the tickets and the two of us go to New York. We get to the apartment and there is turkey she has made, there is ham that she has made, and she is all gussied up. I walk in, throw my suitcase on the floor and say, 'Tell me about my father.' She ignores me and asks my friend if he would like something to drink. I say, 'I want to know about my father.' My friend asks for a beer, and she brings it in a mug. She says that she has theater tickets for the two of us for that night. I say, 'What about my father?'

"She sits down demurely, crosses her legs and says, 'You know about your father.' I said I do not know about my father. Tell me everything about him. Start at the top. What was his name? She says that I know his name.

"By this time my friend is trying to hide behind his mug because he thinks I'm being rude, but I don't care. I ask her when they got married, and she says that she honestly can't remember. I ask her where they got married, and she says she honestly can't remember. That was it. The whole trip to New York was for nothing."

There was a familiarity to Robert's confrontation with his mother that made me uneasy. If I pushed him on why he incessantly badgered his mother when there was little hope of obtaining any information from her, I would have to account to myself for why I had once treated my mother in the same fashion. As a dodge, I idly inquired about the way in which his approach had differed from mine. "Robert," I asked, "why did you bring a friend halfway across the United States to witness this?"

"I don't know." He shrugged. "As a shield, maybe?"

"A shield?" I puzzled. "A shield against what?"

Robert turned his hands up at me and raised his voice. "I told you I don't know," he said. "What the hell's the big deal about that?"

I didn't understand why Robert was overreacting, but I also didn't want to risk spoiling the mood of an interview in which we had yet to talk about the subject's reunion with his father, so I let the point drop.

"While all of this was going on," Robert said, "I wasn't getting any help from anyone. My friends at college were telling me that I should leave it alone—that it might be better if I didn't know my father. Older people, the parents of students, would give me all of this business about, 'Robert, she is your mother, why are you doing this to her? Your mother wouldn't lie to you. Why can't you believe her.'

"I was beginning to feel I should forget about it, and then I got a letter from my mother saying that she had just traveled fourteen hundred miles across three states to find a man who had been in the service with my father. She said that if I didn't believe her, this man would tell me the truth about my father, and that I would be hearing from him. I get a letter from the guy and he says, 'Your father was fine. I don't know what your mother is talking about.' I wrote my mother and told her that, and she replied by saying the man who wrote to me was an alcoholic and a coward.

"I decided at that point to contact the army. I wrote them a letter and said that there was this man, and he had the same name as me, and he had been in the service, and I thought he was my father. I asked if the army had any records on him."

Robert stopped talking and leaned over to search through his box. He found the document he was seeking and began reading from it without looking up. "This is the letter I got back," he said. "It's dated April of 1966, and it says that my father was a career officer who retired in 1962, and it lists the permanent address he gave them."

Robert sat back in his chair and held the letter at arms length. He stared at it for a long moment, then kept his eyes fixed on the paper when he began to talk again. It was as though he were speaking to the letter and conversing with a character from his past that it contained, rather than with me.

"I didn't write to that address for fifteen years. I said to myself at the time, 'I've got this now if I ever want to use it. It was like a talisman—if I had a real crisis in my life, I could use it. But there was another side to it. The address was also like a bomb, and I was afraid of what might happen if it went off."

Robert looked up, gestured at me with the letter in his hand and said in an agitated voice, "A lot of it is fear of what the fuck is going to happen if I use this. I mean, what if I contact him and he doesn't want to know me? That is going to be really tragic . . . horrible . . . awful. What if he says, go the hell away and leave me alone—if I wanted to have anything to do with you, I wouldn't have left in the first place?"

There it was, I thought, confirmation of what I had suspected. The reason people weren't contacting their living fathers was dread that they would discover their fa-

thers had left because of *them* and not because of their
mothers.

"About then I began seeing this woman who was going
to become my wife. I was drifting along and not getting
anywhere. I needed somebody to make my life solid. She
was in high school when I started seeing her. She was five
years younger than me, and everyone told me I was rob-
bing the cradle. Her parents weren't crazy about me, and
I most especially didn't get along with her father.

"We went out for three years and she wouldn't sleep
with me. Those were bad times. I couldn't get a decent
job in Kansas, and my girlfriend kept saying that she
wanted to get out of the Midwest, so we came to New
York and lived with my mother."

"You took your girlfriend to New York to live with
your mother?" I asked, trying to conceal my astonishment.

"Yeah," Robert said and looked away. "Maybe it was
the 'I'm bringing a girl home tonight, please don't be there'
routine again."

"You weren't married at this time," I said, "so I guess
that means you stayed in separate rooms?"

Robert thought for a minute and said, "You know, I
can't remember. We lived there for a year, and it is like
an entire year is gone from my memory."

"You honestly can't recall whether you and your
girlfriend slept in the same bedroom in your mother's
apartment?" I said.

"No."

"Well, were there enough bedrooms in the apartment so each of you could have had your own room?"

Robert shook with laughter. "No," he said, "and I
guess that means that my wife-to-be slept in the same
bedroom with my mother."

I felt my head jerk automatically. This man—who
had charged that his mother had figuratively seduced him
as a child—had delivered his virginal fiancée to his moth-

er's apartment in New York and then installed the woman in the same bedroom with his mother! It was too bizarre to believe.

Robert had gone off to college, cut the cord from his mother, gotten his hands on an address for the father he had been consumed with finding since childhood, acquired a future mate, and then had proceeded, not to contact his father, but to return with his future bride to his mother and the turmoil of their anguished relationship.

It was inconceivable to me—too like some perverse twist on *Oedipus Rex* in which the son, rather than marrying his mother, continually brings women he wants to sleep with home to his mother so he can't sleep with either the woman or his mother.

There did seem, however, to be a consistency of sorts to the tale. Robert's two incidents of bringing women he desired into his mother's home both occurred around the time of his unearthing of his father's address. It was as though, having turned to his mother as a child for solace over his father's absence, he then tried, when faced with the trauma of reuniting with his father, to replace his mother with other comforting women. And he sought to make those women as motherlike as possible by bringing them into his childhood home and thus rendering them sexually enticing but ultimately unavailable, as his mother had been.

"I hardly ever saw my mother after I got married. She would write me notes and I would ignore them; she would call me and give me crap about never getting to see me. We invited my mother and her sister to our place one night after we had been married for about five years. My wife was into a whole nostalgia thing about her family. She had put pictures of her grandparents and great-grandparents around the house. My mother was looking at the pictures and she threw something out at me about my father, just as she had when I was a kid. She said that my father had come home from the war with a couple of medals, but that he was such a coward that he couldn't have earned them. She said he must have bought them or stolen them. Something snapped in me and I decided right then—that was it—I was going to contact my father."

I asked Robert why, given the thousand invectives his mother had hurled at his father, this one suddenly caused him to use the address for his father that he had been carrying around for fifteen years, but he ignored me. He had hunched forward and was again digging in his box of documents. I knew he was going to produce a copy of the letter he had written to his father.

"Here it is," Robert said, as he looked over a carbon of the original letter.

I tried to imagine what, if I were Robert, I would have written in a first letter to my father. How would I begin? Would it be presumptuous or simply too blunt to begin: Dear Dad? Would I try to brace him against the shock of the announcement of myself in the letter by writing our common last name in large letters in the upper left corner of the envelope? And since I was a writer like Robert, wouldn't I want to impress my dad with my skill with words? This would probably be the most important writing assignment Robert ever had, and, if I were him, I imagined I would have spent hours drafting, editing and polishing the work.

Robert finished reading the letter and handed it over to me. I thought he had given me a draft or an outline of the letter he had actually sent to his father. The writing was extremely choppy—sentences ran together and portions of it didn't make sense at all. Most surprising of all, Robert hadn't announced in the opening line that he was writing because he was the recipient's son. He didn't reveal that until the closing sentences, and then in one of the most confusing paragraphs of the letter.

"Robert," I said, "you are almost to the end of the

letter before you say that the reason you are writing to this man is because he is your father, and the phrasing you use there is easy to misread. You say, 'For most of my life I was cut off from you . . . through no doing of my own . . . I am your son . . . the one I gather she wouldn't let you see.' With the way you structured that, it almost sounds like you are saying 'through no doing of my own I am your son.' What do you think about that?"

There was a long silence as Robert continued rummaging through the box. I waited him out this time for what seemed like four or five minutes. Finally, without looking up, he said, "A lot of confusion. I meant, 'Through no doing of your own I had no contact with you.' Robert paused for a moment to consider what he had said, sighed and then continued. 'Through no doing of *my* own I had no contact with you.' That's what I meant."

"Listen to what you just said, Robert. In fact, how did you know at this point that your mother had kept your father away and that he hadn't stayed away of his own accord?"

Robert shook his head and handed me the return letter from his father. "I can't answer you," he said. "I guess I'm just blocking all of this stuff out."

The letter Robert received from his father was an amazingly calm and composed reply from a man who was obviously quite pleased to hear from his son. "I wish you had written to me long ago," he wrote. "It has always been my fondest dream that I would hear from you. Your mother was always very bitter. I hope she enjoys good health and happiness. Please don't blame her. It was all my misconduct that caused the divorce, even though I loved her very much. In spite of all of the past unpleasantness, I will always have a warm spot in my heart for her. So you can see, I wouldn't try to hurt her."

"You couldn't have asked for a nicer letter from your father," I said.

"It was a beautiful letter. So all of that shit about

what's going to happen if he rejects me was right out the window. He did want to see me! He did want to know me! I was real happy, but I was also real tender.

"I told him not to call me because I wasn't ready to talk to him yet. I explain that in this letter," Robert said and began reading from one of the dozens of carbons in his lap. " 'The child is the father of the man, and, when you contact me, you contact the earliest part of me. I wanted you then because the place was awful. I was raised by three women and all of that. It is too late. The nightmare is over. It is too late for you to tend to the child.'

"It was real hard for a while. In one of his letters he said that he had taken me for my first haircut and that I hadn't liked it. My wife read that and said you guys must have been good buddies. I broke down into tears. It was an odd physical sensation, like a baby crying—involuntary gagging, my face all squeezed up. It was just like a baby. I kept crying and crying. It was like the adult couldn't get the child to stop crying. It just had to die out. That happened three or four times—real violent crying jags in response to his letters.

"I sent him a photograph of me and two other kids on the Staten Island ferry. I was in the middle and there was a blond kid on either side of me. My father wrote back and asked if I was the blond kid on the left. As I was writing back to him, I broke down real bad. 'He doesn't know me; he doesn't even recognize me.' Violent, fucking raging tears.

"Then I hear this honking outside and it's the mailman. I think it's snowing. The mailman calls me nature boy because I used to go out for the mail without my shoes on. So I say to myself that I have to get composed and go out and get the mail. And I'm on the floor trying to put my rubbers on and I'm just gagging and crying and sobbing and I can't stop."

"But Robert," I said, "how could your father have

recognized you in the picture when he never saw you as a child?"

"It was the child thinking like a child," he said. "The child didn't have adult rationality. The child thought a father would always be able to recognize his son. The child wanted his father to know him. That's what killed me, because I had to say years later—"

Robert abruptly stopped talking and began flipping through his letters again. "Here," he said, "is the letter I sent back to him. 'I'm the one in the middle. The one with the facial characteristics that might remind you of her. I thought you would know. Maybe I wished that you would know. I'm sorry.' Oh, God, the tears."

Robert handed a sheaf of letters to me that were dated one day after another for weeks. "What were all of these letters about?" I asked. "It looks like you were socking your father with every accusation that your mother ever made against him."

"There were a lot of problems. It was all of the childhood stuff: She says you didn't pay support, did you? She says you beat her, did you? Why didn't you try harder to contact me? I didn't know who to believe. I went of my own volition and tracked down his army pay records that showed he had paid support. He got angry when I asked about the medals, but generally he didn't mind answering questions, and he had answers for everything."

"When did you tell your mother that you had contacted your father," I asked.

"It's funny," Robert said after a long pause. "In January I contacted my father and started seeing a shrink, and by September my wife and I had separated. Connecting with my father was the beginning of the end of my marriage. It was like I traded a rock for a rock, and, once I found the real rock, losing her wasn't so bad. It was like people changing . . . I was ready for it . . . I had been screwing around . . . What was the question?"

Here was Robert linking, almost unconsciously it seemed, his relationship with a woman to his relationship with his father, and doing it to avoid answering a question about informing his mother that he had contacted his father. I knew that there was something there, but I still wasn't certain what it was. "When did you tell your mother?" I repeated.

"I'm not sure," he said. "She wrote to me one time and started all of this crap about my father again, and I told her she better knock it off because I had been in touch with my father and I knew about all of her lies. I said this thing you told me is not true, and that is not true.

"She wrote back with all of this, 'You'll never know what he did to me' nonsense, and I told her that I didn't want to hear another word from her about my father. Then, after claiming for thirty years that she didn't know where my father was, she immediately called him and started writing to him. She sent him a bouquet of roses with a note saying 'Thank you for being a friend to Robert.' She sent me his love letters from forty years before that she still had. She crossed out parts of them. I sent them to my father, because I didn't want them. He wrote to me, all excited, and said, 'You didn't keep copies of these did you?' The amazing part was that my mother never got on me about my father after that."

And so, after almost four decades, Robert and his mother had come full circle. All the love and hatred, sexuality and tenderness, and resentment and rage that his mother had misdirected at Robert, as her surrogate husband, was aborted when her former husband reappeared. There was even the symbolic passing of the love letters from mother to son to father. All that remained was for Robert, as an adult, to meet his father for what was essentially the first time.

"How did you finally meet your father?" I asked.

"After I had been writing to him for a couple of

months, he sent me a note and said this was enough, that
he was going to call me and come for a visit. The phone
rings one day and I answer it, and he says, 'Robert,' and
I say yeah, and he says, 'It's your Dad.' and I'm like, what
the hell is this? He has the same voice that I have—deeper,
with a bit of a twang—but it is the same voice. It was a
very mature conversation—How are you? . . . How are
you? Maybe five minutes. He says he is coming to visit for
a weekend in three weeks. Then I hang up and the tears
start."

"What was it like before your father came, once you
knew he was coming?" I asked.

Robert went for his box again. "Did I show you the
pictures of the two of us together?" he asked and produced a photo album, which he then spent ten minutes
narrating for me.

"What was it like when you saw your father for the
first time?" I asked.

"He had a big smile on his face. All I had of him was
a picture to know what to look for. He was walking through
the airport, and he was this *great, big,* strapping bull moose
of a man. We spent most of the time sitting around talking. . . . The whole thing was the kid, the kid. The only
way I could respond to him was as a child. At the end of
the weekend, we drove him into New York to introduce
him to my brother-in-law and his girlfriend. I wanted to
show him off to everyone. It felt great. Everybody who
met him said he was a great person to have for a father.

"We ate dinner at my brother-in-law's, and then I
started feeling sick. My brother-in-law was subletting an
apartment from a family with kids, so I went into one of
the kid's rooms and laid down on this little bed. The room
was pitch dark, and, without thinking about it, I started
saying quietly, 'I want my father to come in here and see
how I'm doing. I want my daddy to come in. Where is
my daddy?' "

"Suddenly the door opens and this giant looming

figure is standing there in the shadows of the doorway. He says in a deep voice, 'Robert, are you okay?' I say, 'Yes, Daddy,' and I start feeling better right away. I just wanted him to do that.

"Then he had to leave to go to the airport. I started feeling weak again, but I knew he had a flight to catch, so I got up and put my coat on. My wife and I walked him down to the street to get a cab. He said it was silly for us to go all the way out to the airport with him, that he would just ride out by himself. I was hoping a cab wouldn't come right away, but one did as soon as we reached the curb. We flagged it and the cabby pulled over.

"My father opened the back door and put his bags in, and then he turned around to say good-bye. I put my arms out to give my father a hug, and I don't know what happened—I am in his arms, and he is hugging me, and I just burst into violent tears and started choking and gagging . . . I go to jello . . . The cab is waiting, and my wife is standing there, and my spine disappears . . . I can't hold myself up. My legs give way. I collapse into his arms and I can't stop crying and my daddy is holding on to me. It's the kid again—the kid has taken over and he's not old enough to stand up by himself and I can't get him to stop crying. I keep saying, 'Good-bye, Daddy. Good-bye, Daddy. Come see me again soon.'

"My daddy just holds onto me because he doesn't know what else to do. He doesn't say anything. He just holds me until I am able to stop crying and stand up. Then he gets in the cab and it pulls away and I stand there waving good-bye until the cab is out of sight."

CHAPTER

8

Robert sat motionless and gazed at his box of papers with sad eyes. "I didn't know you wanted all of this," he said. "I thought you were after general stuff. I haven't talked to anyone about that visit before." I nodded in understanding and waited a respectful time before leaving.

As Robert led me out, I expected his step would have the momentary lightness of a man who had shifted his load from right shoulder to left. Instead, he shuffled more than walked, as though his telling of the reemergence of the two year old had aged him.

"Can we talk again?" I asked.

"Sure."

I called Robert four times during his last week in Philadelphia, but he was perpetually occupied. I knew it was time to write my article. Robert, alone of all my respondents, had shown me, or perhaps had submitted to my obstinacy about seeing, the core of his sadness. I had assumed the demeanor of a psychological voyeur to win this glimpse—skulking around and pushing back curtains that obscured private dramas, rather than limiting myself to peering in when I happened upon closures that had been left ajar.

I had viewed the unhealed childhood love wound that was the missing fathers' sanctuary, and I wasn't likely to encounter it again. I had learned that Robert and the others had been denied the affection and recognition and protection of the father during their most helpless time, and their stepfathers hadn't been the men to substitute at the task.

I began my prewriting ritual several weeks later—sneaking up on the typewriter by rereading notes, transcripts and outlines in the vicinity of the machine so that, at the moment when my brain seemed destined to burst with research, I would be at the keyboard and the first page of bond would be half-filled with words.

The telephone rang. It was Stuart, a man who, as a child, had lost his father to the Second World War. He had heard about my project and he wanted to talk.

"I appreciate your calling," I said immediately, "but I wasn't planning to do more interviews."

"I'd really like to talk to you," Stuart said, "and I'm only working part-time right now, so I could be available at your convenience."

The irony of an unwanted interview being thrust on me, after two years of begging people to speak into the microphone, wasn't lure enough. I asked Stuart his address, hoping for a reply that I could brand too distant. Instead I received what felt like an electric shock over the phone. Stuart, unknown to him, lived in the same six-unit apartment house Robert had just vacated. The coincidence was irresistible; I made an appointment for the next day.

Stuart had asked for William Wartman when he phoned, but I announced myself as Bill when I rang the buzzer at his building. Stuart had told me he wasn't working that day, and I thought it curious that he appeared in the doorway wearing a starched white shirt with a tie pulled tight to the collar. Stuart gave me a pleasant smile as we shook hands. "Shall we call each other Stuart and Bill then?" he asked.

Stuart's formality lingered in his posture as he sat and precisely crossed one leg over the other, but he launched into his tale as abruptly as if the spirit of revelation had wafted up from Robert's former living quarters one floor below. Stuart's father had been taken as a prisoner of war by the Japanese in the Philippines. "My mother knew where my father was being held," he said, "and I think she got letters from him. I may have even seen those letters at one time, but I don't think I ever read them.

"Then she lost touch with him. One day word came that my father and a thousand other Americans had been put in the hold of a Japanese freighter just before the Philippines were liberated. They were put down into this compartment in an unmarked ship to be taken back to Japan to be used as laborers. On the way there the ship was torpedoed mistakenly by an American submarine . . . emotions are very high for me here . . . and about five people survived. They were locked down there in this boat and only about five people were able to get free and live. So my father is somewhere on the bottom of the Pacific Ocean."

Stuart said, "Excuse me, but I could use a glass of wine. Will you join me?" and left the room. I surveyed the surroundings in his absence and my eyes stopped at a tricycle and an overflowing toy box in the corner. Stuart had mentioned that he had a family, but the playthings seemed alien in the room. Few of the people I had interviewed had children, and, excluding myself, I had come to assume that fatherless adults were childless people.

Stuart returned with two filled goblets and a box of paper tissues. He dried his eyes without self-consciousness and asked where we had been in the conversation.

"Did your mother ever talk about your father?" I said.

"Yes, she was very free about that. She didn't dwell or get weepy eyed, but she had a scrapbook she would take out from time to time, usually when my stepfather wasn't home. When I asked about my father, she would always answer me. My mother tended to romanticize her stories, I suspect. It was like a ritual, using the same descriptions, the same anecdotes, the same phrasing about who my father was. It was almost as if she couldn't stray from that language or the emotions were too much. Many times, though, my mother would want to talk about my father and I wouldn't. I would be terribly afraid."

"What was your stepfather like?"

"I am the son of a strong, dominant mother and a weak, passive stepfather. In feelings of love and nonlove, my feelings for my stepfather are nothing but love. He was always my dad, and there is no doubt that I received anything less than one hundred percent love from him. He had a very good relationship with my mother—one very different, apparently, from the one she had with my father—and I grew up in what I perceived to be a very normal home.

"I had one serious problem with my stepfather. I was inherently very masculine, and I would have loved to have been in sports. But my mother, because I was the son of her husband who had died, didn't want me to die. She was overly protective and made me into a very bookish mama's boy. Climbing trees or getting in fights? No, Stuart wasn't to do that.

"My stepfather, maybe not wanting me to say, 'You're not my real father, get lost,' never stepped in. He didn't have the guts to tell my mother, 'Leave the kid alone. This is natural. Get your hands off of him.' I lost a lot of respect for my stepfather as a result.

"That aside, I couldn't have asked for a man to provide me with a better sense of humor. I was a very serious little boy, but my stepfather got me to express some wit. And he insisted I keep my father's family name. He never made me feel I was someone else's child, yet he also respected my father's memory."

The interview was turning into a waste of time, and I impatiently tried to prod Stuart along by nodding my head repeatedly in contrived agreement. The man had lost his father, but, measured by the sorrowful tales I had heard, his was essentially cheerful. His mother hadn't been so disturbed by the loss of her husband that she denied the man's existence, and he had had a stepfather who was kind, loving and reasonably secure in his role of parent by marriage.

Many of my interviewees had illustrated how the past can create its own absolution for those in search of self-exoneration. My search had begun as an effort to discover whether fathers were so irrefutably important to their offsprings that the childrens' lives were eternally altered in the wake. I had learned that absence provokes craving, and that few men without biological links seemed destined to supply the desired sustenance, but this neediness was being converted into unremitting self-pity over every minor inequity life had dealt to the afflicted.

"So what's the problem?" I asked. "You were a little disappointed with your stepfather? Far worse things have happened to people. You had everything the others I have talked to lacked. Your mother preserved your father's image and you had a stepfather who loved you as his own. I have to tell you, quite honestly, I don't think your father's death has impoverished your life very greatly."

"What I have just told you is the rational part. The unconscious part is more complicated. My feelings for my father were locked away in cold storage for a long, long time. I went into therapy for two years when I was thirty-one. It was a period of real enlightenment and of clearing out garbage for me."

Stuart paused to take a long sip of white wine. I could see tears pooling in his eyes.

"I remember telling the shrink in one session that I never mentioned my father's name . . . Christ, thinking about this still makes me cry . . . that I never mentioned my father's name on Sunday in my prayers. . . . Here was this man who was loving and caring . . . and I hated him . . . this is a bitch . . . I despised him . . . and I kept all of this inside of me when I was a child going to church and an adult going to church. . . . When it came time to remember the dead, I couldn't say my father's name because . . . I hated him.

"I hated my father for not being there for me, for not warding off my mother from making me a milque-toast, nonsexual, nonmacho boy because she didn't want me to be killed. She wanted me not to fight, not to be aggressive, not to compete in sports. I had to cope with my mother myself and I was inadequate to the task.

"When I discovered these feelings I was ashamed. I was blaming a man who had been dead since 1944, and I realized for the first time that he had done nothing wrong. He loved me and cared for me and was trying to look out for my best interests. . . . But, when I was a kid, all I was thinking was: Where are you when I need you—right now? Somebody has to help me. You, I need you. Where are you? I need you to get this woman off of my back. I want to assert my masculinity and she will not let me.

"I found myself becoming aware of things I didn't even know I was feeling. That devastated me. I believed my father had deserted me until then. Once I understood the craziness in putting all of this on him, I was really transformed.

"I have remembered my father in my prayers every

Sunday since then. That day unlocked me and made me realize my father wasn't responsible for his death. It allowed me to feel proud and curious about my father, but it took me a long time to get to that point. It wasn't until I was able to say, 'My God, I really hate him,' that the taboo was removed.

"After that I knew my father had a place in life, and I was able to feel connected with him. I had swept under the carpet all of the heroic parts of my father my mother had told me about. My father was a man who went out and defended his country, his wife and his child, and he died doing that. I couldn't be angry at him.

"I never thought about this before therapy. I don't even remember noticing if other kids had their real fathers living with them when I was growing up. I knew that my stepfather wasn't my real father, but we conducted our life like, 'So what?' I felt I was a part of a normal and secure family, and my father had nothing to do with my life."

"Wasn't it inevitable, though," I asked, "that going into therapy would focus you on your father's death? Didn't that supply a reservoir of causation for every complaint you had?"

"I don't think so. I wasn't consciously aware my going into therapy had anything to do with my father. I started when a four-year relationship ended. I had been living with this woman and, while we loved each other, we never talked of marriage. I believe that was because, before therapy, I didn't have an image of myself as a husband and father. I couldn't certify a marriage relationship. I wanted to be married, but the idea stunned and scared me. I had slept with a number of women, but I felt inadequate to be a father. Now that I am a father, I understand what was behind this.

"There is only one man whose sperm united with my mother's egg and created me, a man who had his own unique characteristics and style, and I don't know him.

No matter how fine a stepfather I had, no matter how close he came to the perfect father, he would not be my father. It's really almost a spiritual feeling. Now that I am a father, it is as though I am compelled to think about my own father.

"I have thought about my father more and more since my daughter was born. The thinking and feeling started after therapy, but it also has something to do with getting older. I am now older than my father was when he died. One day I just realized that. As I get older I think a lot about who my father was. I wonder what characteristics I have that my father had. In a way I gave my dad something with my daughter. I'm sure he would be delighted with her. Wouldn't it be great if some element of my father was in both my daughter and me? I love that idea.

"Even if I were to die now, I would feel better that I have a child. It's a certification that my father's life was and continues. I'm forty-two years old now, and there isn't a day in my life that I don't think about my father."

The following Sunday, Cathy and I were having scrambled eggs, coffee and bread that had to be heated in the oven broiler because she had packed the toaster in preparation for her imminent thousand-mile move. We had gone out for a few months in the fall and broken off when I began seeing someone else. Then Cathy called in early April to say she was leaving the area, and I returned to her bed for the excessive abandonment and reserve of an affair with a four-week life span.

"I don't know what to think about this guy Stuart," I said as I hurried through breakfast. "He made a convincing case for the importance of real fathers, but it is so easy to explain away what he said. He had masculinity problems he wants to hang on his father's death, he is suspiciously religious and he is too professionally sincere for my skeptical nature. How can you give credence to somebody like that?"

"I haven't said anything about this before," Cathy said and put down her coffee, "but I can't believe you're being so dense."

Cathy's tone surprised me. She was ten years my junior, and it was her characteristic deference more than anything that had gradually cooled my attraction to her.

"I've known from the first weekend you stayed here that I could never compete with your son. If I had complained about the way you rushed out on Sunday mornings, you would have given me an instant ultimatum, and if I had blocked the door you would have walked over me. How can you think your fierceness about that boy stems from anything *but* your being his father?"

Cathy made me realize that I had never considered how the women I was involved with felt about my son, because I had never perceived them as entering into my relationship with him. I could remember introducing only two women to him, and then it had been on a single occasion each. My instinct was that my time with my son was our time, and it wasn't fair to him to share it with others.

I had been building my writing career, and I didn't want to get married, both because I didn't want the vocation-altering financial responsibilities that came with marriage, and because the pain of my separation from my son was not something I was in a hurry to risk with children in another failed marriage.

So my relationship with my son became something apart from, and decidedly more stable than, my relationships with women. There were women I was monogamous with for several years or more, and there were romances I was sad to see end, but there was something near sacred to me in the knowledge that my bond with my son would never be affected by compatibility problems or conflicting goals or even boredom. Regardless of anything, my son was my son, and I would always love him and share parts of my life with him.

My sensitivity to my son became more acute as he reached puberty, and my responsiveness to him and my awareness of his needs increased—probably because that age had been a most difficult time for me. I remembered the confusion and stridency, the terrible loneliness of feeling life was an incomprehensible puzzle that no one around me could possible solve.

Joe—having been called Billy by my family until I was in my twenties, I was mindful to drop the *y* from my son's name when he became a teenager—grew restless with our going to the library, and I didn't like spending bright afternoons in darkened movie theaters, so I began searching for a new activity for us. One day my son mentioned that he had played golf with his friends, and I said, "Let's you and I play golf," guessing it would be delightful touring the manicured courses with enough diversion to keep us busy but with enough placidity to encourage conversations.

Joe and I played golf after I left Cathy's that Sunday. We were still new to the game and hit the ball as ineptly as all neophytes do, but my hacks into the turf and long slicing drives didn't rile me as usual. I was beginning to write the article in my head, and Stuart's remarks, with Cathy's amplifications, had jarred me into thinking about where Joe fit into my investigation.

I had recognized by the time my son started school that there was a reparational aspect to my relationship with him. I would gaze at Joey at each stage of his young life and see him trailed by a shadow that was not his own— one that haunted me. The faded silhouette that was fixed behind him was the untended remains of my own childhood, and I would pick details from it—a hug or word of encouragement or praise that had been missing—and impulsively force that thing on my son, usually fighting against a rush of tears.

I called Joey every week, dragging conversation out of him when he didn't want to talk, and concluded each time with "See you on Sunday." I was ever alert to regularity, and on the rare week when I hadn't reached him on the phone my first question on Sunday would be "You knew I was coming, didn't you?"

Sometimes my action would be a non sequitur, as when Joey would climb into the car full of news from his recent extended vacation at the beach, and I would impulsively interrupt him to blurt out, "It's really good to see you." At those times my son would look at me with confusion on his brow that yielded to a brilliant smile. I would see that look and shiver with the relief of someone who had just had ice placed on a burn.

Joey was confident enough of our bond to take it casually, and I envied him that. I was ad-libbing, making every choice up as we went along, and I was often concerned I was going to do something wrong. Achievement in school hadn't been strongly promoted in my home, so I tried to give that to my son. Yet when did support become pressure? If I didn't know, I would be reduced to explaining my confusion to my son. He would tell me it was all right to be unsure and not to worry about it.

Joey though it odd that I brooded over these things. Of course he knew I was going to show up, and yes he knew I loved him and he was important to me. There was a modicum of selfishness to what I did. I was indirectly making a belated gift to myself when I bestowed on my son the knowledge that all he ever needed to do for me was to be himself, but both of us were fortified by it.

Joe was heading down the fifteenth fairway, just ahead of me, when I noticed he was walking heavily on the inside panels of his high-top sneakers. The outer edges of the rubber soles were cutting through the grass on the perpendicular like rudders, and the aluminum air-circulation grommets on the inner canvas sides had become part of his footprint.

"Joe," I called out. "What's wrong with your shoes? Why are you walking on the insides of them that way?"

He looked down at his feet and then turned to face me. "They're loose, but that's what happens when my sneaks get old," he said. "I wear down the inside edges first, and then my feet shift in them."

"That's weird," I said. "Who's your father?"

"You must be," he said, "because your running shoes are worn the same way."

I lifted a foot, turned it sideways and realized that Joe was right—my shoes were turning toward the inside. I laughed and remembered a day, six or seven years earlier, when I had insisted on testing my son's new skateboard.

Joey was dexterous on the board, speeding across the slick surface of a deserted tennis court, cutting figure eights and fancy turns with ease that disguised the difficulty of the maneuvers. When my son rolled up to me, I told him to give his father a turn.

I positioned my right foot on the board, balanced my weight on it and then pushed off with my left. The skateboard, minus me, shot into the air and then dropped, while I momentarily levitated three feet over the surface of the courts before crashing onto my back. The impact forced the wind from my lungs, and I sprawled on the ground, questioning what had happened to my breath and the adroitness of my youth.

My son bent over me and, recognizing that loss of aplomb outranked injury as a concern, said, "Don't worry about it, Dad. The same exact thing happened to me the first time I got on a board."

An argument could be made that my son and I understood each other well without discussion simply because we had spent a good deal of time together. The counterargument, and the one I favored this peaceful April afternoon, was that our special link was that we were each a part of the other. I was the maker of him, and he was the healer of me.

As we walked from the eighteenth green to the car, I dispensed with the gentle kidding that traditionally closed our games. I wouldn't make outlandish excuses for having lost or threaten not to buy dinner for someone who had defeated me by cheating. I grabbed my son hard by the shoulder and said, "You know, Joe, I'm really glad you're my son."

My mother was about to retire from her job, and she was selling the home I grew up in to have an addition built onto my younger sister's home as her new apartment. I hadn't left many of my belongings at my mother's, but it was time to claim or discard what remained from my past. I went through my mother's bedroom to the walk-in closet that contained the staircase to the attic. I turned on the light and climbed the stairs in the hunched posture that was needed to avoid the carpet of nails that protruded through the shingles on the sharply pitched roof.

The attic was hospitable only during spring and fall. Summer incursions would precipitate the sweat of a steam room, and I had seen my breath when I made winter visits to retrieve ice skates. The room was comfortable this day, however, and I sat on the landing to search among the last artifacts of a time that felt ages removed from the present.

I wanted to preserve my set of Lionel trains and the tracks, model-village homes and stores and other accessories that complimented them. I grinned at the memory of the hours I had spent creating the village—with green plastic flakes for grass and parakeet seed for the roadways—that stretched over the train platform each Christmas.

I also wanted my ice skates, although the chance I

would use them was as remote as my putting the trains
up any holiday soon. I uncovered little else I wanted there
until, in moving about a collection of old board games, I
discovered a twelve-inch square, six-inch deep cardboard
box. I recognized it as a carton of photographs my mother
used to keep in the top of her closet when I was a child.
I pulled the box out and slid the top off. There appeared
to be several hundred pictures inside. I couldn't remember the last time I looked at those photos, and I was uncertain of what I would find.

Most of the photographs were thirty-or-more-year-
old, black-and-white snapshots, and my father was in a
number of them. There were pictures of him standing
alone, arrow straight with his hands gathered behind his
back. They were posed portraits that had been taken—
probably by my mother of her fiancé—in the backyards
of my father's parents' home in the Germantown section
of Philadelphia or, not far from where I sat, alongside
what had been my mother's parents' house. I guessed that
my father would have been in his midtwenties in the shots,
and, in his double-breasted jackets and three-piece suits,
I was pleased to see he bore a tremendous resemblance
to F. Scott Fitzgerald.

I found pictures of my parents with other people
their age—holding hands in a park; my mother in saddle
shoes with a bow in her hair; mugging for the camera at
the beach; laughing; my mother always on my father's
arm. The wedding pictures—my father in tails, his left
hand around his bride's waist; my mother glowing in a
long white dress with the veil that flowed down her back
gathered at her feet. The happy young couple starting
their new life.

Then my father with a baby—my older sister, Helen
Marie. It's winter and she's in her snowsuit. My father
grasps her to his chest in the little square of grass behind
his parent's row house. It's summer and my father has
his shirt off and he is balancing Helen Marie on his head

with his skinny arms. Then it's autumn and long shadows fall on the front steps of our house in Germantown. Helen Marie is on my father's lap, and his cheeks are slack as though he is dazed, but my mother grabs at his arm and smiles with the pride of her family.

Then there is a picture of my parents with two children—and one of them is me. This can't be. My mother always said my father got sick just after I was born, and there were no pictures of us together. But there is one and I have it now. It's from Christmas, right here in the house where I grew up. We are on the floor in front of the Christmas tree, and this time my father has *me* in his arms. He's sitting on the floor with his long spidery legs bunched up at his side, and my head is resting against his chest. My father has his hand against my hips to secure me, and he is smiling at the camera.

It's a picture of me with my father, and I can't believe my good fortune in finding this wealth. I imagine the situation. My father is driving his family to visit his in-laws for Christmas. He takes one hand off the wheel and puts it on my mother's leg and says, "Helen, your folks are going to be amazed to see how Billy has grown. He'll be going to school before any of us know it."

Then we are pulling into the driveway in Parkside, and my grandmother hears the car on the gravel and is at the door, calling to my grandfather, "Frank, Helen is here with her family. Come see the children." My father pulls my hat down over my ears to protect me from the cold. He calls out, "Merry Christmas," as he climbs from the car with me in his arms and hurries us into the warmth of the house.

Something is causing my back to tingle from the base of my spine to the top of my skull as I think about this scene. I can feel that my nostrils have pulled open. There isn't enough oxygen in the attic, and what I do draw is leaking out. The first swell of something stronger than me is pushing me to the floor. I don't want to be up here anymore. I clutch the picture and slide down the stairs quickly on my backside, afraid all the while that the nails in the roof are going to gash my face.

I slam and bolt the attic door and then drive back to Philadelphia with my photograph. I put the picture on my desk and don't look at it for a couple of days. The photo feels safe when I go back to it, so I tape it to the wall next to my typewriter and start writing. The words come quickly, and I've got a finished piece in two days.

I call the *Philadelphia Inquirer* in late April and ask if they want a Father's Day story for their Sunday magazine. They say they're interested, but they have a long lead time so send it right away. I put it in the mail that day and am relieved. This is an article I am glad to have over.

The managing editor calls and says she wants it and asks for a paragraph more, a paragraph more. I add a couple of pages and everything's fine.

It's a story with a happy-face ending about how I once thought my father was in prison, and how I stopped thinking about him when I found out that he wasn't. Then I had started thinking about him again, and I interviewed these other people, and it made me really happy when I found the picture of me with my dad.

There weren't any problems until my editor called and said she wanted to run the photo of me and my dad with the piece, and could I bring it over so she could send it to the printer?

I refused, saying there was no way I was going to let that photograph out of my sight, but my editor swore nothing would happen to the picture—that the boss at the printing company would personally supervise its handling—so I gave it to her.

When I delivered the picture she wanted to know how old I was in it, and I couldn't answer. I recognized the child in the photo as me, but I couldn't reason further about it. I took a pencil and made up a chart of when I was born and when my father died, and how many Christmases had fallen in between. My editor asked me if I thought it was this Christmas or that one, and I pointed to that one.

I didn't think about the story much until the Monday before Father's Day when my editor called to say pre-publication copies of the magazine were available. I said it was thoughtful of her to phone, and I'd be right over. Everyone was busy when I arrived, so I grabbed some copies of the magazine off of a pile and opened one to my story.

The first things I sought out were the parts I hadn't written—the headlines and the caption for the picture. I looked at the photograph—my father and I's photo-graph—pasted across the top of the page and read, "The author, seventeenth months old in this photograph, was two when his father died. He would wait about thirty years, however, before retrieving this photo from his mother's box of pictures and beginning to reconnect with the past and part of himself."

It wasn't until I saw my words in print that it oc-curred to me that, in selling this article, I had gone public on a topic that had been so intensely painful and buried that, for many years, I couldn't even acknowledge having feelings about my father's death. Soon, strangers would have access to these emotions for the dollar price of the Sunday paper. I found a chair in a remote section of the building and began reading to learn if I had made my vulnerability as public in the article as it seemed my edi-tor had in her caption.

It was far worse than I had feared. There was nee-diness and pain sloshed up and down the columns. My interview subjects couldn't be identified, but I couldn't have been more naked—both my name and photograph were prominent on the pages. I wasn't ready for this. I had to corner my editor, return her money and insist the maga-zine pull the story. That imperative was hardly formed, however, before reality intervened. There were over one million copies of the magazine in print; the newspaper would never destroy them.

I seldom shared my most deeply held feelings with anyone. In six days, hundreds of thousands of strangers would laugh at "Peanuts" and "Doonesbury" on the comic pages, then turn to the magazine and digest my soul along with their breakfasts. And there was nothing I could do to prevent it.

CHAPTER

9

I picked my son up at noon on Father's Day. "Have you seen it?" I asked as he came out onto the front porch.

"I went to the store last night and got the Saturday evening edition," he said.

"And?"

"It's great. I loved it," Joe said and kissed me on the cheek. My teenager and I had tacit understanding on the matter of kissing his father. He would kiss me hello and goodbye, as I asked, as long as no witnesses were present. If anyone else was near, especially one of his friends, I was not even to consider it.

Joe and I had been talking about this article since I

had first conceived the idea, and, although he was mentioned only once in the story, I had offered to let him see it in manuscript form. He had said no, that he wanted to wait until it was published and then buy it in the store.

I hadn't, however, offered my mother such a preview. I had told her the story might make her sad, and she might not like it because of that. She had asked to see it before publication, but I had balked. My mother was hurt and angered, but I had offered her numerous opportunities to speak on this topic, and she had unstintingly declined. I perceived her belated interest as an eleventh-hour attempt at censorship. I didn't believe that was a maternal prerogative.

There wasn't anything derogatory about my mother in the article. I had only presented my version of the truth—that she had been greatly pained by my father's death, and, as a result, she had never wanted to talk about him. Still, given her past stoicism, I couldn't guess what her response to the article was going to be.

My family knew of my continued attachment to the project. I would occasionally recount scenes from my interviews when we were together, and they would listen politely, but that was all. Helen Marie would sometimes ask questions, but my mother and my younger sister, Anne, would have nothing to say. I maintained a faint hope that one day I would find the triggering word that would free their tongues, but I had gone forward as if this were a road I was destined to travel alone.

"Have you talked to Grandmom yet?" Joe asked as we set off on a trip to Parkside.

"No," I said, "and I'm nervous about seeing her."

"Why?"

"I'm not sure. Maybe it's because of the clashes we've had on this subject, or maybe it's just because she's my mother. Somehow, having her like this is important to me."

My mother had the magazine on a table next to her when my son and I arrived.

"Well?" I asked, looking for signs in her face. But there were none, save pleasantness.

"It's beautiful," she said. "People who recognized me in the picture have been calling all morning. I don't know how they could tell it was me, I look so sad. That's the way I was feeling too. Your father had been sick for a year then."

I was aware that my mother and Helen Marie were in that picture—I had asked for their permission to print it with the story—but I hadn't thought about it beyond that. I had been so delighted in finding a photograph of my father and me together that I had considered it our picture, with my mother and sister forming a backdrop for us. I sat down next to my mother on the couch and studied the left side of the picture in the magazine, where my mother rested on the floor behind Helen Marie.

My mother looked to be consciously diverting her eyes from the camera in the photograph, and the listlessness on her face seemed to explain why. My mother must have known my father was dying even as the shutter clicked. My father lived for eleven months more, but, given the malignancy of his tumor and the medical technology of 1949, death would have been a difficult prospect to ignore. I wonder if the alarm of the inevitable showed in my mother's eyes that holiday, and if she had looked down from the camera so she wouldn't be confronted with it when the film was returned from the drugstore.

I closed the magazine, looked at my mother and tried to imagine what her morning had been like. She had been alone in the house, studying the picture of my father and her that ran like a banner over their son's words. My mother surely had many fond memories of her time with my father, and I wondered whether some of them had managed to crowd out the painful remembrances as she read. Once again, I was troubled that my mother and I had become adversaries over someone we both loved.

"I'm sure you were sad a lot then, Mom," I said. "I'm sorry if I pushed you too much to remember things you didn't want to remember. It's just . . . it was important for me to find out about this."

"I know, Bill," she said. "It's been a long time."

Helen Marie called shortly after we arrived. "It was wonderful," she said when I got on the phone.

"Thanks. I'm glad you liked it."

"I did," she said, "but it was hard to finish. I was crying so much I had to keep stopping."

I almost apologized to Helen Marie for making her cry, but her tone said it wasn't necessary. There was a gratifying softness in my sister's voice that told me she had welcomed the sanction my article had given her to cry about our father.

Anne called during the afternoon, followed by aunts and uncles and cousins. It was a good Father's Day. My son was with me, and my inquiry into my father's death had, after beginning so destructively, come to a harmonious conclusion.

The incessant ringing of the telephone vibrated against my front door as I turned the key in the lock at ten o'clock that night. I didn't hurry to answer it. I was tired and it was a long walk to the receiver. I tried to ignore the sound while I calmly relocked the door and put my keys on the table. The phone was still bleating when I got into the kitchen. I answered it more to stop the clamor than out of a desire to talk with anyone.

"Hello?"

"Are you the man who wrote the article?" a young female voice asked. I rubbed my eyes with my free hand to interrupt the displeasure I felt before I spoke it. I was listed in the phone book, but no one had ever used that as a means to call me at home after I had published something.

"Yes, I am," I said.

"I never knew my father," the woman began in a

heavy working-class Philadelphia accent. "My mother either didn't know who the man was or she wouldn't tell me. Now I'm married, and I have a baby. But my husband just died of a disease I can't even pronounce, so my son won't have a father either. I'm not sure why I called you, but I felt like I had to. I've been calling you all day."

The telephone felt outsized in my hand as I stretched the cord to sit on top of a radiator. I searched for something comforting or sympathetic to say but found nothing. I had talked to some people and written a few thousand words. I hadn't meant to volunteer for this kind of responsibility.

"I'm sorry this has happened to you," I said finally. "I know how difficult it is. I wish I could do something, but I don't know what that would be."

"If you could talk to me, like you talked to those people you wrote about, that would help me."

I could hear the woman crying at the other end of the line. "I'm not doing anymore interviews," I said. "I'm finished with this topic. And I know I don't have any answers for you. I'm just a writer—I don't know how to help you. Maybe your husband's doctor could recommend someone for you to talk to. Or is there a mental health center in your neighborhood?"

We talked for a few minutes before I wished my caller good luck and hung up.

My arm was trembling as I returned the phone to its cradle. There had been many highly charged moments during my interviews, but they had always come with warning. I had known the territory I was entering when I walked into someone's home with a tape recorder. There had been preliminaries on the phone and various forms of conversational foreplay during the start of the interviews—before the mania came. The abruptness of this telephone call had been like having a sidewalk grate give way as I stepped on it.

I mixed a strong gin and tonic, extinguished the lights

and started for my bedroom. The phone blared again before I got there.

"Are you Mr. Wartman?" the caller, another young woman, asked. I said that I was.

"Oh, thank God," she said. "I have to talk to you. My father died when I was three and my brother was one. Last year my brother committed suicide, and I know it was because my father died. I must talk to you. You understand."

"No," I protested, "I don't understand anything. It wouldn't help you to talk to me. You need to talk to someone professional, someone who has training."

"Shrinks can't help," she interjected. "They don't understand. My brother had shrinks and look what happened to him."

This woman wasn't going to be talked off of the phone, but I didn't want to be rude. My writing had provoked this; I owed her civility at least. I told the woman that she would be the first one I would call if I decided to interview more people but made no commitment beyond that.

I disconnected the telephone and went to bed. I thought it would be safe to reconnect the device the following morning—it was Monday, people were at work—but the calls resumed. The first was from a man who didn't even inquire if he had reached the correct party.

"Did you have any brothers?" I heard a voice say when I picked up the receiver.

"Excuse me?" I asked.

"Brothers. Did you have any brothers?"

"Who is this? What is this about?"

"I read that article you wrote yesterday in the paper," the man said. I could hear office sounds—conversations and clicking typewriters—in the background. "You said you had all these problems because your father died. That's because you didn't have any brothers. My father died when I was a kid, but I came from a big Italian family. My older brothers were like fathers to me. My grand-father was around all of the time. And I went to Catholic school where there were priests.

"If those people you talked to had good strong fam-ilies with a lot of discipline in them, they wouldn't have had those troubles. I know about this. My father died when I was a kid, but it hasn't messed up my life."

"Look," I said, "thank you for calling, but I'm not doing any more interviews."

"Interview?" the man asked, stunned. "Who said anything about an interview?"

"If you didn't call to volunteer for an interview, then why did you call?"

The line was silent for a moment, until the man banged the receiver down and severed our connection.

The calls continued all morning and I was reminded that the most salient characteristic of a family with an ab-sent father was the absence of conversation about the man. Distraught widows and outraged deserted women im-posed moratoriums on talk in the the hope that the sub-ject, like the man, would disappear. Instead, the men took up residence in their children, where the women couldn't see them and the children always did.

I decided to go for a walk to escape the needy pleas that were being piped into my home. I found something extending through the mail slot when I reached the front door. It was a note that read, "I hope you don't feel like I've invaded your privacy too horribly. I haven't been able to reach you on the phone, so I got your address from the phone book. My father died and I have to talk to you. . . ."

I tried not to get upset. I told myself it would pass in a few days. When the mail arrived on Tuesday, there was an envelope with the name of my street abbreviated as it was in the phone book and without a zip code. The note inside began, "Human scum like you doesn't deserve to live. You better keep your eyes open or you might not be breathing much longer. Someone could be watching you."

I panicked and called the police. Two patrolmen arrived, examined the letter and took me to the West Philadelphia detective bureau to file a report. I paced back and forth in the brutally plain and soiled waiting room until a detective was available. Each man who was led through in handcuffs, and each woman who came to post bail with screaming children and the trials of the world etched into her face, increased my distress.

The detective who summoned me to his dented metal desk saw my concern and advised me not to worry, that people wrote threatening letters frequently but seldom acted on them. I said I was sure he was right and that the letter wouldn't have bothered me if it hadn't been preceded by the phone calls.

The detective read the letter and asked, "What about your article would have caused someone to write this?"

"The people who called said that I touched a nerve in them. I guess this person's nerve was more exposed than the others'."

"Do you think it was a man or a woman?" he asked.

"I've been wondering about that myself," I said. "It could be either. It could be from a man who left his family and feels guilty, from a woman who didn't want to hear that her ex-husband is important to their kids or even from a person who grew up without a father and didn't want to be reminded of the past. If I've learned anything from this project, it's that everybody has strong feelings about fathers. People love them or hate them. I haven't met anyone who was indifferent."

During the following weeks I received a number of letters that had been sent to me in care of the newspaper. They were generous and satisfying notes from a diverse group of people who hadn't known their fathers.

Many people wrote brief communiqués to acknowledge a shared experience. "I read your story through wet eyes and with a lump in my throat," one woman said, "knowing all too well what it is like to have your father die when you're a child."

Others identified with certain interviewees or characteristics that I had written about: "After my father died I developed into an extremely self-sufficient woman, the sort who can accomplish just about anything to which she sets herself. But, oh, the cravings for protection are sometimes overwhelming, as is the insecurity that apparently comes from its absence."

One woman found release in the article: "My father died four months before I was born, and he was never talked about by my mother. I fantasized about him, wrote letters to him and addressed them to heaven, and prayed that it was a mistake and he would return one day.

"No one, ever, in my whole life, anywhere, gave me a clue that it was okay to hurt because I never knew my father.

"Today I have a son and a daughter, and when I see my husband and my daughter together I think 'that is what it could have been like for me.'

"I will keep your article always. Thank you for telling me my pain is valid."

But for one man it had come too late: "I was very intrigued and greatly astonished by your article. I only wish you had written it ten years ago."

Those who had telephoned frightened me with their demands, their intrusiveness and their attempts to make me into the all-knowing man they probably thought their fathers were. It wasn't like that with the people who had taken the time to write; their letters replenished rather than drained me. I had tried to make sense of and share one aspect of my life in the article, and my correspondents responded in kind, acknowledging what I had said and modulating it with their own perceptions.

The project was over, and I had learned a great deal, especially from the people I had spoken with. The interviews had been the most difficult to arrange and conduct I had ever done. Nonetheless, people were amazingly forthcoming and tolerant of my insistent questioning. I was astounded by the stories I had heard and transformed in my thinking about the significance of a father to a person's identity, confidence and notion of safety in the world. The work had changed the way I thought about myself and my life.

On the Friday before Christmas of 1983, I drove to the Camden, New Jersey, campus of Rutgers University at one o'clock. I had been teaching writing courses there for the past year, and I would have a paycheck waiting for me. Classes had ended several weeks before for the long semester break, and the campus was quiet. I went to the English department, got my check from the secretary and collected the accumulated mail from my mailbox. The box was littered with advertising brochures from textbook publishers and junk mail from insurance companies. I sorted through it as I walked down the narrow tiled corridor to the alcove where my office was located.

Amidst the third-class mail was a bright red envelope in the square shape of a Christmas card. It was addressed to me in care of, rather than at, Rutgers—as a stranger would send mail. The stamp hadn't been canceled, and there was no postmark or return address on the exterior. I wondered who it could be from. The *Inquirer* had mentioned where I taught in the magazine, and I had received some letters at school over the summer, but the last had arrived months before.

I let myself into my office and flipped the lights on with my right elbow. I dropped the rest of my mail onto the desk and sat down to open the envelope without taking my coat off. It was a card with two poinsettias on the front under the words, "Remembering you at Christmas." I didn't recognize the name that was inside, but there was a long note that had been written in a careful hand with a fountain pen.

Dear Mr. Wartman. I planned on writing to you in June when your most stirring article about the loss of your dad appeared in the Sunday magazine, but time has a way of getting away from us. I kept the article and have read it many times.

I remember your family well, especially your dad. We were neighbors on Beechwood Street. My husband and I lived a few doors from your grandparents, and the same distance from your home on the corner. I have memories of your dad and his brother growing up and going out on dates. Then of course the big day—your dad's wedding day. How happy he looked that morning. Then a few years later how pleased we were when we heard your dad and his new wife were buying a house on our block.

We had done the same thing. My husband was raised in the neighborhood and we had bought our first house near his parents' home.

I can remember how proud your dad was of his two little ones—holding you in his arm and holding your sister by the hand as he walked you up the street to visit his folks.

Then the terrible shock when we heard about his illness! We could see him failing every day. The happy smile was gone and we could see the fear and worry in his eyes. His last trip home from the hospital with his head bandaged made us feel so sad and useless. We knew that the end would be soon.

Through all of this your mother in her quiet, silent way suffered alone. We all prayed for her, so young and what a terrible sorrow to carry.

The day of the funeral we will never forget. Why would God take such a good man, so early in his life, with so much to live for? He had a wonderful wife, two lovely children and his own home. What a wonderful start your parents had.

We moved from Beechwood Street many years

ago. We left there with memories of many good times and very sad times. Your dad's death was one of the saddest. My husband passed away several years ago at age sixty-five. God was good to us and we had a long happy life together.

Thank you for writing the article. I am sure your dad is very proud of you.

The grief that was released had been crammed away for so long I couldn't recognize it as my own. Tears and utterances and mucous emanated from my head with such force I worried I would lose consciousness if I cried any harder. Then it would subside, only to begin again.

Each time I reread the card a new image would engulf me—my father at his wedding; my father taking us to visit his parents; my father with his head bandaged; my father dying; my father knowing I had written that story for us and being proud—and then sorrow would pound me as if I had never cried before.

The pressure was too measureless to strain against. I didn't consider running or resisting. I had learned, without knowing how, that I could release the pain and my life wouldn't dissipate with it. I locked the door, wrapped my arms around myself to pull my heavy winter coat close against the chill and cried until I didn't have another tear.

I recognized then that all of my interviews and research had been a conceit, an intricate charade I had worked on myself. I had thought I could use my intelligence to disarm the feelings that had been inexorably ripping loose from their containments since my thirtieth birthday, five years before. I had questioned others, analyzed them and tried their distress on for fit—as if in hearing others' grief I could dispel my own.

All of my endeavors had been abstractions. I had sought to make Mike's and Susan's and Janice's and the others' fathers mine, and they weren't and never would be. I had committed the same transgression as the re-

searchers whose work I had spurned at the inception of
my search. I had created a laboratory glass slide of a father, one I could mourn theoretically.

Discovering the picture in the attic marked the onset
of recognition. My father was so remote from my life then
that seeing us together in the photograph was the first
psychically admissable evidence I had that my father actually had lived—that he had courted my mother, danced
at his wedding and conceived and loved his son. But a
picture is finally only a mechanical representation waiting
for meaning, and I couldn't supply it then. The discovery
was too shocking, the memory too remote.

The woman who sent the card was a living witness
to the events she related, and her images had a testimon-
ial authenticity that the camera's couldn't. Her note put
me in my father's arms, in my grandfather's house with
my father, and, in whatever way two year olds perceive
the world, in our house knowing my father was missing.

I would have dismissed the possibility of—or need
for—such a reconnection with my father as hysterical
nonsense a few years before, as questionable speculation
a few months ago. But when that card undid me, I knew
it was truth.

It was time for me to abandon the counterfeit emotions and to travel inward, to find my father, as Robert
and Stuart had in their ways. Sitting in my office, defeated by exhaustion, I found new sympathy for my interviewees' reluctance. Disinterring the dead was not
something a person did willfully. One had to find one's
self in a position of no choice.

There were two steps awaiting me. I had half considered them before, in the way I thought about remar-
rying and having children—as dreamy visions I toyed with
in the minutes between waking and casting off the blan-
kets on winter mornings. Now I was compelled to act. I
would contact my father's only surviving blood relative—
his brother, my Uncle Jeff, a man I had last seen at Helen

Marie's wedding sixteen years earlier. I would also visit my father's grave, a site I hadn't been to in twenty years.

My Uncle Jeff had been transferred from Philadelphia to Pittsburgh years earlier by the food company with which he had spent his entire career. My Uncle Jeff and my mother shared no love, and our families had had little contact even when we lived close by. I had never exchanged a word with the man about my father. I had no notion how he would respond to a request from his distant nephew for information about his long-dead brother. I knew my mother would interpret my decision to contact my uncle as betrayal. I also knew that, like my interviewees who had debated contact with their living father, I was going to be shattered if Uncle Jeff turned me away.

A journey to the cemetery could be as simple as communicating with my uncle could be complex. My father was buried in Holy Sepulcher Cemetery in the far northwestern corner of Philadelphia. I need only consult a map, enter my car and drive. But oh, that prospect immobilized me. It had required the picture and the Christmas card to persuade me that my father had lived. I suspected only the grave would bring forth full comprehension of his death.

It was early evening when I rode the elevator to the first floor. I went to the parking lot with my collar up, my hands burrowed deep into my pockets. I often cursed winter, but that night the bitter air had no bite. It felt sharp and clean against my cheeks. I was humbled and calm.

I thought about the magnificent gift the woman's note had become as I cut through the Christmas shopping traffic. It had provoked a catharsis that promised to restore the splendor of my feelings. I would never be as afraid of sadness and happiness as I had been before that day. I wouldn't be as quick to consider the worst possible manifestation of each encounter until spontaneity was obliterated. I was beginning to face down the actuality of my father's death. So far, the horror of it hadn't killed me.

I wanted to thank my correspondent, but I couldn't. The woman had intentionally omitted a return address from her message. I rejected the impulse to begin thumbing telephone directories—the recollection of my unsolicited supplicants precluded that. I could only accept that I had received the rarest kind of offering, one that came without a price. I would always be appreciative of that woman, and I could only trust she had known that when she took pen in hand.

The *Philadelphia Inquirer* called in May of 1984 to say another magazine wanted to buy reprint rights to my Father's Day article, and the paper had given them my phone number. Not many writers are going to retire on secondary sales income, but, in a profession where grocery money can be elusive, any sum received without having to put a word on paper is manna.

My pleasure was increased when the editor called shortly afterward. She had enjoyed the piece so much when she saw it in the *Inquirer,* she said, that she had been waiting for a year to buy it.

"Where is your paper located?" I asked.

"Pittsburgh," she said.

"Pittsburgh?" I shouted. "Pittsburgh, Pennsylvania?"

"Yes," she said. "Is something wrong?"

"My father's only brother lives in Pittsburgh. I haven't seen him in years, and I've been thinking about contacting him. The irony in someone from Pittsburgh, of all the cities in the country, publishing the article is incredible.

"I've been wanting to write to my uncle but avoiding it. I've been waiting for something to compel me, and now you have. I'll have to contact him before you run the article."

I considered what I was going to say to my uncle for

three weeks. I was concerned he would think I had arranged to have the article published in his backyard as an embarrassment. My uncle hadn't been involved in my life since his brother died, and that would be evident to readers—my uncle wasn't present or alluded to in the article. It was chance the Pittsburgh editor had called me, but I wasn't certain my uncle would believe that.

I also mulled over what personal things I might tell him to increase my chances of getting a favorable response. One of the few memories I had of Uncle Jeff's house in Philadelphia was an oil painting of Christ's face in which thickened paint had been pushed on the canvas with a blade, rather than stroked on with a brush. Peaks of liturgical red and purple paint rose from the surface so the picture resembled a topographical map.

The painting had captivated me as a child and, given the endless lure about signs from God the priests and nuns circulated, it fostered the notion that my uncle must have been blessed to have such a dramatic picture in his home. I concluded from that remembrance that I would have to present my unCatholic-like divorce carefully.

I also remembered Uncle Jeff as a crew cut, spit-shined wingtips, former marine whose career was in sales. He drank nothing but water when he visited us in Parkside, and, while ingesting it, he would hold forth with conviction on the marked superiority of suburban water over its urban counterpart. Uncle Jeff was quick to make a joke or talk sports, but he wouldn't be anxious to dredge up difficult memories. He was a hail-fellow-well-met extrovert; he would recoil at the first sign of emotionalism.

As I debated these points with myself and tried to remember my uncle, I recognized our only connection, outside of his brother, seemed to be that we had graduated from the same university.

When I avoided writing until the letter couldn't be delayed further, I knew how avidly I believed my uncle wouldn't be happy to receive my message and how much that distressed me. My uncle's previous lack of concern wasn't a good omen. But he had had four children of his own to raise, an hour's driving time separated us and he had no blood relations with my family. I had never had childhood expectations of him as I did of my Uncle Bill, so I never felt that he had disappointed me. Now, I needed him.

I had never bothered Uncle Jeff before. How could he turn me away the first time? Besides, I reasoned, childhood analogies didn't apply. The grown son of his dead brother was approaching him as an adult. He would recognize his duty to his brother. My uncle was only in his early sixties, but, nonetheless, he would sense the number of pages left on his calendar were shrinking, and he would want to resolve familial affairs while he could.

He would be delighted to hear from me, pleased at the prospect of seeing his nephew and meeting my son for the first time. He'd want to hear about our lives, tell me about his children and reminisce about my father. Joe and I would fly to Pittsburgh for the weekend—I had seen discount airfares advertised in the travel section last Sunday—and it would be a mutually rich and rewarding convocation of three generations of men who carried some of the same genes.

I would return with vibrant images of my father—as a school boy, at home with his parents, as a brother, as a man who knew he was dying. My perplexing isolation from my father would be ended. And I would regain a portion of my life that had been lost—my father's family.

"Dear Uncle Jeff," I began the note in early June. "After not having seen you for so long, I hope my letter won't come as too much of a shock. I'm writing now because a magazine article I wrote about my having grown up without a father is going to appear in Pittsburgh on Father's Day, and I wanted to let you know about it in advance so you wouldn't have an even bigger shock if you happened upon the article without warning.

"For the past few years I have been talking to people about the experience of growing up without knowing their fathers. Last Father's Day I published an article on this topic in the *Philadelphia Inquirer* Sunday magazine. The editor of the Pittsburgh magazine saw the article last year and bought reprint rights from me to run it in her magazine this year.

"This project had been a rewarding one for me. The subject is still so painful for my mother that she is unable to talk about my father, so I grew up knowing little about him. After the article appeared in the *Inquirer,* a woman who had lived on Beechwood Street contacted me to say that she had known you and my father as children and that she remembered when my father died.

"I don't know how you will feel about this, but I would really like to talk to you about my father some time. I realize that he has been dead for many years now, and that nothing is going to change that, but I know so little about him that, to me, it sometimes feels as if he never existed. Hearing about my father from you could help make him seem more like a real person to me.

"I have been making my living as a professional writer for some years now, and I also teach writing in college and run a writer's organization. I live close to the University of Pennsylvania where I, and I think you, went to college. My son is now a sixteen-year-old, six-footer, and, while I'm divorced, he lives nearby and I see him quite frequently. He looks very much like me, which is to say he looks like a Wartman.

"I hope that you like my article."

I signed it "Best Regards, Bill Wartman."

I put the letter aside for a few days, then went back and did some polishing. When I was satisfied with the prose, I wrote a clean copy and appended my address and telephone number to the bottom. I didn't want to risk having the letter damaged if kids put water or firecrackers in the local mail-deposit box on my corner, so I delivered it to the central post office at Thirtieth Street.

I figured the best I could hope for was a call on Father's Day when the piece ran. When that didn't happen, I waited for a brief note in the following weeks. It didn't come either.

My uncle never acknowledged or responded to the letter.

CHAPTER 10

My mother had been incensed when I told her, in advance of the Pittsburgh magazine sale, that I was going to contact her brother-in-law. "He won't talk to you," she had said bitterly. "That guy never did anything for anyone. Look at the way he battled with his mother."

My mother's case against my uncle, as I understood it, seemed to be based largely on the nature of his relationship with Grandmother Wartman. Mom Mom, as we called our father's mother, was a diminutive but feisty German woman with bad eyes and a sharp tongue to which she gave full rein. Mom Mom, perhaps because of her vision rather than indifference, ignored people's reactions to the pronouncements she delivered in a voice ringing with exclamation. She had been the only member of my extended family who had supported me in my divorce initially, and she routinely expressed that unsolicited and unappreciated conviction at family gatherings.

Mom Mom had outlived her husband by twenty years, surviving falls and illnesses unscathed. She seemed indestructible. "I should have died years ago," she would say with characteristic bluntness, as she peered at the floor through her thick glasses and hobbled forward on a cane as I guided her to the dinner table. She was near ninety when she died.

I remember Mom Mom as an uncomplicated, if unequivocal, woman who found irony everywhere and who always seemed to favor me over my sisters. Nonetheless, family stories of antagonism between Uncle Jeff and Mom Mom, including a wedding-day fight Mom Mom had with Uncle Jeff's new bride, Mary, made it easier for me, if not my mother, to appreciate why Uncle Jeff might not have remained a devoted son.

For the duration of our childhoods, amidst all the requisites of working and raising three children, my mother had spent many Sunday afternoons fighting the traffic on City Line Avenue driving us to Germantown to visit our paternal grandparents. Even after we children were grown, my mother continued to chauffeur Mom Mom to and from our family's activities until the woman died. My mother was generous to her mother-in-law. And she believed, on Mom Mom's word, that Uncle Jeff was neglectful of his mother, and this angered her.

When I decided I wanted to talk to Uncle Jeff, I disregarded judgments about him entirely. I didn't care what he had or had not done. I only wanted particulars from him, not moral guidance. But I again found myself in opposition to my mother's wishes.

The quality of my mother that salvaged our relationship during disagreements was her ability to recognize my superior stubbornness. Regardless of her degree of obstinacy on an issue, if I took an equally obstinate contrary position, and announced I was going to do what I wanted to do, whether she concurred or not, she would ultimately be accepting, if not approving, of my resolution.

Each time I spoke with my mother during the summer of 1984, she asked if I had heard from Uncle Jeff. "Not yet," I would say. My mother took this as confirmation of her expectations, but I was convinced that eventually my uncle would see me. The tenacity of family bonds I had witnessed in my interviews caused me to believe that no one, no matter how disengaged, could finally resist continued appeals from a dead sibling's child.

I would need to be persistent with my uncle and overcome some unidentified resistance. I was prepared to do that, but my inclination to grant him a blanket pardon was faltering. I had been willing to absolve him of any responsibility to me as a child, but his indifference to my correspondence as an adult caused me to question my prior benevolence.

I had allowed my mother her solitude regarding my father because she seemed unable to speak without exorbitant pain. I couldn't imagine my uncle had suffered similar emotional paralysis—his insensitivity to my letter demonstrated that excessive tenderness was not his infirmity.

If my uncle wouldn't see me of his own volition, I decided, I'd travel to Pittsburgh uninvited. I'd drive west out of Philadelphia at daybreak, hurry across the state and converge on my uncle's street in early evening. I'd park a few houses away and keep his place under surveillance until he pulled into the driveway after work. I'd cruise down the block, get a confirming look, then ease away to allow him to get into the house and pour a drink.

I wouldn't park at the curb when I came back. I'd
steer into the driveway behind his car, as if that were my
due. Uncle Jeff would see my headlights bounce off of
the picture window in the family room and jump out of
his reclining chair. "Mary," he'd call out to his wife, "who
the hell is that pulling into our driveway?"

I'd go up the walk with my head tilted so he couldn't
identify me and give the door two solid raps. My uncle
would edge back the curtain on one of the two columns
of small windows that flanked the door and suspiciously
look around the knickknacks that my aunt had placed
there.

I'd detect the movement and spin to catch his glance.
First his eyes would be questioning, then his eyelids would
fly back in distress and his pupils would flash the glassy
chaos of an animal caught in human light.

He'd yank the curtain back and call out, "Mary, Jesus Christ, it's Billy Wartman. Billy Wartman is standing
out there knocking on our goddamn front door. Can you
believe this? Billy Wartman from Philadelphia pulls into
the driveway and knocks on the goddamn door, just like
that!"

"Well, let him in," a female voice would say.

"Like hell I will," would be the rejoinder. "That kid
can't mean anything but trouble. I'm not letting him into
my house. Close the drapes and lock the doors. He'll get
tired of standing out there and leave."

"That's what you think," I'd call out threateningly
and go retrieve my sleeping bag from the trunk. I'd un-
roll it on the cement square outside the door then bang
on one of the little windows.

"You're going to talk to me whether you want to or
not, you bastard," I'd yell. "You've ignored me for thirty
years, but you're not going to anymore. I'm your dead
brother's son. You owe me! You will talk to me, or I'll
kick your ass the second you walk out of the door."

A satisfied smile, one reflecting the pleasures of retaliation, would come to my lips as I played out that scenario in my mind. I'd feel powerful and vindicated. Then the ancient vulnerability that would have provoked such a journey always edged forward a question. What if Uncle Jeff went for the telephone, and a police cruiser arrived?

A heavy man with sergeant's stripes and blush skin from high blood pressure would walk across the lawn with his right hand finger-deep in his back pocket. His thin hair would be solid white and smell of Vitalis. He would see the respectable clothing I had worn to visit my uncle and know I wasn't going to be trouble.

"What's the problem, son?" he would ask gently.

"I'm here to talk to my uncle," I'd say, "but he won't let me in."

"There isn't any law that says a man has to talk to his nephew."

"But this is different. I'm trying to find out about my father. He's been dead for thirty years and I don't know anything about him. My uncle is the only one I can come to. Nobody else can help me. Is this too much to ask—for a nephew to want his uncle to give him a few hours of his time to help him learn about his father?"

"In most cases it wouldn't be," the sergeant would say, "but in this case it appears it is. If the man doesn't want to talk to you, he doesn't have to. I'm sure he has his reasons. Why don't you call it a day and go on home now, son?"

"I can't do that," I'd say, water in my eyes, my voice getting thick. "I have to find out about my father."

"Come on, son," he would say and begin gathering up my sleeping bag. "Let's get you into your car and back on the road before your uncle sees you out here crying. What would he think of a great big drink-of-water like you crying in public like a baby? If you leave now, I won't even write this one up. No one will know you were here. You'll save yourself a lot of embarrassment."

I'd let the sergeant lead me to the car, then I'd look weakly at the house. "Fuck you, Uncle Jeff," I'd say before I left. "You're nobody to me."

While I was wrestling with the dangers of a trip to Pittsburgh, an improbability occurred. My mother informed me, in spite of her opposition to my proposed dealings with Uncle Jeff, that a notice had appeared in a local newspaper concerning my uncle's oldest son. My cousin, who hadn't lived near Philadelphia in many years, was getting married in September to a woman who lived close to the suburban borough where I had grown up.

Uncle Jeff would be in my territory. There were only a few motels in the area; I could scout around, find out where he was staying and confront him. But the specific date of the nuptial wasn't given, and it was, after all, going to be a wedding weekend. I couldn't disrupt the occasion regardless of my anger. I decided to trust human nature and write my uncle a stronger letter.

"Dear Uncle Jeff," I wrote on September third. "I was disappointed that I didn't hear from you after I wrote in June. I assume your silence means you feel you don't want to talk with me about my father as I asked. While I am puzzled by that, if circumstances were any different I would respect your wishes and not trouble you any further. But, there are several factors involved that compel me to keep trying to reach you. I hope a more detailed explanation of why I want to talk to you will enable you to understand why I can't just let this pass.

"The primary cause for my persistence is you are the only one I can come to about this. You are literally the only person still living who knew my father well both as a child and a young man. There isn't anyone else I can talk with to learn more about my father. Even if you don't remember much about him, what you do remember is more than anyone else can tell me.

"If you saw my article you probably noted that one of the things that bothered me the most about growing up without a father was knowing so little about him.

Everyone believed the best way to protect me from the pain of my father's death was not to talk about him. While that may have seemed to have been the best way when I was a child, I am now an adult who is caught in the same bind. I still don't know very much about my father, and my need to know about him has only intensified with time.

"The picture of my father and me that accompanied my article is priceless to me. Every bit of information I get about my father puts more life into that picture and helps me recreate an image of my father for myself and my son. There are few other things in my life that have been as rewarding as 'finding' my father after all of these years. Your knowledge of my father would be invaluable to me.

"I saw in a local paper that your oldest son is getting married in the area soon. Couldn't you please take a small amount of time at the end of that weekend to meet with me before you leave town? I don't know what your concerns over talking with me are, but you have my word that I will do whatever I can to eliminate them. Again, I'm sorry to be persistent about this, but I hope you can understand both how important this is to me and that you are the only person I can come to.

"Although this is an emotional subject for me, it isn't that I can't talk about it without going to pieces. What I would like to do is have a regular old everyday conversation with you about what you remember about my father. I don't want to involve you in this in any other way than to get some information from you."

I retraced my path to the central post office, deposited the letter and resumed my wait, certain that I had made an appeal my uncle couldn't resist. The telephone never rang.

I came home to make dinner with a friend at six o'clock on the evening of October 1. I paused to scan the mail quickly before going to the kitchen and halted at an envelope of expensive personal stationery. The blue paper was hand addressed, the postmark was Pittsburgh. I flipped it over. The name printed on the back flap was that of my uncle's wife, my Aunt Mary.

"Oh, my God," I said in shock.

My companion asked what was wrong, but I could only shake my head. There shouldn't have been anything troublesome in receiving the acknowledgement I had been seeking since June, but the pounding of my heart told me there was.

I studied the envelope, unsure about opening it. I thought of my interview with Robert and how, after getting his father's address, he had carried it around unused for fifteen years. "It was like a bomb," he had said. "What happens if it goes off?"

"This is from my aunt in Pittsburgh," I explained to my friend. "I've written to her husband twice in the past four months trying to get him to talk to me about my father. I haven't heard from him. I didn't think he was going to answer me."

"Let's sit down," I said and gestured toward the couch. "I feel like I've been blindsided. I'm going to need a minute to recover and to prepare to read this. I'll explain it to you later. I'm not going to be able to talk right now."

I took long deep breaths and released them slowly to shunt energy through my lungs. I handled the envelope and considered which would be worse—my aunt saying my uncle would see me, or her saying that he wouldn't?

I ran my finger gently under the flap and pulled the folded pages free. I held the letter loosely as I read it, trying to dampen the responses it would provoke.

My aunt began the long letter by explaining that she hadn't received my last message until she had returned from the wedding. She said that she was living in Pittsburgh alone because Uncle Jeff had been transferred to New Jersey, that they hadn't been able to sell their old house and their new one wasn't completed. My uncle hadn't been able to get back to me, she said, because of all of the confusion. "I haven't even told him of your second letter," she added.

"When your mother returned to her family after your father's death, it was a happy home she took you to. Your Grandmother Glatts is a wonderful, kind woman. After rearing her own family, she undertook the rearing of you, your sister and a new baby. You children received more attention than you could ever know. Your Uncle Bill adored you and was a second father to you. He got a job for your mother and was always with you.

"Your dad was extremely close to his mother. He was very mild and quiet. Your dad and Uncle Jeff were like black and white, very different and not real close. Growing up, Jeff was always getting into fights in the playground and was into baseball and tennis. They didn't seem to do much together. When your dad became ill, Uncle Jeff said Bill was too good to suffer, and that it should have happened to him.

"Your dad was the apple of his mother's eye and catered to her always. Uncle Jeff was for his father. When Grandpop Wartman got cancer, Uncle Jeff was heartbroken. He carried both your dad and then his father into the hospital for cobalt treatments. When your Grandmother Wartman lost a son and her husband, she made great demands on Jeff, and he is not one to cater.

"When you were growing up, all said you were like your Uncle Jeff and looked like him. Don't know you'll want to hear this! Let us get settled in our new house, and I *promise* Uncle Jeff will see you. Give me time and I'll work it out."

I put the letter down with uneasy relief. "My uncle is going to see me," I said.

"Soon?" my friend asked.

"When they move into their new house. It's supposed to be done by Christmas. My aunt said she would contact me."

"You must be excited."

"I guess I am," I said, "but it's also like I'm afraid to be excited. Most of all I feel confused. Let's eat and talk about something else."

My thoughts kept drifting away from the conversation all evening, as I wondered what I had gotten myself in for. Would the meeting bring happiness or sadness, benefit or futility? And why did the prospect of seeing my uncle suddenly seem so ominous?

My aunt had said that my Uncle Bill had adored me and was a second father to me. I believed my aunt; there was no reason for her to do my Uncle Bill's bidding. Why, though, hadn't I remembered him that way? I recalled being paid merely token attention. Perhaps my memory had been selective, and I had chosen to remember Uncle Bill as neglectful. Now it appeared that was only part of the story.

My aunt's letter was dislocating me. It was blurring the lines I had circumscribed between myself and the people she had spoken of. Why would I have been hasty with my uncle Bill? What end would have been served by unfairness? And why was it unsettling that Uncle Jeff was going to talk with me? Was it because our meeting would force me to redefine my relationship with Uncle Jeff as well? How could creating an affiliation from ashes be frightening?

I found myself thinking about my Pop Pop Wartman later that evening. My grandparents had moved the few blocks from Beechwood Street to Price Street when I was about six, and most of my memories were of visiting them there. My grandfather had been a Republican committeeman and held city jobs, until the party machine that had controlled Philadelphia for the first half of the twentieth century was defeated in the 1951 election. My grandfather was sixty-one then, and he only worked occasionally after that.

Row house neighborhoods within Germantown had two distinguishing characteristics: the distance the homes were set back from the street and the exterior construction materials, either brick or fieldstone. The houses on Price Street were midrange. They were perched on aboveground basements and garages that elevated the first stories of the houses fifteen feet about street level, and the brick buildings were set back from the street another twenty-five feet. The fieldstone front porches, which all of the houses had, were accessed by climbing two flights of ten cement steps. The porches provided a majestic view of the street, and it was on his porch that Pop Pop practiced his favorite pastime.

Pop Pop hated pigeons, and their omnipresence in his neighborhood distressed him. He addressed the infestation by making it his retirement project to police the area abutting his porch with a slingshot. Pop Pop shot objects at pigeons the way other men played cards or did woodworking—he took it seriously.

When we visited Pop Pop in fair weather, he would slip his newest slingshot—one he had exactingly crafted from a Y-shaped section of tree branch, wide rubber bands and a bit of leather for the ammunition pouch—into the pocket of a light jacket. Then he would motion for me to follow him out onto the front porch.

Pop Pop would drop into one of the metal porch chairs and pull his glasses off to polish the lenses with a handkerchief. He'd call out to neighbors who walked down the street, seeming every bit the dutiful grandfather entertaining his grandson. All the while he would be studying the tires of the cars parked at the curb. When a pigeon appeared from behind one, Pop Pop would hastily remove his ordnance and take aim, sighting through the uprights of his weapon before letting the elastic band fly.

Pop Pop's projectiles of choice were marbles he purchased especially for these missions. They were, he would tell me in confidence, possessed of superior aerodynamic qualities over the common jagged-surface pebbles one found lying about.

Pop Pop wasn't an expert marksman. He seldom scored more than a cloud of street dust where the chunk of glass hit the tarmac a foot or more wide of a bird. The pigeons recognized the enemy when they encountered him, however, and they would scurry off to a safer haven in a rush of feather. Pop Pop would laugh derisively and say, "I'd like to hear what that bird has to say to his brother when he gets down the street."

Pop Pop would continue his amusement until Mom Mom came to the screen door and caught him in the act. "Bill Wartman," she'd holler, "put that slingshot away before the SPCA comes and arrests you."

Pop Pop would tap me on the shoulder and say with a wink, "Let's get away from all of these women." We would escape by walking to the arboretum several blocks away to have a catch. I'd be pleased with the change of venue. I always felt sorry for the pigeons but never wanted to say so.

When we got to the park, we'd take our spots, twenty paces apart, facing each other. Pop Pop would lean forward with his pitch and wing the ball to me at a good clip. I wasn't a muscular or fearless child. I'd be careful to catch the ball in the webbing of the glove, between the thumb and index finger, but it would always sting my palm nevertheless.

I don't know if I winced from the impact, but Pop Pop would ask if he was throwing too hard for me. "Oh, no," I'd say real fast, afraid that our game would end.

The sensation of being a young boy in the solitary company of an adult male relative was exquisite. It was the means for receiving intelligence essential to avoid being a dopey little boy all your life. It was learning how to be a man—knowing who you were and what the world expected—from someone you thought was good at it and who cared enough about you to want you to learn well.

That evening I realized Joe and I had duplicated this ritual in a park three miles from the one I had visited with Pop Pop. We traveled there when the temperature was inhospitable to golf but not to an excursion. We had fallen into the journeys spontaneously, deciding once on the spur of the moment to visit a section of Fairmount Park near Valley Green Inn.

It was a narrow swatch of woodland that was cut by a stream with sharply pitched banks. We'd walk down one side of the river on the pedestrian path, and return on the densely wooded side, ducking and bending through the vegetation. Joe and I went there often, but I don't remember us exchanging a single word of significance on those days. Yet no matter how insolvent I was at the time, or what magnitude of travails were afflicting me, I always concluded those walks feeling the balance of my life was tipped to the positive side.

I didn't have those male audiences often when I was a child, and when I did, I never took any chances on messing them up. I didn't speak up for the pigeons, or ask Pop Pop to put a little more loft on the ball, because, I recognized now, I was afraid I was going to blow it.

I had been a boy who eternally believed he was going to drive men away. I didn't understand men, and I was comfortable with them only in the posture of an afflicted supplicant. I had intuited that people who received everything they were offered without objection were always in demand, because they were never any trouble. I adopted that model I dealt with men.

The possibility that Uncle Jeff would discontinue his silence spooked me. If I had chosen to remember that Uncle Bill and Pop Pop and Uncle Jeff ignored me, and they acted at their own pleasure, I was a victim. If they did pay attention and I chose to ignore it, then I liked being a victim. It was risk free. Victims were blameless and couldn't have shortcomings. Everything that happened to them was the result of others' pathologies. I had asked Uncle Jeff for something and it sounded as though he was going to give it to me. If I was going to cease being a victim with men, I would have to recompose how I saw myself in relation to them.

But if the letter caused me to question my relationships with men, I also found, as I perused the document during subsequent weeks, much about the links between men and women. Part of the story of growing up without one's biological father was the saga of displacement between the males and females of a family in the father's wake. Sons and daughters lost an intermediary between them and their mothers, and wives lost a marital counterpart.

My mother, Aunt Mary and Mom Mom—and the mothers of all of my interviewees—were women of prefeminist generations. They presumed their dealings with familial men operated within prescribed guidelines. Men dealt with the world, women with domesticity. The women gave the whole of themselves to their husbands and families at marriage, and they had specific notions about what was due them in return. When husbands and fathers defaulted by dying or disappearing, however, the wives/ mothers sometimes looked to their male offsprings to meet the terms of the fathers' agreements.

Aunt Mary's cautious letter implied that my uncle had refused to see me when he had received my first note in June. There were, after all, postal boxes in New Jersey where he could have deposited a letter, or even a post card, to me. My aunt now intended, as a kindness to me, to change Uncle Jeff's mind. She was the sentimental, emotional half of her marriage, and my appeal had touched her as it could not her husband. Uncle Jeff was the gruff provider of the family, Aunt Mary the gentle nurturer.

She would act as my agent, gauging my uncle's moods and waiting for his disposition to be correct. When it was, she would tell him of my second letter. She would make my case as doggedly as necessary to win my claim, and she was so confident she would secure my uncle's acquiescence she had pledged it in advance. Uncle Jeff, despite his misgivings, would accede to his wife because he loved her and needed her. It was part of their marriage deal that he would occasionally allow himself to be persuaded.

It was one matter for a partner to make such requests of a husband and another for a mother to ask it of a son—particularly an adult son. One of my nuns' favorite Bible stories in grammar school had been the Marriage Feast of Cana. Their telling of the St. John Gospel emphasized that Christ had refused to replenish the wine at the reception—by miraculously transforming water into wine—until he was asked to do so by his mother. When the Blessed Mother made the entreaty, they said, he dismissed her, saying it was not yet his time to begin performing miracles. But the Virgin Mary, knowing that her son would indulge her, unobtrusively told the servants to follow whatever instructions Jesus gave them. Jesus, sure enough, went on to quietly create extraordinary wine for the festivities. The moral of the story, according to my nuns, was if the Son of God couldn't refuse his mother, how could any man?

I found some sympathy for Uncle Jeff in his dealings with Mom Mom that Aunt Mary had described in her letter. I knew of the expectations that traditional mothers, once they lost their husbands, could transfer to their sons. Part of this was necessity. Women alone with children had tremendous obligations forced on them, and survival demanded cooperation from everyone. Yet there was another, less pragmatic aspect to mother-son dependency that I had heard of in my interviews and in which my mother and I had some history.

Uncle Jeff had been a family man when he became

Mom Mom's last surviving male, and she, apparently, transferred her expectations of her husband onto her son. Uncle Jeff, also apparently, had expressed his unwillingness to satisfy those desires, for reasons unknown, and the battle lines between mother and son were drawn.

Little boys cannot decline their mothers as easily as men, nor are they as apt to want to. The jettisoned mantel of "man of the house" was a tantalizing cloak for a boy to resist when it lay on the hearth unclaimed. Some of the men I had spoken to, as well as myself, had grasped it gleefully during our childhoods.

Playing at little man of the house fed into the greatest child's wish of all—to escape childhood entirely and become an instant grown-up. Childhood isn't an end but a germinating period for that magical day when you become a real person like your parents. One didn't have to practice by playing house when the father was missing; one could live house.

Stuart had told me during our interview that his mother and stepfather had come to him when he was eight and asked if he would like to have a little brother or sister. Stuart said no, and his parents never had a child, presumably because Stuart didn't want to share his domain with a sibling. "That's the kind of prince I was," he said. "Eight years old and my word ruled."

Appropriating the father role also paid a bonus. Not only were boys given the priceless opportunity to become premature adults, but they would also win a special place in their mothers' hearts. They could become mommies' lilliputian surrogate husbands, sometimes serving as mommies' escorts and gaining other special privileges.

It struck me that this had been the essence of Robert's talk about his mother's seductiveness. It wasn't the mother wanting sexually to corrupt the child but desiring to create a special bond between herself and the little boy who was the last remnant of the man she had loved and lost. Little girls were supposed to want to be the apple of their daddies' eyes, but little boys certainly didn't mind being their mothers' elfin Prince Charmings.

My sisters had remained children when we were growing up. They helped with the housework but never had outside jobs, while my mother kept watch over them. I got, or perhaps seized, the right to look out for myself and be self-sufficient. While aspects of that were heady stuff that I willingly embraced, I wondered if, like Stuart, I wasn't a precious little prince who got his own way too easily and too completely.

I thought I had relished the role, granting me, as it did, a place of apartness from my sisters. I took care of the car and made house repairs, while exacting in exchange total autonomy, as though I were turning my paycheck over to my mother rather than disposing of it myself. In reviewing the past, however, I now wondered if being a miniature father didn't entail a disappointing foreshortening of childhood. I considered if I hadn't missed being able to be just a kid, and if one aspect of my excursion into my father's death wasn't my seeking the childhood I had lost to responsibility.

I had accepted the notion, which surfaced in my father's absence, that I was indeed an unformed man who should protect and help the women, without making other than domestic demands. I arrogantly separated myself from my mother's control when I didn't know anywhere near as much as I had convinced myself I did. I extorted enormous leeway as an adolescent. I answered to no one.

If I sometimes got into trouble, I had, for the most part, been an overly responsible child. I began working to support myself at an early age, and I had put myself through college by hook and crook. All the time I was doing this I was earning my mother's tacit approval by being her little man.

My mother's endorsement stood in the stead of the consensus I failed to receive from men. I cultivated a talent for pleasing women with facility. And as I thought about the qualities of the women I had dated seriously, I began to understand that my mother was the woman I had dated longest.

I also wondered if some of the anger I had felt toward my mother when she refused to talk about my father didn't have its roots elsewhere. Could I have been angry at her for allowing me to be husband replacement—a result of feeling guilty if I didn't take care of her, while resenting it when I did?

I knew that I had identified some misdirected feelings on my mother's part. I was familiar with the anger my mother held toward Uncle Jeff, because that wrath had once been directed toward me. My mother had been furious at me when I got divorced. Although she came to understand the marriage had been a mistake, the recognition was slow in coming.

I believe that, to my mother, both my Uncle Jeff and I were Wartman men who left women—as her Wartman man, my father, had left her. Because she had not dealt with my father's death completely, and hadn't passed through the normal stage of anger at the person who has deserted the survivors, my uncle and I were, I believed, the recipients of anger that was actually directed at my father.

CHAPTER

11

Aunt Mary sent a Christmas card wishing me well and explaining their new house still wasn't completed. She would, she promised, be in touch as soon as they were settled. It was just as well, I thought. The holidays were always busy enough without the added trauma of a reunion. Late winter would be an excellent time for a visit, a means of escaping the drab present with a detour into the unknown past.

Spring, after Aunt Mary hadn't contacted me, also struck me as a perfectly proper time to call on relatives. When I didn't hear from her then, I couldn't identify any objection to a summer journey. The delay was understandable. It would be trying for an older couple to relocate after a long hibernation, what with all the packing and unpacking, the breaking and making of friendships.

Perhaps my uncle was being especially obtuse, and Aunt Mary was having difficulty making a clearing in his mood into which she could insert my plea. But the more I considered this possibility, the less it satisfied me. Why did Aunt Mary have to work wifely magic to secure me a hearing with my father's brother? Why did an uncle-nephew rendezvous require that a deal be cut, like some familial trade agreement?

Uncle Jeff could have spurned my initial inquiry because of his animosity toward my mother, but, if he knew about the second letter, the rationalization no longer held. I was his sole petitioner now. We were dealing, through Aunt Mary, only with each other. This man had no case with me, legitimate or otherwise. I had committed no encroachments against him. I hadn't seen him often enough to have had the opportunity.

As the months continued to pass, I began to surmise Aunt Mary's word might be as thin as the extenuation she had offered when Uncle Jeff had disregarded my first letter, and my resolve was intensified. This man, my uncle, would talk to me, if only to specify his objection to talking. I would call on him, invited or not.

He would be harder to stalk this time. Aunt Mary had—coincidentally?—only divulged the state on their new residence, and it happened to be the most densely populated province in the country. Nonetheless, I would find that bastard and he would answer to me.

My son went into the hospital in July to have minor elective surgery performed on a deviated septum. I have never been admitted to a hospital. I always get the willies the moment I step inside the front door of one—when the scent of infirmity closes in on me, and I begin to worry I will contract a disease by osmosis and they will make me stay.

Joe wasn't concerned about the operation. He was having trouble breathing and wanted the procedure performed. He has my nose, only worse. I used to wake up with my pillowcase caked with dried blood from nosebleeds, but they halted when I was eleven or twelve. His have continued. Veins in his nose have already been cauterized to staunch the blood. Now he blows his nose excessively in the morning to clear it, so he doesn't have to breathe through his mouth all day.

This will be corrected by the surgeon and his knife. It's part of the program of modern medicine. Joe will be back on the street in a few days with a nose that works. It's silly, but one aspect of the enterprise nags me. The surgery is to be performed in the same hospital in which my father died.

I arrive at the hospital sleepless at seven on the morning of the operation to see my son, who has spent the previous night there, before he is taken away. Joe's mother is present. We are not friends, and the tension is tangible when we are forced together.

I watch my son being wheeled out of the room on the gurney. He is struggling against a ridiculously skimpy hospital gown to maintain his dignity, while I fight against the apprehension that is making my tongue swell and my palms sweat. I promise myself that I am not going to get alarmed. I am not going to dwell on the dangers inherent in anesthesia or the multivariate forms of human error.

I buy a newspaper and go to the hospital cafeteria to have breakfast. I select the extra-large container of coffee to accompany my eggs and sausage then walk to a distant table. I don't want to be disturbed or asked to move to another location. I will get lost in the food and the news, and then look up to see my son is due out of surgery any

minute. I'll have to hurry to the waiting room to hear the
surgeon say that the procedure went perfectly. There will
be no lowering of his voice, no professional regret in his
eyes.

My son is not out of surgery when I arrive in the
waiting room at the appointed time. Not to worry, what
gets completed on schedule today?

My son is not out of surgery at thirty minutes beyond schedule. I am patrolling the carpet between the
waiting room and the surgery, certain the doors will fly
open on my next approach. A doctor will emerge in a
rush and remove a green mask to reveal a smile.

My son is not out of surgery at forty-five minutes
beyond schedule, and I have found a civilian family coun-
selor. She is a well-meaning older woman who volunteers
her time to say generically soothing words to the families
of the afflicted. I tell her I want to know, immediately,
what is going on in the operating room. She says this information is not made available.

I plant my hands on her desk and lean forward until
our eyes are at the same level, six inches apart. "In this
case it will be," I say. The weight of my voice startles her
and she hurries down the hall. She returns with the news
that the procedure had been successfully completed. The
doctor will be out momentarily.

I am dizzy with relief and hear little of what the doctor says concerning extra bone and cartilage that had to
be removed. It's over and it's right. I couldn't comprehend anything else.

I mastered two hours of sleep that night and four
the next, as Joe began recovering from the operation. I
took my son home on the third day. There was a metal
splint on his nose and his face was bandaged, but my heart
resumed its normal rhythm when we were clear of the
building. I excitedly pointed across the street to show Joe
my new car, one I have been describing to him for the
past week. It was a used, five-year-old but showroom-

condition German sports car I had bought with money I borrowed from my mother.

We crawled through dense traffic in the city, but, when we exited the toll booth of the bridge into New Jersey, the highway before us was empty. I released the clutch and ran the engine up to six thousand RPMs in each gear. The whine of the engine was the poetry of precision, the lift of the front end at each gear change the embodiment of acceleration. We rocketed down the highway, the car tracking flatly though curves in the road.

Joe smiled at me from under his surgical dressing. I knew what he was thinking. Until this week I had been driving a pathetic, rusting Japanese station wagon that burned oil faster than gasoline. My son had survived the hospital my father had died in, and we were tearing down the highway in a great car.

"This is terrific," Joe said.

"Yeah," I said, "I know what you mean."

The phone woke me early on a Saturday morning in November. I opened my eyes and tried to orient myself. It was 7:45. I had been to a party the evening before and had not returned home until three in the morning. Why was someone calling this early? Let it ring. No, a call coming that early could be important—trouble in the family. I had to answer it.

I grumbled hello into the mouthpiece.

"Billy?" a voice boomed.

"No," I said, exasperated that I had crawled out of bed for this. "You have the wrong number. There isn't any Billy here."

"Billy," I heard, "this is your Uncle Jeff down in New Jersey."

What was this man talking about? I don't have an Uncle Jeff. Uncle Jeff? . . . Uncle Jeff! It was *that* Uncle Jeff, the man I had despaired of ever hearing from.

"Oh, hi, Uncle Jeff," I said, shakily. What should I say next? 'Thanks for calling?' No, that wasn't right. 'I didn't think I was going to hear from you,' or, 'It's about time?'

"How are you?" I asked.

"Why don't you come to dinner tomorrow?" my uncle said abruptly.

"Tomorrow," I repeated and tried to remember when tomorrow was. I couldn't think; this was happening too fast. My uncle had called and, wham, he was summoning me to an audience the next day. I had been troubling over this call for a year and a half, but I wasn't prepared for it to arrive. It was unfolding with an appalling lack of ceremony.

"My son and I were supposed to play golf tomorrow," I said. "I suppose we could change our plans and come there. Okay, I'll come and bring my son."

"Mary," my uncle shouted to his wife, "he says he's going to come and bring his boy with him. They were going to play golf, but they're going to come here instead."

"Fine," I heard my aunt holler, "tell them to come early and spend the day."

"Yeah," Uncle Jeff repeated, "come early. You don't have to wait until dinner time."

I'd been trying to get this man to talk to me for eighteen months. Now he calls me before eight o'clock on a Saturday morning, invited me to dinner with a day's notice and specifies my arrival time. "I don't pick my son up until twelve," I said. "It will be afternoon before we arrive."

"Tell your son not to get all dressed up," Uncle Jeff said.

"You don't have to worry about that," I replied. "Teenagers today never get dressed up as you mean it."

There was a long silence. "Write these directions

down," he said and outlined the route from Philadelphia to the coast.

"Tell him to watch for the left turn for Route 9. You can drive right past without seeing it," Aunt Mary shouted in the background.

"Yeah, that cutoff for 9 comes at you fast," Uncle Jeff said. "Watch for the hardware store followed by the diner. It's right after that."

We said goodbye and hung up. The conversation had lasted about three minutes.

I walked back to bed unsteadily and buried myself under the covers. The heat of the electric blanket on the sheets was a balm against my hangover and the disturbances of the telephone. I closed my eyes and felt through the bedding for the second pillow. The pillow had gotten pushed under the covers during the night, and it retained the warmth of a steamy radiator. I turned on my side, hugged the pillow tightly and courted sleep to elude the voice from the phone.

The tears came in seconds. They were astonishingly gentle. My chest didn't heave; my breathing didn't turn to gasps. Small streams of water ran softly but steadily from my eyes for a few minutes and then stopped. It continued that way all morning and afternoon, as if a pressure-relief valve were periodically bleeding off a potentially dangerous excess. I spent the day in bed, feeling wounded. Whenever a tear cycle started and I wondered why I was weeping, I'd find myself repeating out loud, "My God, this is finally going to be over."

"I was pretty upset after I got the call yesterday," I said to my son as we drove past the endless plains of shopping malls and housing developments that are suburban New Jersey. "I might need your help with the conversation if it's like that today."

"Okay, Dad," Joe said. "Why do you think he finally called?"

"I don't believe I'll ever know that. It's my guess that Aunt Mary kept after him, but I'd certainly like to know why it took him this long to call."

"What do you expect to find out today, anyway?"

"I'd like to find out what my father was like. What kind of person he was. What his dreams were. How he handled his illness. Things like that."

"Do you think Uncle Jeff will remember much of that?" Joe asked.

"I'm sure he remembers it. The question is whether he will talk about it. He was really nervous on the phone yesterday. This may end up being an ice-breaking visit. I may have to come back before he will loosen up."

"What's the most you could hope for today?" Joe asked.

"Where did you learn to ask questions like that?" I asked and smiled at my son. "The best I will let myself hope for is not very much. Some of the people I interviewed contacted relatives after I talked to them, and I know from them not to expect the world to change.

"Robert, the guy I interviewed who wrote to his father, took a job in Chicago where his father lived. I've talked to him when he's been back in Philadelphia, and he was very vague about what happened between him and his father after the move. He sounded disappointed.

"I've also seen Mike. He swore he'd never contact his father, but he went to visit him after our interviews. He drove a thousand miles nonstop, stayed at his father's place for a day and a half and then drove the thousand miles back. He said he and his father were so frantic they could hardly talk.

"Mike got married after that and his father came to the wedding. He got a kick out of it being the first time his parents had been in the same room in thirty years. He said he calls his father from time to time, and they mostly talk about football. I asked him if he was dissatisfied that he and his father hadn't become closer. Mike said, 'No, I never reckoned he suddenly was going to want to play catch with me.' "

Forty minutes into our ride we stopped at a back-roads pizza joint to have steak sandwiches. Joe was possessed of a teenager's appetite, and I didn't want him to arrive hungry. The cook lost our order, with only two other customers in the store, and we waited twenty minutes for the food.

We were at the edge of the Pine Barrens. Omnipresent shopping plazas yielded to periodic clusters of liquor stores, gas stations, dairy bars and seasonal fruit and vegetable stands. The isolated roads became deserted as we neared the shore. The concrete ribbons through the sandy soil and miles of uniform-height pine trees were crowded with beach traffic from June to September, but we rarely saw another driver. Towns were rarer still. The landscape was dotted with the ornamentations of rural south—random shack-houses with cannibalized cars alongside huge television antenna dishes.

I was doing seventy miles an hour, studying the rearview mirror and worrying there was going to be a radar trap camouflaged beyond the next crest in the road. The trip was taking longer than I had expected. It had been a point of honor not to arrive early, but it was getting into late afternoon and Uncle Jeff might interpret our tardiness as intentional rudeness.

As we emerged from the Pine Barrens and neared Uncle Jeff's, the suffixes on the housing developments' names became "towne," and the seafood restaurants, which were finished in unpainted wood, had fishing nets, lobster traps and other nautical artifacts strung across the outside walls.

Uncle Jeff's neighborhood was a nice upper middle-class pocket of homes with stone fronts. His place was a small, square, one-story affair with a flashy rock driveway and a wooden deck along the back. Everything about the outside of the house was just so.

I pulled into the driveway and parked my car in a highly visible spot near the door. I had taken care to have it washed that morning, and it looked expensive. "Okay, Joe," I said to my son, "let's do it."

Aunt Mary answers the door and kisses my son and me on the cheek. She is older and heavier, but still blond and sturdy looking. She is smiling warmly and seems pleased to see us. I give her the bouquet of cut flowers I bought on Saturday. I can see my uncle over her shoulder, with short, thinning hair combed forward and a paunch straining against his polo shirt. He is standing expectantly with his hands in his pockets.

My uncle comes forward and shakes my hand. "Jeff, this is Billy's son, Joe," Aunt Mary says. Uncle Jeff shakes Joe's hand and looks us over.

My uncle is about 5′9″, a good five inches shorter than me and smaller than I remember. "I'm surprised you're not taller, Billy," Uncle Jeff says. "I expected you to be bigger."

"Your boy looks just like you," Aunt Mary says to me.

I slide my arm around my son's shoulders. Joe grins, anticipating the line I am about to deliver. "Yeah, the lucky kid," I say.

"What grade are you in, Joe?" Aunt Mary asks.

Joe says he is a senior in high school and, after Aunt Mary asks, that he wants to study engineering in college.

"Where do you want him to go to college?" Uncle Jeff asks me.

I'm confused by the question. "I want him to go to college wherever he wants to go to college," I say.

My aunt and uncle stare at me in horror, and I understand they have taken my answer to mean I don't love my son enough to have selected an Ivy League college for him to attend. I smile, glad for the opportunity to show them I will not be touched by their opinions. "He's going to college for himself," I say, "not me."

My uncle leads us into an oblong recreation room where the couch and all the chairs are stretched out along the left wall, fronting a large color television on the right wall. The set is tuned to a professional football game, the volume is high. My son and I sit on the couch at the far end of the room and turn to our right to face my aunt and uncle.

My aunt brings beer, soda and visiting-company snacks, as Uncle Jeff darts his eyes from the television to the conversation. He has one leg hanging over the arm of his chair, but his shoulders and back are stiff. He twists his head toward us when he speaks, but his body remains uncomfortably fixed in the chair.

Uncle Jeff names the large salaries his sons are making in the banking business and asks what I am doing. I have already told him this in my letters, but I say writing and teaching. "What kind of life is that?" he asks. "How are you ever going to make any money?"

"Time is more important to me than money," I say. "I've always been able to do pretty much what I wanted to do when I wanted to do it. I'm not good at taking orders from people. If I have control of my time, I can find ways to make money."

"That's what you should have done, Jeff," Aunt Mary says. "Look at all of the crap you've had to put up with in your job. You should have been your own boss."

I had come fantasizing that my uncle would be in the upper management of his company. He had a business degree, and Mom Mom always went on about his "big job." I soon learn, however, that Uncle Jeff is a regional sales manager. He still spends much of his time putting miles on his company car, and he answers to superiors who are younger than himself. I am disappointed for myself that my uncle doesn't have a prominent job.

Uncle Jeff talks more about his sons than his daughters, except to recount the time one girl got a C on her report. Uncle Jeff put her in the car, drove her to a K mart and asked her if she wanted to work there for the rest of her life.

"How old are you now?" Uncle Jeff asks me.

"Thirty-seven."

"Thirty-seven? That means your life is half-over," he says.

I resist the urge to tell him that his life is ninety percent over.

"I feel exactly like I did forty years ago," Uncle Jeff says. "It's hard to understand that you get old. Time passes, but you don't feel any different."

"How's your mother?" Aunt Mary asks.

"She's fine," I say. "She's getting ready to retire."

"Your article in the Pittsburgh magazine was wonderful," Aunt Mary says. "My friends saw your name and asked if I knew you. I said, 'I sure do, he's my nephew.'"

Uncle Jeff's eyes flee to the football game when my aunt mentions the magazine story.

I mention the Christmas card I got from the woman who had lived on Beechwood Street and say how helpful it was to me. "My mother still won't talk about my father," I say.

"Why won't your mother talk about him?" Aunt Mary asks.

"She says she can't remember," I say.

Uncle Jeff, who has been studying the tv, looks over. "I can just hear your mother saying that," he says. "That sounds just like her."

"What do you mean by that?" I accuse.

"Your mother was in terrible shape after your father died," Aunt Mary says. "She wore black for months. It didn't seem like she was ever going to get over your father's death."

"Given the circumstances," I say in a raised voice, "it doesn't seem odd to me my mother was upset. Did you expect her to be happy?"

Easy boy, I say to myself. That's not what you are here for.

"How come a handsome bachelor like you isn't married?" Aunt Mary asks.

Her question catches me off guard. I have never thought of myself as a bachelor, and I'm not sure how a bachelor answers such a question. "When the time was right, the woman was wrong. When the woman was right, the time was wrong," I say, and she smiles that my homily is acceptable.

"You should get married," she says. "It's okay to be single when you are young, but you get lonely when you are in your fifties."

We are into our third beers when my uncle says to me, "Don't you smoke? I thought I smelled smoke on you when you walked in."

I have been craving a cigarette for the past hour, but there are no ashtrays around and I am worried about lighting one up. "I smoke," I say, "but I'm trying to quit."

"How the hell can you smoke when your Grandpop Wartman died of lung cancer? Don't you remember what he went through? Lung cancer is the quickest cancer there is. Your grandpop was dead three months after they found it. I saw one of my boys smoking outside the house, and I told him to put that thing out before I broke his neck."

I go to the bathroom and smoke a cigarette under the exhaust fan while I'm in there.

Uncle Jeff takes Joe and me on a tour of the house. The inside is compact and not as embellished as the exterior. He says it is the same house they had an architect build for them in Pittsburgh, but while the outside is sleek and impressive, the inside is cramped and ordinary—insubstantial in the manner of modern plasterboard homes. It is a perfectly nice retirement house for a middle-class couple that has raised children and sent them to college. I expected more.

Uncle Jeff takes us into the master bedroom and I feel odd and uncomfortable, like a child who has entered a place that was forbidden to him. I'm afraid I'm going to get the carpet dirty or disturb something, and the adults will know I was there. My father's brother has invited me into the room, and he is standing a few feet away with my son, but it is as though I am an infant and it is 1950.

Aunt Mary turns off the television while we are in the bedroom. Uncle Jeff snaps it back on when we return then goes for more beers, our fourth or fifth before dinner.

Uncle Jeff puts cheese on a cracker and impulsively begins talking about my father for the first time. He says that my father didn't want to go to Catholic high school, so my father went to public school, while Uncle Jeff went to Catholic school.

"Tell the truth," Aunt Mary says. "Your father said there wasn't enough money for both of you to go to Catholic school. You said you wanted to go, and Bill said he didn't mind going to public school."

"Your father worked at Strawbridge and Clothier's department store warehouse for a while," Uncle Jeff says. "He used to get depressed when he was there, and Grandpop Wartman said later that may have been because of the tumor.

"Your father was playing behind the house on Beechwood Street with a bunch of kids when he was seven or eight. The kids were crashing through hedges and pushing each other. A brick whacked your father in the head. The kids were shoving through the hedges. They couldn't see each other because the hedge was thick. The brick whacked him in the back of the head.

"His head was bleeding and it wouldn't stop. Your grandfather had to take him to the hospital. That was a big thing. It was during the Depression and nobody had any money. Going to see a doctor wasn't something you did. Nobody could afford it. But your grandfather was worried because of the bleeding.

"He took your father over to the hospital and they had to wait for hours. The doctors said he had a concussion. He seemed okay after that, but I always said that getting whacked with the brick when he was a kid was how your father got the tumor.

"The kids were pushing through hedges and he got whacked with this brick right here in the back of his head," Uncle Jeff says and rubs the bottom of his hair line. "He got whacked with that brick and I always said that was what did it to him.

"You never know about that cancer. Something happens and twenty years later you've got it and you're dead. I said that as soon as we found out about your father. I remembered when he got whacked with that brick. Right in the back of the head. The kids were pushing through the hedges and the brick whacked him. The brick whacked him good."

The beer is working on me and I'm sedated. I know enough about medicine to recognize that malignant brain cancer isn't caused by a blow to the head, but I don't want to argue. Uncle Jeff is possessed by his theory and I don't want to hear him repeating himself anymore. I'm not going to fight about this. It's taken him hours and almost a six-pack to say anything about my father. Let him go.

"Why did my father have a medical deferment during the war?" I ask.

Uncle Jeff avoids my eyes while he considers his answer then looks up. "The doctors said he was psychotic," he says flatly.

"What?" I sputter in disbelief.

"He took some test at the induction center and the doctors said your father was psychotic." Uncle Jeff looks off, sorry that he had to give me this shameful information.

"That's not possible," I say. "Do you know what it means to be psychotic? Psychotics are people who lose touch with reality. Are you going to tell me my father worked, got married and conceived three children while he was psychotic?"

Uncle Jeff regards me flatly. "That's what the doctors said."

I'm getting angry. I want to tell Uncle Jeff what a fool he is. First he thinks my father's tumor was caused by a brick, then he says that he had a serious mental illness. I want to explain to my uncle how primitive psychological testing was in the 1940s, especially when it was conducted in assembly-line fashion by the army during a time of war. I want to lecture him on the primitiveness of a psychiatric medical establishment that routinely performed lobotomies on patients. I want to ask him how he can be so dumb, but then I realize that it would be pointless. I want to go home.

We have pot roast, mashed potatoes, corn and apple sauce for dinner. Aunt Mary asks me to select a bottle of wine from the several she has available, saying she doesn't know anything about wine. Uncle Jeff and Aunt Mary are very talkative during dinner. The topic is their lives, and the table becomes a verbal battlefield as they cut each other off and finish each other's sentences. I smile and swing my eyes from one to the other, unable to get a word into the overheated air.

An hour later, Uncle Jeff notices that I am not talking and says summarily, "They've listened to us for long enough. Let them go home."

"We have a long ride," I say.

"Bring Joe back over Christmas when our kids are visiting," Aunt Mary says. "Let him meet all of his cousins."

"We'll come," I say. "I would like to see the rest of my family."

"Thanks for coming," Uncle Jeff says. "Visit us again anytime."

"They were nice people," Joe said on the ride home. I hesitated a moment and then agreed. We were there for five hours, but my uncle said almost nothing about my father. I decided that was all right. The silence had been broken. I would get more next time.

"Dear Uncle Jeff and Aunt Mary," I began a thank-you note on Monday. "Many thanks for all of your kindness and hospitality on Sunday. Joe and I both enjoyed our visit very much. . . ."

The brick. I suddenly realized Uncle Jeff had never said who threw the brick. He kept going on about the brick, but he never said who threw it. He knew all the details of the incident, and he was obsessed with talking about it. There could be only one explanation. Uncle Jeff threw the brick. Uncle Jeff threw the brick that he thinks caused his brother's tumor. Uncle Jeff thinks he killed my father.

It explained everything—his distance when we were kids, his spurning my letter, his apprehension during our visit and his blurted quasi confession. He had conceded the circumstances of what he saw as my father's murder, but had not related that he was the assassin.

My uncle has been walking around with the accountability for his brother's death on his conscience for thirty years. That was why he had finally agreed to see me—to

face the nephew he had deprived of a father and to fur-
tively acknowledge culpability for my loss.

Uncle Jeff had gone as far with his disclosure as his
courage would take him. I wondered if he had wanted
me to confront him—to demand to know the identity of
the person who had issued the brick that had smashed
into my father's head? Had he needed an accusation to
push him over the edge into a full confession?

I faintly recalled something that had seemed odd in
Aunt Mary's first letter to me the previous year. I found
the letter and reread it. "When your dad became ill," she
had written, "Uncle Jeff said Bill was too good to suffer,
and that it should have happened to him."

Uncle Jeff wasn't someone who would offer to bear
his brother's burden quickly. I could remember him buying me ice cream cones at the corner store when we had
visited Beechwood Street. "Hurry up and eat that before
we get home," he'd tell me. "I don't want your sisters to
see it. They'll start hollering for one too."

Only guilt could have compelled Uncle Jeff to wish
to receive my father's illness. Guilt so bad it made him
hate himself. Guilt so bad it made him wish for death as
an escape.

Yet Uncle Jeff hadn't been able to die for his brother.
He had lived with his guilt, and it had probably faded as
time passed. He had moved to another city, raised his
family, put his children through school and forgotten the
past. Then, just when the image of my father shrieking
in pain from the impact of the brick had become inaudi-
ble, his dead brother's son wrote an article mourning the
loss of his father and had published it in the murderer's
home town newspaper. Uncle Jeff must have thought I
was his brother's ghost stalking him with a typewriter.

I had to tell Uncle Jeff that he hadn't done it; that
bricks didn't cause tumors. I had to grant him the forgiveness of the son for a death of which he was innocent.
This was not, however, absolution that could be dis-

pensed over the telephone. If I asked him flat out if he threw the brick, he would deny it, thinking that I wanted to berate him. I would first have to defuse the question by convincing him that masonry didn't cause cancer.

I would have to wait until I went to visit him at Christmas. I would take him aside from his family and ask quietly. I would be able to do that in a few weeks. Both my aunt and uncle had been anxious for us to return. I would be able to clear my uncle's conscience. I would hear from them soon and then grant him forgiveness.

"Dear Bill," Aunt Mary wrote in their Christmas card. "I hope you and Joe have a very happy holiday! Ours will be very busy." She then detailed the numerous comings and goings she and Uncle Jeff had planned, concluding with an oblique reference to my possibly visiting sometime during January.

Well, Wartman, I said to myself, this isn't going to be "Ozzie and Harriet Find Their Long-Lost Nephew." I still wanted to hear about my father, though, and now I held the key that might unlock my uncle's memory. If I could tell him he wasn't a murderer, he'd have to talk to me out of gratitude.

I waited until after New Year's, then placed the call. My uncle's oldest son was living near me in Philadelphia, and my aunt had told me that he and his wife were expecting a baby in January. My aunt and uncle would be coming to my territory frequently during the coming weeks. It would be easy for them to say yes.

A woman answered the phone when I called. I didn't know if it was my aunt or one of her daughters, so I didn't say "Is this Aunt Mary?" I just asked if it was Mary.

"Yes," she said.

"Hi, this is Bill Wartman."

"Your Uncle Jeff isn't here," she said.

"Oh, well, I don't know that I need to speak to him. The reason I'm calling," I said, "is that I know you are going to be coming to Philadelphia soon to visit your new grandchild. I'd really like to see you again. We didn't talk about my father much last time. It would really be helpful to me if we could get together again. Why don't you call me when you're coming up to the hospital? I could meet you for lunch or dinner."

"That's a great idea, Billy," she said. "I'll tell your Uncle Jeff you called, and we'll let you know when we are going to be in town."

I was moderately hopeful when I hung up. Lunch in a neutral restaurant couldn't feel that risky to Uncle Jeff. He had seen me once and I hadn't accused him of murder. Maybe he was anxious to tell me the rest of the story of the brick. Sure, I'd see him again soon and we'd get this resolved.

CHAPTER

12

My mother telephoned me three days after my journey to New Jersey. "Did you ever hear from your Uncle Jeff?" she asked early in the conversation.

"Actually," I said, "Joe and I went to see him this past Sunday."

"Well, the old son of a gun surprised me," she said. "I never thought he'd call you."

I told my mother I believed Aunt Mary was the person most responsible for the welcome accorded us and then recounted the events of the day.

"Mom," I said, "Uncle Jeff claims Dad had a medical deferment because he was diagnosed as being psychotic."

"That's nonsense," she said. "I was with your father for many years, and if anything like that had been wrong with him, I would have known. There was never anything wrong with your father's mind, even when he had the tumor."

"How long did you know Dad?" I asked.

"I met your father in 1940 at Auntie Glatts's house, when I was eighteen. He wrote to me the next week and asked me to go to a dance. We were always together after that. Sometimes we only saw each other every couple of weeks. Your father didn't have a car, so it was hard for him to get around. We went together for five years, and we were married for six years.

"Your father worked at Bendix during the war and then at Strawbridge's until your grandfather got him a job with the city as a draftsman. He was measuring something at City Hall when he had his first fall in September of 1948. He started getting headaches after that, but the doctors couldn't find anything. Then they discovered the tumor. The first operation was in February of 1949. He was sick on and off for the next year and a half. He went back into the hospital in early October of 1950 and never came out. They did two or three operations in a row to relieve the pressure from the tumor, but he died shortly afterward."

"I didn't know Dad was a draftsman," I said. "Joe was telling me on Sunday how much he liked the drafting course he was taking in school. I haven't been able to understand his interest in engineering. Maybe he got it from Dad."

"How is Joe?" she asked.

"Fine," I said. "He's taking this new acne medicine that really dries him out, but otherwise he's doing fine. That's something else I don't understand. My acne was gone by the time I was sixteen, but his keeps coming back."

"Your father had trouble with acne when he was in his twenties," my mother said.

"Why didn't you tell me any of this before, Mom?"

"I didn't think of it," she said.

I told my mother Uncle Jeff's theory about the brick that was tossed by the anonymous person. "I think Uncle Jeff threw the brick, Mom, and that he believes he killed Dad."

"Oh, Bill," she said, "I don't know where you get your ideas sometimes."

I knew my speculation about Uncle Jeff was at least feasible because, until recently, I had shared my uncle's guilt. Like him, I thought I was the one responsible for my father's death.

As a child I had groped for an explanation of why we were the only family around without a father. I knew there had to be a reason. Without any explication, the world was far too capricious and dangerous. A child could never feel safe. If a father—an adult who knew how to cope with the enormous forces around him—could die without cause, then what could happen to a child? How could he have any certainty he would awaken in the morning, when he crawled into an enormous bed and closed his eyes for the night?

Somewhere, amidst the hush of silence on my father, there had to be a rationale for his death. I kept looking until I found it in one of my mother's standard lines— "Your father got sick just after you were born."

If my father had gotten sick right after I was born, then my birth had precipitated his illness and death. The proof was on my birth certificate. William Harmer Wartman III, it read. Harmer—someone who harmed people—was my middle name. I was born to injure and cause pain. My destiny had first been fulfilled with my father. My parents had given me the name as a caveat to others—don't say we didn't warn you. Tragically, my father had failed to heed his own cautionary.

I never used the name Harmer, afraid others would unearth my secret. If I was required to produce my birth certificate, I'd instruct the teacher or coach or administrator who asked for it, "Don't write my middle name down. That's a mistake. My name is just William Wartman."

The Catholic church ultimately provided me with redemption from the name that branded me a father-killer. During second grade, our nun undertook a classroom review of the saints and their lure in preparation for the ceremony marking our confirmation as Catholics. Each of us was to select the name of a saint—as the nuns selected saints' names to replace their own—as a "confirmation name." The saint whose name I chose, the nun said, would become my second guardian angel, watching over and protecting me in a world fraught with near occasions of sin.

The nun said Saint Joseph, the earthly father of Jesus, was known as the patron saint of lost causes. When a soul seemed doomed to everlasting damnation in Purgatory or Hell, she counseled, Saint Joseph could sometimes make a case before God and get special consideration. Failing that, she said, celestial rumor had it that Saint Joseph, who had been a carpenter by trade, had built a trap door in the floor of his heavenly abode, through which he smuggled refugees from wickedness named Joseph into their eternal reward.

I certainly qualified as a lost cause, having had the Original Sin on my soul bloated by the murder of my father. I couldn't fathom the quantity of penance I would have to perform to atone for those sins. I knew straightaway that Saint Joseph was the saint for me. I adopted Joseph as my middle name, replacing Harmer, and hoped for the best.

My conjectured role in my father's death had surfaced, amidst many tears, during psychotherapy. I had sought refuge on the couch twice during the past five years, when I felt the need for a guide through the alien territory of my psyche that was my father's life and death.

The patricide fantasy had been slowly extricated from the encoding of my memory and transformed into words that I expelled with the thrust of vomit. I retched them out in painful contractions then laughed at their absurdity and their dogmatic quaintness. Then I felt anger at myself for having permitted illusion to cast a controlling spell over aspects of my childhood.

I was so convinced of my culpability for my father's death that I had once wanted to die to make amends. The *Baltimore Catechism* we memorized admonished us that the purpose of this life was to earn eternal life in the hereafter. Such a reward seemed an unlikely prospect for me, unless Saint Joseph interceded. Then a nun told us, in third or fourth grade, that martyrs for Catholicism were guaranteed admission to heaven, regardless of their prior transgressions against God's laws.

"I wish there was a religious war going on somewhere," I told my mother after dinner that evening.

"Why in heaven's name would you ever say something like that, Billy?" she asked.

"I could go fight and die in the war," I said as my mother looked on in astonishment, "and then I would go straight to heaven."

My mother hadn't said anything then, and she was quiet now as I laid out my theory about Uncle Jeff. My mother knew that I had been in therapy, and I told her how, when I was a child, I had twisted her phrasing about the timing of my father's illness into a much-needed explanation for his death.

"That seems unbelievable, Bill," she said. "I guess it's hard to imagine what happens in a child's mind. I remember Helen Marie once told a nun her father wasn't dead. She said he was working out of town and living near his job. The nun knew that wasn't true, and she called me and repeated what Helen Marie had said. Helen Marie probably doesn't even remember having said that."

One Saturday I went in search of the house I had lived in with my father on Beechwood Street. It was located midway between my residence and my father's cemetery. Beechwood Street was an intermediary stop on a journey I wasn't ready to complete yet.

I had prepared for the trip by locating our house number, 5767, in my father's death notice, which ran once in each of the two major newspapers in Philadelphia. It was a modest nine lines, detailing survivors and funeral information. The headline emblazoned in two-inch letters on the cover of that day's *Philadelphia Bulletin* read "Berserk Vet armed with 2 guns kills 5, wounds 4 on rampage in 2 N.J. villages."

I paused at the microfilm machine in the library to wonder if some of the crazed vet's victims were fathers, and if it had made a difference to their children that their fathers' deaths had been reported on the front page, rather than in the alphabetized listings at the rear of the paper?

I drove to Beechwood Street with Alice, a woman who was in my life for the second time. The first liaison had ended six years earlier, after three years of involvement. We had continued to write to each other sporadically after the breakup, even after she married. Now she was only months separated from her husband, the divorce not yet in the hands of the lawyers. I was coming off of a two-year affair, one inertia had sustained long beyond its actual conclusion. I had always had difficulty ending relationships. I usually forced the woman to say the final words by flagrantly neglecting her.

Alice and I had been in love at various times, in varying degrees, sometimes seriously. Yet there was a rub. Alice and I were from different socioeconomic backgrounds, as the absence or presence of money was currently called. Alice's family had been privileged for generations. I had worked in a gas station, while her ancestors had been charter stockholders in oil companies.

I had made constant, defensive, pseudo joking references to this disparity when we began spending time together. I found never-ending opportunities to introduce our variant lineages into every conversation, no matter how innocuous, until Alice angrily ordered me to stop.

The money that Alice's family had was of no interest to me in and of itself. Rather, I was fascinated with the life it had allowed them to develop. Her father regaled me with stories of Edith Wharton's New York, an era I had only read of but one in which he had known the players. Her mother had a keen social conscience and a love of Russian literature. We became archrival debaters and Scrabble players. I got on splendidly with her parents and spent many happy hours in their company.

Alice and I had been on and off our last time around. On when she graduated from college and we discussed sharing quarters, and off when I declined and she left for graduate school. I had said that I wasn't ready for living together. Perhaps there were risks attached to being intensely in love with someone that I was unable to assume.

This time Alice and I knew there would be a denouement. We had history—nothing about either of us was unknown to the other—and we could no longer be described as young adults. We would be married quickly, or the individual speculations we had entertained for nearly a decade would be put to rest forever.

Alice had written from her new apartment sixty miles away to inform me of her separation and to suggest we have a friendly visit. Within two months, we were each inadvertently saying "our place," when we meant to speak of my place or hers. Her marriage was ended and I was free. It was insane but intoxicating, trying to reimagine the past.

"I told a friend you were a writer," Alice said during the first weekend we spent together, the second time around. "She said to me, 'Oh, a creative person who works at home. That's like your father. Isn't he a sculptor with a studio behind the house?' "

"I was amazed," Alice said. "I never saw that connection before."

Old issues reappeared frequently, partially because they had never been resolved and partially because the confusion of our autonomous lives compelled us to halt what was unfolding. We needed to batter each other off. We managed it well, each of us having honed our pugilistic talents during our separation. Everything had been glossed over last time. Now, without reflecting on the consequences, or perhaps courting them, everything was voiced.

"Why should I want to marry you?" Alice challenged me once as we got into her car after a morning of disagreement. "It's not like you have a lot of money."

"But, Alice," I answered, pausing at the top of my conversational backswing to achieve maximum velocity on the follow-through, "if I had a lot of money, what would I need you for?"

I had brought Alice along on the drive to Beechwood Street because I knew what we were going to find. I was certain Beechwood Street would be a microcosm of the worst that poverty could create for people in an old densely populated section of an eastern city.

My grandparents had fled Beechwood Street thirty years earlier to escape an influx of people of fewer means and different skin color than themselves. There was nothing compelling enough about the vicinity to have encouraged prosperous folks—black or white—to reclaim the neighborhood since.

I wouldn't have invited Alice to Beechwood Street the first time we were together. I had tried to "pass" then, to assimilate myself into her world as if I were a native. This time I wanted her to taste the grit. I was uncertain if she would be affected by it, but I needed to document to myself that I had the equilibrium to take her there.

The neighborhood was a tangle of narrow one-way streets. Beechwood, like many streets in Philadelphia, runs for a few blocks, dead-ends, then resumes after a short distance. Drivers must jog down side streets, while keeping their course in mind, to navigate the noncontiguous sections.

We passed down tiny streets where two-story brick row houses with sagging porches and broken steps crowded the sidewalks. On other roads the houses were mismatched, some having been demolished and replaced by newer dwellings of nondescript utilitarian design. It was a weekend, and bored teenagers were strutting around and gathering on corners. Trash adorned every open space. Medical and dental services were being administered in a squat cinderblock building with a No Appointment Necessary sign.

We came to a corner where a boarded-up pink stucco-covered house had a brightly colored mural painted on the side. Adjacent to it was a low-slung industrial building. A roofing truck was double-parked in the street, blocking our passage, until the driver, who was standing twenty feet away with his raised left arm braced against a wall, finished urinating.

"Not the sort of area that makes you want to jump out and take a walking tour, is it?" I said to Alice.

"No," she said evenly, "it's not a pretty sight."

The traffic flow on Beechwood Street become one-way against us when we reached the 5700 block, so I circled to the left. We approached a cement playground I remembered from visiting my grandparents. It was contained by a six-foot fence of closely spaced iron stakes with sharply pointed tops, designed to discourage children from climbing or to impale them if they did. The fence had been coated with off-green paint at one time, but much of it had yielded to rust.

The playground sat behind a recreation center with few windows. Those that hadn't been replaced with glass blocks were covered with grating which was painted the same faded green. An additional fence, this a twelve-foot,

chain link one, also with a partial green veneer, seg-
mented the school yard from the backyards of the Beechwood Street houses. The last barricade was probably intended to keep solidly hit balls from banging into the
houses. Tall weeds erupted from breaks in the concrete
ground cover. The playground looked as though it hadn't
heard the excited squeals of a victorious team in years.

We swing down my block. I am cheered that the
houses are in better repair, nicer than those on the surrounding streets. Many residents have installed aluminum siding over the eaves at the junction of the front
brick wall and the roof and on the dormer windows that
jut out over the porches. Some of the porches themselves
have been enclosed, and wrought iron decorates the pe-
rimeters of those that haven't been. The houses are two
short cement flights of stairs back from the street, with
miniature grass patches substituting for yards. It is not
the suburban dream, but it could be home.

But then, wait, something is wrong. The corner house,
5767, our house . . . someone has broken a window . . .
two windows . . . all the windows. The house is abandoned, boarded up. There is graffiti on the walls. No one
lives there. Have vandals looted the interior? Have the
copper pipes been torn from the ceiling of the cellar? Have
the bathroom fixtures been smashed? Is the house over-
run with rats?

I feel as though my past has been fouled. How could
this have happened? The woman who had lived on the
street had told me in the Christmas card how happy she
had been when she learned my father was moving into
this house with his family. Three generations of Wart-
mans had lived on this block when my sister and I resided
here. Now our house stands vacant like a hulk of urban
jetsam.

I want to bang on someone's door and ask who is
responsible for this. Who owns this building, and why have

they forsaken it? Why haven't the neighbors, who look after their own homes, demanded that my house be restored? Why haven't they found a young family to fix it up and move in?

I knew I had no right to ask these questions of anyone, that the memory of my past was another person's current reality, so I drove away. I was on Chew Avenue, pursuing a path back to my present neighborhood, before I realized I hadn't spoken to Alice since we had turned onto the 5700 block of Beechwood Street. I hadn't solicited her opinion about the house, coughed up excuses for it or expressed regret. I was pleased by that.

The house wasn't me. It was a building where I had lived with my family when I was an infant. It was a neighborhood I had passed through on the way to another place. I was what I was. I had been where I had been. Those were the facts.

I looked over at Alice. She was gazing out the side window, her expression featureless. I didn't inquire about, or try to imagine, what she was thinking. It didn't matter. We wouldn't be seeing each other much longer anyway. "What do you want to eat for dinner tonight?" I asked.

It was December of 1986. Christmas card time. I hadn't heard from Aunt Mary or Uncle Jeff since my call eleven months earlier. My uncle would have been on the phone eons ago if he had known what I had to offer him. He still didn't know he was wrong about the brick and his supposed slaughter of my father.

Poor Uncle Jeff, the anguish he must have wrestled with. I wanted to tell him it was okay, that he could ease up on himself, but the guy kept avoiding me because of his guilt.

I reminded myself what shame could do to a man whenever Uncle Jeff's being so distant started to eat at me. I'd catch myself wondering what I had done to him when he didn't call, but then I'd remember it was all a misunderstanding.

I decided to take the initiative one final time. The blow to my pride was worth it. I still wanted to talk to him about my father. I sent Aunt Mary and Uncle Jeff a card offering holiday wishes from my son and me and added a last appeal.

I'd like to come visit you again to talk about my father, I wrote. The information I got from you last time was very useful. Uncle Jeff said he thought my father's having been hit by a brick had caused his tumor. You might be interested to hear that I have spoken to several medical experts about that, and they assured me there wasn't any connection between the blow and my father's tumor. I'll call you after the holidays to see if we can get together.

I was certain this would do it. The brick was out on the table now—Uncle Jeff, don't worry, you didn't kill my father. God, he was going to be relieved.

The day I mailed my card, I received a card from my aunt. She wrote that she and my uncle hadn't been to Philadelphia much because their daughter-in-law had gone back to work after giving birth, but that I should visit them in New Jersey. I thought that was strange. She had sent their card before they had received mine. I wondered how she talked my Uncle Jeff into letting me visit?

Maybe Uncle Jeff had come clean with Aunt Mary. Perhaps she had kept bugging him. "Jeff," she might have said, "Billy Wartman needs to see you again. I've reminded you a dozen times."

Uncle Jeff, sensing that he wasn't going to escape his wife's insistence on my behalf, might have told her everything. "Mary," he probably said, "I was the one who threw that brick. We were kids out there playing. You know how kids pick up things and chuck them. I didn't mean to hit

Bill. It was an accident, I swear to you. I didn't want to kill my brother. It was a mistake."

Aunt Mary, in her compassion and wisdom, would have told her husband what he had to do. "You have to explain to Billy Wartman," she would say. "He will understand the circumstances and forgive you. But you must tell him. You owe him that."

I didn't call Uncle Jeff until mid-March. I knew he was going to be glad to hear from me after getting the absolving Christmas card. Besides, he hadn't seen me in fourteen months. Aunt Mary's card had said, "Let's not lose touch."

I smiled as I picked up the phone. Then, with three numerals of Uncle Jeff's number punched into the phone, an ancient dread gripped me. It was 9:15 P.M. Was it too late to call? Perhaps I should wait until another day? Keep dialing, Wartman, I said to myself.

"Yes, sir?" a man answered.

"Hi. Is this Jeff?"

"Yes, sir."

"Hi. This is Bill Wartman up in Philadelphia."

"Hey, how you doing, Billy?" my uncle said. "Christ, I though you died or something when we didn't hear from you."

"No, no, I'm still here."

"How's your son doing?"

"Fine. He's in Villanova now."

"No kidding. You got him into a good school. Do you want to come down and see us?"

"Yeah, I do."

"Sure. When do you want to come?"

"Are you going to be around this weekend?"

"Sure."

"How about on Sunday afternoon?"

"No problem. How's your job and everything?"

"Good. I'm looking around at other teaching jobs now."

"That's good. You know, it's amazing when you get that *New York Times* and see that education page and see the jobs that are open. One college wants a guy that's head of admissions, or they want a guy to head a department. They're big ads, the boxed ones. There's a lot of movement.

"I don't have to tell you, though. You've been in the writing business long enough to know what's going on. Did you know I used to work at the old *Philadelphia Record* after I got out of high school? I used to know that sportswriter—what the hell's his name—Smith?"

"Red Smith?"

"Yeah. Red Smith. I knew all of those guys. It's not good that there's only one big newspaper in Philadelphia now. Those people at the *Inquirer* are in the Newspaper Guild. If you could hook onto something like a newspaper job then you'd be set. It's just a thought."

"I'm not really interested in newspaper work," I said. "Too many daily deadlines. That's no fun."

"You young guys. With all of this AIDS around I'm glad I'm sixty-seven. It makes you wonder what the hell's going on out there. How old are you now?

"Thirty-eight."

"Thirty-eight. Jesus, I can't believe that. That's almost forty. Doesn't life begin at forty? I'll be sixty-seven this December and I'm still working. I'm having too much fun to retire. They need me. I got a region here and we got the troops going. Every time I turn around they are giving me increases. What the hell am I going to do, sit around here? Throw away big money? What am I, crazy?

"I don't need work, but if they're throwing the money at me and I'm enjoying what I'm doing . . . I don't feel any different than when I was thirty or forty. If you like

your work it isn't work. It's like the baseball player. He's
playing a boy's game. If a guy fits in and likes his job,
hell, age doesn't matter. He'll work until he dies. He needs
it. When you can still contribute and the company knows
you're contributing, that's all you need. If you're not contributing today, then at sixty-two they start putting you
into the program to get you out.

"People at your age, at forty, you're in the prime of
your life. If you can hook onto something big or something like that. But I'm glad you called. And, yeah, we'll
be glad to have you down. Are you going to bring your
son?"

"I don't know. His work load at school is really heavy."

"Our oldest son, since we last saw you, he had a little
girl and his wife is pregnant again. So we've got things
going for us. Okay, Billy, thanks for calling."

"Don't forget, now. I'm coming Sunday afternoon."

"Yeah, yeah, thanks for calling."

This was wonderful. My Uncle Jeff was going to see
me and we'd get everything straightened out. He'd probably still be reluctant to own up to the brick, but I'd make
it easy for him, let him know it wasn't something that
troubled me.

He'd say, "Christ, I was so happy when I got the
card from you. This thing has been eating at my gut for
thirty years. Every time I saw your mother alone with you
kids it killed me—thinking I was responsible for her not
having a husband and you kids not having a father.

"It's all over now," I'd say. "Let's forget about it."

Uncle Jeff would get out his good whisky and we'd
have a drink or two. Then he'd start telling me these
wonderful stories about my father and what a great guy
he was. It would go on all afternoon like that.

Then, when I was getting ready to leave, he'd say,
"Tell you what. Bring your mother and your sisters and
their kids down with you next time. We'll get our kids

together, and we'll have this great big Wartman family reunion. Christ, what would it be, twenty or twenty-five people?

"We'll have a Wartman family barbecue out in the backyard here. We'll put up the volleyball net and get out the badminton stuff. We'll get a half-keg of beer and cook hot dogs and hamburgers on the grill out there. We'll get out our old pictures and see how everybody has fallen apart as they have gotten older.

"We'll do it in June, that way the weather will be good and you kids can go down to the beach first, and us old folks can drive over to the bay and look at the boats in the harbor. What do you think about that, Billy? Has your Uncle Jeff got a hot idea here or not?"

"Yes," I'd say, all excited. "This is a perfect idea. I will have to do some fast talking to get my mother to come down here, but I'll pull it off. I'll tell her everything is okay now. That I've gotten it all straightened out, and we're going to be a family again. Then maybe you and Aunt Mary can come visit my family in Pennsylvania over Christmas."

"Okay," Uncle Jeff would say, "you get things arranged on your end, and I'll get my kids lined up."

I'd drive home happier than I had been in a long time.

CHAPTER 13

Uncle Jeff invited me into his house, yelling the news of my arrival to Aunt Mary over the noise of the basketball game on the television. We sat on the couch, talked basketball for a moment, and then Uncle Jeff began specifying the even larger sums of money his sons were extracting from the financial world this year.

Aunt Mary entered the family room and greeted me. "Billy," she said, as struck as if she had never seen me before, "you look just like somebody on television."

"People keep telling me I look like the guy who plays Jeff Colby on one of the soap operas," I said.

"Yes," she said. "John James who plays Jeff on "The Colby's."

"Too bad you don't have his money," Uncle Jeff said.

"You could be his twin," Aunt Mary said.

"There you go," Uncle Jeff said. "Move out to California and get a job as his double."

I started to grin at my uncle's joke but stopped when I saw earnestness in his eyes. "I should give up being a writer and become a human mannequin?" I asked.

Uncle Jeff said money was money and went on to detail the deftness of his sons' career paths. It was a rerun. I had heard the same saga, almost word for word, during my last visit.

"If you went out to California," Uncle Jeff said, "you might make connections and get work writing movies. Or are you too old to break into a new field?"

"Writing is different from the businesses you're used to," I said. "Talent is usually the most important qualification for a writer."

"Our oldest son's company is sending him to a conference in Switzerland," Aunt Mary said.

I didn't want to be impolite to my aunt and uncle— I didn't see anything wrong with parents being proud of their children—but I also didn't want to be subjected to another installment of the upward mobility of the Wartman clan. I though if I gently let them know they weren't impressing me, they'd get the hint.

"Switzerland is a beautiful country," I said, "but I prefer the south of France."

"Oh, have you been to Europe?" Aunt Mary asked.

"Remember I told you about that trip when I was here last year?"

"No," Aunt Mary said, frowning. "How long were you there?"

"A month."

"Well, aren't you good to yourself," Aunt Mary said.

"Our youngest boy spent his honeymoon in France," Uncle Jeff said.

I did a quick calculation. Uncle Jeff's youngest son

hadn't been married at the time of my last visit. He must have gotten married during the past year. I hadn't been invited to the wedding.

"Yes, and his college roommate got married last summer," Aunt Mary, having done her own calculation, quickly interjected. "Now, there was a wedding."

"It cost thirty grand," Uncle Jeff said. "Can you imagine that—thirty big ones for a wedding?"

"I have never seen such food in my life," Aunt Mary said. "The girl was Jewish and they had both Jewish and American food. Tables and tables of it."

"You should have seen this country club where the reception was held," Uncle Jeff said. "Christ, was that place ritzy. There were some beautiful golf clubs near us when we lived in Pittsburgh. You're a golfer—you should have visited us in Pittsburgh."

I struggled to keep my grin from becoming a smirk. "I guess I should have," I said.

" Are you still teaching?" Uncle Jeff asked.

"Yeah, I talked to you on the phone about that the other night," I said.

"Did your mother ever retire?" Aunt Mary asked.

"Yes, remember I told you the last time I was here that she was about to leave her job?"

"I'm still working, you know," Uncle Jeff said.

"Right, you told me on the phone."

"When you're a good man they never want to let you go," Uncle Jeff said. "They keep giving me increases, one after the other. What the hell? Am I going to sit around the house and turn down money? I've got my territory here and I'm breaking in some new kids they hired."

"That's his specialty," Aunt Mary said, "grooming young sales talent."

"Our oldest boy bought himself a new house in the suburbs and two fancy cars," Uncle Jeff said.

"He's working on one hundred percent commission now," Aunt Mary said. "I told him I didn't know how he

could stand that, not knowing how much his next paycheck was going to be. I want to know how much I'm
going to get and when I'm going to get it. But he said,
'Mom, I receive five job offers a week. What do I have to
worry about? Headhunters are always after me.' "

I had the misfortune of being positioned between
my aunt and uncle. I sat there whipping my head from
side to side, smiling and nodding. I didn't know which
one to look at when they both talked at the same time. I
tried keeping my gaze on one of them in the hope the
other would shut up, but the other would keep talking,
so I kept swiveling until the muscles in my neck started
tightening up.

It could have been comical, but the slip about the
wedding was grating on me. I thought about asking, quite
casually, when their son had gotten married. I would have
enjoyed watching them squirm.

This day was supposed to end with plans being made
for a family reunion. I didn't see how that was going to
happen when these people didn't even invite me to my
cousin's wedding. And, after all of the trouble I went to
in making contact with them. Something was going wrong.
Maybe it would be different after Uncle Jeff and I talked
about the brick.

We were sitting next to each other on the couch. He
wasn't paying as much attention to the television this time.
I would say something in a minute about needing to talk
about my father. Then we would have this intimate male
conversation. The reunion was a sure thing after that.

There was a momentary break in the conversation,
and I snatched it. "I need to use the bathroom," I said,
"but can I ask you some questions about my father when
I come back?"

Aunt Mary hopped out of her chair and said, "I have
to get dinner ready. You guys go ahead and talk."

The television was turned off when I returned to the
family room, and Uncle Jeff had even remained on the

couch. I took those to be prophetic signs. Uncle Jeff was ready to talk seriously this time. Aunt Mary was playing a portable tv in the kitchen, but it wasn't that loud.

"Could you tell me any stories you remember about my father?" I said and sat down near Uncle Jeff.

"The big thing was we were poor. It was during the Depression and nobody had any money. My father was a committeeman. He was probably making eighteen hundred dollars a year in the thirties. We used to walk to school because we couldn't afford the fifteen cents for the trolley.

"Your father and I graduated from eighth grade together. Your father was a year older than me, so he must have been held back a year. We went to Olney for a year because Pop Pop was out of work then. He couldn't pay the seventy-five dollar tuition for us at LaSalle High.

"Nobody ever had any money. Nobody ever had anything. My parents rented the house on Beechwood Street from the woman who owned the ice cream store at Chew and Chelten. My father used to go over to the store to pay the rent, and they would give him a container of ice cream. He'd come back home with the ice cream and wake us up if we were in bed. That was the only time we had ice cream.

"Everything then was who you knew. If you wanted a job as a policeman, you gave money to the committeeman and he took it to the ward leader. My father didn't get any of that money. He was just the bag man. It was the same thing if you wanted your street paved or something. You had to grease some politician's palm.

"Nobody had any money for anything. You had to walk everywhere because you couldn't afford fifteen cents for the trolley. All I ever wanted to do was to go to a good college. That's all I ever wanted. Nothing was going to stop me from getting it."

"What kind of things do you remember about my father? What kind of person was he?"

"Your father would come home from work and complain that people were talking about him and saying things behind his back. I think he was schizophrenic. Isn't that what you call it? He had trouble getting along with people at work. He used to come home and complain. Me, I never cared what anybody thought. You can't worry about whether people are going to like you or not. Ninety-nine percent of the people in the world don't have any brains anyway. Why worry about them?

"I've always been that way. I was just telling a young girl at work about this. You can't worry about what people think about you. You have to get people's attention— hit them with a two-by-four if you have to, to get their attention, then you close the deal."

I let Uncle Jeff's revised psychiatric diagnosis of my father pass. "Did my father do badly in school?" I asked.

"No, but he wasn't motivated like me. All I ever wanted to do was to go to a good college and make sure my kids did the same."

"Didn't my father want to go to college?"

"Your father was more into mechanical things. He went for his army physical and they gave him some kind of medical deferment. He worked at Bendix during the war. He made out well working at the plant there, but he lost out when the war was over.

"I always said your father got his tumor because he got whacked on the head with a brick when he was a kid."

The brick. I wanted to interrupt my uncle, but he was rolling with his monologue and I couldn't have broken in without getting trampled.

"I was in the marines when your father took sick. I wasn't one to write home much or come home on furlough. I didn't find out about your father until I was discharged.

"The surgeon had sent your Pop Pop a bill for something like five thousand dollars for your father's first operation. Everybody from both families put together a thousand dollars and paid the doctor that much. Then the doctor was dunning your Pop Pop for the rest of the money. I came home from the marines and put on my uniform and went down to his office.

"I gave the doctor whatever I had in my pocket— five hundred bucks or something like that—and told him that was it. I told him the family didn't have any more money and to stop bothering my father.

"Everybody in the Glatts family liked your dad. Billy and Jimmy and Frank and your Grandfather and Grandmother Glatts. Everybody got along. No matter how bad things got, your mother and father were always happy, even with your father so sick. They were perfect for each other.

"Nobody had any money but, because everybody got along, they all pitched in when something like this happened. We didn't know what the hell was going on. What the hell did the average man know about cancer then? People died, they died, that's all there was to it. There wasn't any talk about why it happened. Most of the time the doctors didn't even know.

"They did that operation on your father, but what the hell could that do? The brain is like a sponge. How the hell are they ever going to cut the cancer out of a sponge and get it all? They open you up and the air gets to the cancer, and the cancer spreads like wildfire. That's what happens. The air makes the cancer grow wild when they open you up.

"I used to take time off from my sales route to take your father to the hospital for his cobalt treatments three times a week. The treatment burned his hair all off.

"When your father came home from the hospital somebody gave him a copy of this book. Mary?", Uncle Jeff yelled. "Who was that guy who gave that book to Bill?"

"It was his best friend, Chris," Aunt Mary said and walked in from the kitchen. "We had only told Bill that he had to have an operation on his head. We didn't tell him that he had a tumor. Then, when he came home from the hospital, his best friend Chris walked in with a copy of the *Reader's Digest*. It had a condensation of *Death Be Not Proud* by John Gunther in it. It was about the man's son dying from a brain tumor.

"He gave it to your father and said, 'Hey, Bill, this is just like you.' We all almost died right on the spot. We didn't want Bill to know that he had a tumor, so that he wouldn't worry, and then this guy comes in and says that. We all talked about it at Pop Pop's house up the street later on."

"Your grandfather wouldn't let them do the last operation," Uncle Jeff said. "They did two or three operations, and they wanted to keep doing more, but the family told them no."

"The last time I saw your father in the hospital," Aunt Mary said, "he looked like he was dead. He was sitting up in a chair in a doorway—he was in a ward because nobody had any money and his insurance was gone. His weight was down to nothing, and his cheeks were sunken. I saw him sitting there in that breeze and said, 'My God, he's going to get even sicker.' Sure enough, he died of pneumonia a few days later.

"He would have been better off," Aunt Mary said with a dismissive wave of her arm, "if he had died right away in the beginning. Then he wouldn't have had to suffer."

I had come hoping to get biographical information about my father. What I was being given by Uncle Jeff and Aunt Mary instead was revisionist history. They were telling me how they had overseen my father's illness and death. I questioned much of what they were saying. If they had been involved with and concerned about my father as they now claimed, they never would have distanced themselves from my family as they had after his death.

I also didn't like the spin they were putting on their

tales. They were patronizing my father, talking about him as though he were a child who needed relatives to make all of his decisions for him. My father may not have been a genius, but my aunt and uncle weren't going to be counted among the great minds of the western world either.

What I was hearing was more folklore masquerading as explanations for the unexplainable. People are not supposed to die at the age of thirty-one, and, when they do, the survivors create rationales. Mine was that my birth had caused my father's death. My mother's family said my father was too good to live. Uncle Jeff said it was because he got whacked with a brick, and then the air fanned his tumor. Now, Aunt Mary was saying he caught a chill in the hospital, and topping it off by summarily concluding my father's life would have been improved had it been two years shorter.

I had developed a piercing headache that nagged at me as if it were going to last for hours. I had to keep reminding myself why I had come to see these people who happened to be my relatives. I asked Uncle Jeff if he had any photographs of my father.

"No," he said, "people didn't have money for photographs in those days. You had to buy the film and get it developed. Maybe your father is in some of our wedding pictures."

Uncle Jeff turned on several lamps when he returned from the bedroom with the album. It was early evening by then and the room had gotten progressively darker as we talked, the details of Uncle Jeff's face becoming lost in the shadows. The illumination wasn't much brighter with the lights on. Aunt Mary came in and wanted to turn on more lamps, but I told her I could see fine. I knew what we were going to be talking about soon. Darkness would make it easier.

Uncle Jeff and I were looking at the pictures, trying to find my father, when he stopped at a shot showing the backs of four men from the wedding party who were standing at the altar. "I don't know if one of them is your father or not," he said. "Your father was a skinny guy. He never filled out.

"No, I don't recognize your father in this picture," Uncle Jeff said, turning the page. "I don't think your father was in our wedding. Mary, was Bill in our wedding?"

"Yes," she called from the kitchen. "He was your best man."

My uncle stopped at a picture of my father standing behind the head table at the reception. He had a glass raised in his hand and his mouth was open. My father was offering a toast to his brother and sister-in-law. He had the poised look of a man in a tuxedo who knows his audience is listening attentively to what he had to say. This was not the shell of a man my aunt and uncle were attempting to create.

Dad, I said to myself, I hope you can't hear this. I don't want you to know what these people are saying about you. I don't want you to know that your brother forgot you were the best man at his wedding.

My mother's words were ringing in my ears. "Your Uncle Jeff never cared about your father," she had said. She was right. My uncle wasn't going to remember anything about my father I didn't already know. I didn't think Uncle Jeff's memory was failing him. Rather, I suspected he had never known his brother. I thought that was my uncle's loss rather than my father's. I still wanted to know about the brick, however, if only for my own satisfaction.

I closed the album on the table and turned to Uncle Jeff. "When people die unexpectedly," I said, "everyone tries to find explanations for it. My mother didn't talk about my father, so I made up my own reason. She used to say that my father got sick right after I was born, and I twisted that to mean that my being born had caused my father to die."

"Yeah," he said, "I can see how you might think that."

"It's like what you said about the brick. My father develops a tumor. That's not supposed to happen, so you go back looking for an explanation to make it understandable. 'How can someone that young get a tumor?' you ask yourself. Then you remember my father got hit in the head with that brick, and you conclude the blow caused the tumor."

"I can see that," Uncle Jeff said and looked at me warily. I waited for him to continue—to volunteer something or to ask what the point was—but he didn't.

"Were you there when my father got hit with the brick?" I asked.

"Yeah, I was there," he said quietly.

I hesitated a moment, almost afraid to ask the question. Then I forced it out. "Did you throw the brick?"

Uncle Jeff's eyes narrowed as outrage collected in them. He looked at me hard, as if I were a kid in a playground who had just insulted his mother. His chin was set forward, his shoulders tensed. He sat there quietly— thinking what?—then said in a low voice, "I don't know who threw it. There were a bunch of kids there. The hedge was higher than our heads. The brick just came over the top from the other side."

I couldn't decide whether to believe him or not. "I thought you might have been the one who threw it," I said. "That you might have felt guilty about it afterward, thinking the brick had caused my father's tumor. That the brick had killed him."

"No. I never thought that."

"Well, did you ever think back and feel that you should have seen the brick coming and knocked it out of the way? Or just anything you could have done to change that day?"

"No, I never thought anything like that. I guess I could have visited your family more. I didn't come down to Parkside much."

"You had your own family," I said.

"I had my own family and everyone seemed to be doing fine in Parkside with your mother's people."

Aunt Mary came in with a camera. "Our kids have been asking about you," she said to me. "Let me take a picture of you two guys together on the couch." Uncle Jeff slid closer to me and I produced a synthetic smile for the photographer.

"We have the deed to the cemetery that I will give to you before you leave," Aunt Mary said. "It's only your father and Mom Mom and Pop Pop there, and the plot is for six graves. I'm sure your mother wants to be buried with your father."

"Why do we have the deed?" Uncle Jeff asked.

"From when your mother was buried," Aunt Mary said and then looked at me. "We've been remiss about getting Mom Mom's name put on the headstone. The roads from Pittsburgh were snowed in when she died, and we couldn't get down. Luckily we had a friend in Philadelphia who is an undertaker, and we told him to take care of it for us. We told him just to have private services."

My mother, sisters and I were the only close relatives, other than Uncle Jeff and Aunt Mary, that Mom Mom had when she died four years earlier. My aunt and uncle hadn't notified my mother when Mom Mom died in a nursing home, so we had never known anything about a funeral. If Aunt Mary and Uncle Jeff hadn't left Pittsburgh when Mom Mom died, then Aunt Mary's term "private services" was quite a euphemism. Uncle Jeff's parting memorial to his mother, apparently, had been to have her stuck into a grave with no one in attendance save the person who drove the hearse and the men who tossed the dirt back into the hole.

I looked at my aunt and uncle vacantly. The anxiety and turmoil of the day had prevented me from thinking clearly up to that point. Expectations, remarks and obser-

vations had been coalescing in my head, creating nervous
confusion. But I managed a single clear thought at that
moment. These people, I suddenly realized, these people
I had troubled over and had written pleading letters to,
were among the most vulgar human beings I had ever
met.

My headache had gotten worse. The pain seemed to
be leaking down from the inside surface of my skull into
the roots of my brain. I wanted to get into my car and
flee through the Pine Barrens, to put that primordial
buffer between myself and my relatives. Dinner was almost ready, however, and I couldn't leave without creating a scene. It would be easier to silently endure the meal
than to attempt to explain why I felt as if I wanted to go
home and bathe.

Aunt Mary called me into the kitchen and asked me
to open the champagne we were going to drink with dinner. Then they marveled out loud when I opened the
bottle without losing control of the cork. "I would have
spilled half of it on the floor if I had opened it," Uncle
Jeff said.

They kept doing that to me. Just when I was ready
to start hating them, they would say something nice or
act like they really were pleased that I had come to visit.
Uncle Jeff had dragged two cases of assorted imported
beers his kids had given him for Christmas into the family room when I had arrived. "What kind do you want?"
he asked. "I keep these in the garage for special occasions."

Aunt Mary wasn't Julia Child, but dinner, too, was a
relatively big production—plates full of chicken with
pineapple sauce, rice and asparagus. It was food she had
taken trouble with. "How the hell am I going to eat all of
this?" Uncle Jeff said.

"You'll find a way," Aunt Mary said. "Billy, when it's
the two of us, I can't give him his silverware before I sit

down or he'd be finished eating and leaving the table before I had the first bite of my food.

"You know what probably happened with you, Billy?" Aunt Mary said. "Your mother probably left you alone too much when you were little. She would have been in taking care of your father when he was sick, and then after he died she went on and on till I thought she would never stop grieving. She probably didn't pay any attention to you at all then—I don't know how she could have the way she carried on."

I would have reached over the table and backhanded my aunt hard across the face, had my mother not taught me better manners. How dare this woman, whose husband came home and handed her a paycheck while she was raising her children, speak against my mother? My mother had done without plenty. She had made her children her whole life. This woman couldn't have been my mother's diaper changer.

An epithet was half way out of my mouth before I caught it. I realized again discussion was pointless. These people weren't purposely vicious. They simply didn't know any better. They were like children's wind-up toys. They charged around the room, bouncing off of furniture and running in circles until their springs wound down.

Aunt Mary started dissecting her children's mates during desert. Her verbal scalpel was slashing the air with a sweep that foretold a bloody and hours-long massacre. I gave her two minutes of silent attention, then pushed my chair back from the table without a word. The requirements of politeness had been exceeded.

Aunt Mary and Uncle Jeff sprang from their chairs instantly.

"I have to be going," I said.

"Thanks for coming, Billy," Uncle Jeff said.

"Come down during the summer and spend the weekend," Aunt Mary said.

"We'll call you when the boys are down. You can come play golf with them," Uncle Jeff said.

"Sure," I said. "Thanks for dinner."

The headache lasted until Monday afternoon. When it lifted, I knew that Uncle Jeff hadn't thrown the brick. That story, as my interviewee Robert had said of his behavior during his first meeting with his father, had been created by the kid.

When Billy was little, he couldn't understand why his Uncle Jeff hadn't paid attention to him. When Billy was big, he couldn't understand how his uncle could ignore his letters. Little Billy thought there was something wrong with him that kept his uncle away. Big Billy had a grown-up answer. He thought it was because of guilt over the brick. Big Billy thought once he told Uncle Jeff that he hadn't killed his daddy, they would be a happy family again. Billy couldn't get his daddy back, but, if he was really good, maybe he could get his daddy's brother back for his mommy, his sisters and himself.

I had once worked with a child psychiatrist, writing about educational programs for emotionally disturbed children. The man had told me one of the most difficult aspects of working with children was getting them to accept that they were not always responsible for what happened to them. "It is an awesome thing," he had said, "for children to accept that their fathers or mothers or relatives are bad people of their own accord."

In retrospect, I discovered that, at least in my opinion, my aunt and uncle were, if not bad people, self-obsessed people. My uncle hadn't responded to my letters because, to use his terms, there wasn't any profit in it for him. He didn't care what I wanted and needed. He was consumed with his own life.

Uncle Jeff said he had paid for his kids' undergraduate education and lent them money when they needed it. He had, in fact, quoted the exact dollar figures involved. I believed him. I also believed Aunt Mary when she said they had relocated and assumed a new mortgage late in life because their children said they wanted their parents closer to them.

Aunt Mary and Uncle Jeff loved and supported their children. As I was not their child, and as they couldn't identify anything I could add to their lives, they felt no obligation to me. Rather than avoiding me out of guilt, my aunt and uncle had simply ignored me.

Big Billy thought that was okay with him. He knew he wouldn't trouble about his aunt and uncle again.

CHAPTER

14

I went to see Uncle Jeff yesterday," I said to my mother over the telephone.

"Oh, glory be," she said.

"Do you remember Uncle Jeff paying for Dad's bill the first time he was in the hospital?" I asked.

"No, he did not. If he did, I didn't know about it."

"Uncle Jeff's recollection is that the bill was five thousand dollars. He said the family paid a thousand dollars toward it, and then he went to the doctor, gave him five hundred dollars and told the doctor he wasn't going to get any more money."

"Your dad went into the hospital through a clinic, and as far as I know a bill was never issued. They were told we didn't have any money. I don't know of any bill. When your dad died, I wrote letters. One of the letters I wrote was to that doctor, thanking him for all he had done.

"Your father was in a room with twenty-three other men. I'll never forget that. Twelve beds on each side. I sat in that room every day from morning to night. They had him right inside the door. As bad as he was, he was left in the clinic.

"When he was taken off of the critical list after the first operation, I couldn't even see him every day because of the clinic rules. Weekends and every other day in the afternoons were the only times I was allowed to visit him. You couldn't just walk in. You had to go to a certain place and take a special elevator. There were two tickets for each patient. Only two people were allowed to visit each day, and I would always be afraid someone from the family would get there before me and I wouldn't be able to see him. That's how badly they treated you in a clinic.

"It didn't have anything to do with his recovery. It was because it was a clinic. You weren't allowed in because those were the rules. When he got real bad the last time he was hospitalized, I was allowed in every day, but it was only when he was critical. It was a terrible, terrible thing. I was staying in Parkside for part of the time and I would have to take a train in. Then I just stayed with Mom Mom."

"Did you live in Parkside when you were married?" I asked.

"When we were first married we lived on 26th Street, in an apartment at the very end of the street—242 or something like that. They were brand new apartments. We were the first ones to live in them. We lived there for the first year we were married. Your dad was working at Bendix in Philadelphia. He took a bus and a train to get to work. We didn't have a car until a friend in the family died and we bought his car for a couple of hundred dollars.

"Then Bendix closed the plant near the end of the war, and your father was out of work for a few months. We couldn't pay the rent so we lived with Grandmom and Grandpop for a while. We slept in the sun porch. We put our mattress in there on the floor and we stored our furniture around at different places. I was waiting for Helen Marie then. We were there through the summer.

"Your dad went back to work at Strawbridge's, and we bought the house on Beechwood Street. Then we couldn't get the people out of the house we bought. It was right after the war and there wasn't any housing—you couldn't get people out. We moved to Mom Mom's house on Beechwood Street in September. I was expecting Helen Marie in October. We didn't get into our house until after the new year.

"Your Uncle Jeff came out of the service while we were living at Mom Mom's. But I know he didn't pay that hospital bill. I would have known about it. We paid fifty cents each time we went to see the doctor in the clinic. It was a terrible experience."

"Mom," I said, "if Uncle Jeff came out of the service around the time Helen Marie was born, that was two years before Dad's operation. He said he paid the bill when he came out of the service."

"Jeff was as tight as could be," my mother said. "He didn't care about your father or you children. Jeff and Mary always thought they had more than anybody else. That's why there was never any closeness between your dad and I and Jeff and Mary. After we were married we didn't have anything, and they always thought they had everything. Mary thought she was hot stuff. She always dressed it and acted it."

"Aunt Mary said they were snowed in when Mom

Mom died and they had to have an undertaker hold what she called private services for Mom Mom."

"Snowed in?" my mother said. "How long could they have been snowed in? Your Mom Mom died at Easter. That's how I found out she was dead. I sent her an Easter card and it came back stamped 'deceased.' I called the nursing home and they said Mom Mom had died the week before. That guy is as rotten as they come."

"You're right, Mom," I said. "But I hope you understand I had to find that out for myself. Do you remember a friend of Dad's by the name of Chris?"

"Chris Amato," she said. "He was a friend of your father's."

"Was he a friend of Dad's from school?"

"No, I don't know how your father knew him. He and his wife were older than us. They had children when we were going around together. They lived four blocks or so away, down by LaSalle College. I don't even remember where Chris worked. He sold jewelry on the side. Different people in our family bought jewelry from him through your dad. Chris died a long while ago. I don't know where his wife would be, Madelyn. I don't know if she is still living.

"Wes Sneed was another of your father's friends. He was even in our wedding. We went around with Wes more than Chris. Wes was in the picture when I started going out with your father. Wes went out with a girlfriend of mine for a while, Rosemary Gallagher. She used to go to Philadelphia with me and we would stay overnight at Auntie and Uncle George's. That's how I met your dad— through them. Auntie was your grandpop's sister.

"I haven't heard anything from Wes in years. He moved to New Jersey after his first wife died and he got remarried. I think I went to his first wife's viewing. I'm not sure where he lives in New Jersey. It was Wesley Sneed, and I think he lived near where Helen Marie is. He was an only child. He lived on Lambert Street."

"Uncle Jeff said that when Dad came home from the hospital he didn't know he had a tumor, and Chris came in with a *Reader's Digest* article about a kid with a brain tumor and said to Dad, 'This is like you.' "

"I don't have any idea where he got that from," she said.

"Did Dad know what was going on when he came home from the hospital?"

"Certainly. He knew that he had an operation on his head. He knew that he had a brain tumor. He and I didn't know it was cancerous. I was never told it was cancerous. Mom Mom and Pop Pop were told, but I was never told. I only found out by accident.

"We had to go to an outpatient clinic at the hospital for checkups. We'd have to sit for hours every time we went. You took a number when you got there and waited your turn. Your father was okay for a while and then he started getting worse. I guess it was—he died in November, so I guess it was the summer before that when he was up and down a little bit. I don't know what I said to the doctor about your father's condition at the time, but he said to me, 'Well, you know how these cancers are.' I almost died on the spot. I had no idea your father had cancer. That's how I found out.

"Your father kept asking me if he had cancer, and I kept telling him he didn't. I'm sure in his own mind he knew he did."

"Why would you have thought Dad was going in for treatments if it wasn't cancer?" I asked.

"At that age I didn't know anything about cancer, even though he had to go for X-ray treatments. We would drive down to the hospital from Germantown. It would be every day for a week or a couple of weeks. Then they would take a rest, and then we would have to go again. Your dad would drop me off after we left the hospital. I would take a trolley home and he would go off to work. But in the meantime he was throwing up all over the place.

The treatments made him sick, and we would be riding along and he would start throwing up right as we were riding along. How he went into work I don't know.

"That's how he lost all of his hair. He had these big square bald spots, one on each side of his head and one on the top. They would put things on his head for the X-rays. He wore a hat all of the time, and he combed his hair back over the bald spots, so you couldn't see it in a picture. But he really only had hair in the front, and as it grew he combed it back. Most of the top and the two sides were bare."

"He didn't have any hair for two years?" I asked.

"It was mostly after the X-ray treatments in the beginning, after he had the first operation. It would have been a month or two after. I don't remember going back again for X-ray treatments until the summer before he died.

"But the fact that he was having X-ray treatments didn't mean anything to me. I didn't understand what it was about and no one told me anything about it. I guess it meant something to your father to a certain extent. You didn't hear about X-ray treatment and cancer then. There wasn't stuff out about it. I never came in contact with any of it. The treatments were doing something to what was wrong, that's all they told me.

"Then your dad started going down little by little after the second series of treatments. He had gotten a job at City Hall, and he worked there up until a month before he died. They never took him off the payroll, even when he was in the hospital, because of your Pop Pop. Your dad would go to work when he could. But he only made peanuts.

"He came down sick again in the middle of October and he had to be admitted to the hospital. He never came out. He was in for a month until he died."

"Aunt Mary said he died of pneumonia, but I think that's just something they put on death certificates," I said.

"I'm sure that's it. They called me about five-thirty in the morning. I was at your Mom Mom's at the time because of being at the hospital from morning to night. You children were down in Parkside with Grandmom. He had been in a coma the day before he died. When I went in he was in a coma.

"Here again, I didn't know too much about what a coma was then. I just knew he wasn't responding. His eyes were open, but he wasn't responding to me. He just laid there. And then the next morning a phone call came to your Mom Mom's that he had died. They wanted us to come in and sign papers, but we never went. They wanted to do an autopsy, but we wouldn't let them. What did I start to say? Oh, I don't know if you'd be able to find Wes Sneed or not."

"Mom, did you know Dad was dying, or were you shocked when the hospital called?"

"I guess I knew he had been awful bad in the month he was in the hospital. He had had a couple of more operations in that time. The pressure would get so bad they would have to take him up and open something up to relieve it. The last week or two weeks, he had several operations. I would go to visit him and he would be terrible. I would go in first thing in the morning and sit with him all day. They would have him propped up in chairs or in bed, but he couldn't really talk too much. He was bad and he got worse each day."

"Mom, I said, "when Dad was that sick, how could you not have known he was dying?"

"I probably . . . I probably—in my unconscious mind I maybe knew he was dying. But I would never admit to myself that he was dying. I just thought it wouldn't happen—that it couldn't happen. At twenty-six or twenty-eight years old, with two small children, those kinds of things didn't come into my mind. I truly felt it couldn't happen. The morning of the phone call I was shocked and stunned that it did happen. . . .

"But your father's friend, Wes, I don't know if you would be able to track him down to talk to him or not."

I allowed my mother to change the subject. We talked about our lives, Joe, my sisters and their families. We were on the phone for an hour. It was one of the warmest telephone conversations I had ever had with my mother.

I found the excerpt of *Death Be Not Proud* in the March 1949 edition of *Reader's Digest*. The pages of the magazine were darkened at the edges and fragile with age. I was uncertain if my father had read a copy of the article when the paper was fresh, but I wanted to read it in case he had.

The author was a prominent international journalist who traveled in rarified circles. His son Johnny, who died from a tumor at seventeen, had lived in Europe with his parents for the first seven years of his life. The Gunthers divorced then and established an amicable joint-custody arrangement. Johnny, a precocious and articulate child, attended Deerfield Academy and was planning to enroll at Harvard when he died.

The Gunthers were affluent and well-connected people whose world was remote from the one in which my family had operated. There were no clinics for Johnny. He was ministered to by the most prominent neurosurgeons in New York—men who left their Park Avenue practices to examine the boy in Connecticut on an hour's notice. Yet, for all the doctors' acclaim, their first inquiry to the Gunthers upon identifying the tumor was whether Johnny had ever received a blow to the head.

A surgeon told Johnny he had removed a tumor when the procedure was completed, but no one informed the boy the growth was malignant. "Of course, he did not know the full seriousness of his illness," Johnny's father wrote. "Above all, we had to shield him from definite, explicit knowledge." This protection extended to his father concealing in his apartment, before the boy was released from the hospital, the volume of the *Encyclopedia Britannica* that contained an entry on brain tumors, a deletion Johnny noted immediately.

Nonetheless, Johnny, whose special interest was science, guessed his cancer before the lead shield was removed from his chest at the conclusion of his first sitting beneath the X-ray machine. Even then, however, the word *cancer* was seldom employed by the family. The surgeon had left an opening in Johnny's skull for the tumor to expand through, and the Gunthers discussed the swelling and recession of the malignancy by naming it Johnny's Bump.

I examined a 1948 *New York Times Sunday Magazine* article about a hospital clinic in Manhattan while I was in the library. The story was at the back of the magazine, following pieces entitled, "The Qualities a President Needs," "Communism in Asia" and "The Six Challenges to Peace."

It was the Cold War. Stalin was being denounced by Allied heads of state, communists had taken Manchuria and Jews were battling to establish a homeland in Israel. Unsettling stories about a world in strife pervaded the news sections of the paper. Peace, which had been forced by the burgeoning cloud of the hydrogen bomb, seemed to be in no one's control.

Those stories were read by families whose men, only yesterday, had been appropriated by telegramed governmental greetings and shipped to fates unknown. The men had followed their commanders through rains of shrapnel and returned or not, while the families watched the mail for intelligence on the mens' continued existence. The women worked their war jobs or raised their children, while denied comprehension of the events that killed their husbands and brothers.

The entertainment pages of the *Times* enumerated the few programs that were beginning to appear on television. In that section, among the ads for bulbous refrigerators and romantic films, the paper also ran an article on modern girls—women who wrote filmscripts for westerns, just like men. "Meet the gals who write 'em, not ride 'em," the headline read. The story defined the ladies as "nice, refined gals, most of whom admit they'd probably have to be revived with smelling salts and a loosening of their stays if a horse as much as whinnied in their direction."

The clinic article was a public service piece, noting in a short aside the hospital was seeking donations to continue its services. The doctors interviewed were cheerfully gruff, telling the writer that no, they didn't mind putting in a few hours without pay. The reporter countered that the doctors must be humanitarians. The physicians said that was nonsense—their efforts were in the interest of science, not good will. Where else, they asked, could a young doctor encounter such a challenging miscellany of diseases waiting to be investigated?

The patients were blissfully compliant. They spoke of their gratitude at being attended to for four bits and of the trust they placed in the young men they assigned their health to. "You fellows helped a lot of our boys during the war," a man with emotional troubles told a psychiatrist, "and I'm hoping you'll be able to get me straightened out."

My father's illness befell him at a time when doctors knew better than their patients, parents knew better than their married children and healthy people knew better than the infirm. When the doctors identified my father's cancer, they informed only his parents, who told only my Aunt Mary and Uncle Jeff. When my mother inadvertently fell through the curtain of silence that had been draped around her, she reserved the truth for herself.

Thus, while all of those who loved my father gathered quietly on the ebb of his life, he went to his grave never having regarded his mortality with any of the people who were attempting to spare him the actuality that he was about to die. My God, I thought, what a tragically lonely way for my father to have left this world.

My father inexorably slipped toward eternity while his pregnant wife grasped his hand from a bedside chair. My father knew he was dying—of course he knew he was dying. My mother knew he was dying. Everyone knew he was dying. But no one could voice the words.

My father knew he was leaving us. He didn't want to go. He was fighting as hard as he could. He had prevailed against the cancer for two years. He slicked his remaining hair over the bald spots, put his hat on and went to work, even when the radiation made him sick. He didn't give up. He fought and kept his dignity. He strived for his family. But then the cancer had to win.

Everyone wanted my father to stay. Especially me. But I was too little to talk. I couldn't say it to him. No one wanted my father to go, but everyone was afraid to tell him. They wanted to tell him. My mother wanted to. But she didn't think she should. She did what she thought was best for my father. She didn't want it to be bad for him.

My father lay there, until death consumed him, feeling fear of what was to come, sorrow at what was being lost, anger that he could not alter his fate and hope that the circle would be completed in the end.

I didn't need to know anything else about my father. I knew it all now. My father wasn't a valiant war hero. He never attended college. He didn't set a world record in the one-hundred-yard dash. His career didn't amount to much.

My father died slowly in a crowded hospital ward as my mother and twenty-three transient patients looked on.

The world may have taken little note of his passing, but his wife and children have never forgotten him.

My father was no more or less than my father. There could never be a finer reason for me to love him and to miss him.

My son was on spring break from his freshman year of college. We were going to play our first game of golf since he had started school in September. Our leisurely afternoons together have been replaced by short phone calls and quick dinners every few weeks. Joe sees his girlfriend on weekends now. I miss the old days when Sundays were only for us. My son is a breath from being a fully grown man. His life has become his own. I am working hard to handle the transition gracefully.

Joe had been playing our rounds of golf with a serviceable but tattered set of inherited clubs that obscured one vital element of the game. Golf is a sport that demands a certain measure of elegance. The aesthetics of the game argue that the fairway grass be trimmed, the sand traps be raked and the greens be watered against the sun. Too, a player needs immaculate clubheads—ones free of blight from pocks and scores—if he is to fully savor lofting the dimpled ball through the quiet air.

My Christmas present to Joe had been a new set of clubs. He hadn't had a suspicion what the oblong boxes in my living room concealed until he tore off the green wrapping paper and found the descriptions printed on the packages. His mouth drew open and his eyes pulled wide. "Oh, great! Oh, great!" he repeated a dozen times as he slid the clubs from their confinement and enjoyed them with his eyes.

Joe jumped from his chair into address position over a nonexistent ball as I hurried furniture out of his arc. He waggled the three wood to gauge its flex, then pulled his pitching wedge through a swing that was certain to have produced a birdie from ninety feet out in heavy crosswinds with a tricky green.

I opened my first presents and discovered a blue cotton oxford cloth shirt and complimentary tie that coincided with my tastes so exactly I would have bought them for myself. I fingered the smooth finish of the tie and thanked my son. "This is a wonderful tie," I said. "Did you know it was silk?"

"Sure I knew it was silk," he said. "That's why I bought it for you."

Joe continued his championship round in the living room while I cooked eggs mixed with chunks of smoked ham and sharp cheese and heated sticky cinnamon buns we would gorge ourselves on. We'd each argue that the other should have the last of the pastry then decide to split it. "Merry Christmas, Dad," my son would say when I took him home. "And thanks for the great presents." A week would pass before I would be able to remove the smile from my face.

The weather was unpleasant, cold and overcast, when we played our game on a Friday afternoon in March, but it had its compensations. Joe and I were the only people on the course—a rare pleasure. Polished clubs weren't of much avail that day. We had to hit four balls from the first tee between us before one landed in the fairway. We were out of practice, the creaks in our swings almost audible.

We searched the high grass for each other's misdirected balls, rehit shots and talked. We talked about what we had read in the newspaper, his teachers, my students, women, golf, the play he was to see that night, cars, the validity of scientific method, Aunt Mary and Uncle Jeff, my writing, his courses for next year, a trip we might take together.

I stopped keeping score on the third hole. I praised

my son when he made a putt and said with a laugh, "Thanks, Joe, I rather liked it myself," when he failed to admire my solid drive. Joe had spent two summers selling funnel cakes on the boardwalk at the beach, and I had become the better golfer in his absence from the links.

"You better watch out, Wartman," I had cautioned my son one Sunday at the driving range. "I'm going to be beating you soon."

"That will be the day," he had said.

The day had come, and it returned regularly. My son is working hard now to accept his losses gracefully.

We had never played this course before. It was in such poor condition that putts became airborne as they bounced their way to the cups. The tees were difficult to locate and we got lost going from hole to hole. It was getting late and Joe had to meet his girlfriend, so we skipped holes or played them out of sequence. We struck balls to provide accompaniment for our conversation.

Joe had three opinions—yes, no, yes—during our ride home about whether he had time for us to eat. We stopped at a fast-food place. He ordered two large cheeseburgers, large fries and a shake, then swallowed them as though he had just been released from a prison camp.

My son eats his french fries with ketchup now. For years, whenever we shared an order of potatoes, they would have to be separated on the tray between my pile with ketchup and his without. If one of his fries without bumped one of my fries with, Joe would add the contaminated fry to my catch. Then my son casually heaped ketchup on his fries one Sunday.

"What is this?" I asked.

"I decided I like ketchup on my fries," Joe said offhandedly.

Some months later, ketchup was usurped by mustard and then mayonnaise, which ultimately yielded to ketchup.

My son had told me at Christmas that his girlfriend's gift to him was a ten-gallon hat, apparel not often seen on the streets of Philadelphia. "Oh," I said, uncertain of how to respond. "Why did she choose that?"

"That's what I told her to get me," he said. "I've wanted one for a while."

"Will you wear it at school?" I said.

"No," Joe said easily, "I'll just put it on whenever I feel like it."

Watching my son go about the business of being a boy is second in delight only to talking with him. His lack of self-consciousness is majestic, like a hawk playing with the wind. It gives me boundless pleasure that my son is so free. If I have played even a minor role in this acquisition of his, it is my happiest accomplishment.

My family was dispersed around the back porch and yard of Anne's house when I arrived for dinner on Easter Sunday. My baggage was two bottles of good wine for the dinner table, rather than a tape recorder, and an altered frame of mind. I felt like an abscess on my spirit had been lanced. The fever was beginning to wane as the infection started to heal. The religious holiday held no meaning for me, and I had work to do, but my mother had said, "I hope you're coming for dinner," so I had told her of course I would.

I kissed my mother and hollered Hello to the others, when my oldest nephew, Tommy, asked if we could have a talk. Tommy was a senior in high school and had several scholarship offers from colleges. He's a good student who wants to be a writer, and he wanted my advice on selecting a school. I was pleased to be asked and spent a half hour telling him what I knew.

My mother, sisters and Anne's in-laws were talking about the Pennsylvania lottery when I returned to the

porch. There had been a twenty-million-dollar jackpot recently, and many in the family had purchased tickets in
the sweepstakes.

"Don't you know how bad the odds are in lotteries?"
I demanded with a stridency that came easily. "They only
return about forty cents on the dollar, and, if they gave
away twenty million dollars, they must have sold fifty million tickets. You have a better chance of being hit by a
car."

"You only have to have one ticket to win though,
Bill," my mother said. "I don't mind spending a dollar
for a chance to win that much money."

"But many of the people who buy lottery tickets are
poor and uneducated. They often waste forty or fifty dollars a month of the little money they have, hoping their
lives are going to be changed by magic. It's the most re-
gressive form of taxation there is."

"You're right about that," Anne's father-in-law said.
"I see poor people buying fistfuls of tickets every time I
go to the store."

"Most of the people who win now do it by pooling
their money and buying blocks of tickets," Helen Marie
said. "There were twenty people from one school who
had a share of the winning ticket this time."

"But look what happens then," I said. "Each of them
won only thirteen thousand dollars a year. That's not
enough money to allow them to quit their jobs."

"No," my mother said with a smile, "but it's thirteen
thousand dollars a year more than they had before."

"And," Helen Marie added, "I've read plenty of
newspaper stories saying that winning huge amounts of
money often ruins the winners' lives. I could get by just
fine with a little extra money each year. I don't need a
fortune."

In that moment I understood the wisdom of people
pooling what they had in an attempt to create more than
each of them could have individually. So what if many

times they lost and, when they did win, the outcome wasn't utopian? The losing efforts gave hope that got people up in the morning and brought them home at night. And small but shared rewards might, indeed, be the best life has to offer.

"You're right, folks," I said. "Something is always better than nothing."

I recounted my last visit with Uncle Jeff and Aunt Mary for my sisters, as my mother listened attentively. My father and our lives without him have become more comfortable parts of our conversations. I am the family expert on the topic—I have done the research and the thinking. My mother and sisters listen more than speak because they are still, in many ways, in the place I was before an imagined brain tumor led me into a passage I hadn't known existed. But now, when I call to my family from that place, they hear my voice and are not frightened.

As we talked, Anne's husband drifted to the other end of the porch where his mother and stepfather were chatting. Helen Marie's spouse went into the yard to be with their boys. It was an easy gathering of families within families, a momentary abandonment of acquired bonds to replenish biological ones.

The smaller clusters disbanded after a time, and Helen Marie's husband came onto the porch. I asked him about his job, and he said he had been in Chicago on a business trip the past week.

"How did you get there?" I asked, remembering my brother-in-law's fear of flying.

"I flew," he said. "I'm getting over being afraid of it. I was a little nervous when the plane took off, but I pulled down the window shade and I was fine."

"That's great," I said. "I'm not crazy about flying myself, but it's never as bad as you think it's going to be if you just go ahead and do it."

"Look at those two," Helen Marie said and pointed

at her youngest son, Matt, and Anne's daughter, Corinne, in the yard. Matt, who is much younger than his brothers and my son, takes three-year-old Corinne, the only infant in the family, under his wing at these gatherings. Now Matt was resting on a grassy slope with Corinne stretched out across his legs.

"My big brother never did that for me," Anne said and looked at me.

I was startled by her words. I started to defend myself by saying I hadn't known she had wanted me to act like a big brother. Then I realized I wouldn't have known how to fill that role even if she had asked me. It was another vestige of a boyhood in which men had been in short supply. I couldn't change the past, my only hope was to improve the future.

"You're right," I said. "I guess I never did."

Dinner was a satisfying meal of ham, potato salad and other family favorites. I sat and talked with the adults for a short time after dessert, but I was anxious to escape to the backyard. "Okay, Matt," I hollered when I got there, "let's show these bums how to play whiffle ball."

The rivalry was a long-standing one. Uncle Bill and Matt against the teenagers, Tommy and Chris. I am bigger and stronger than my nephews, and my power paired with Matt's youth makes for highly competitive games against my two older nephews.

We pulled out to an early lead as my teammate and I piled up solid hits to the left and then defended them with dazzling pitching, as we alternated on the mound. But then Tommy and Chris started finding the ball with their bats, and I would be winded and sweaty from chasing flies, ones I was getting too old to shag, when we returned to the plate. My speed on the bases diminished and my curve ball lost some of its hop.

Our lead had diminished to one run when Matt relinquished the mound to me in a final effort to salvage the win. Darkness was closing in on the field, my shirt was soaked with sweat and my breathing was labored. The outlook wasn't good.

Chris hit an opposite field line drive I was too tired to chase, with Tommy on base, and the other guys won. "That's okay, Matt," I said as I draped my arm over his shoulders and we headed in for sodas, "we would have beaten them if they hadn't cheated so badly. Next time, they won't have a chance."

EPILOGUE

H oly Sepulcher Cemetery is more than two hundred acres of the dead. Headstones reverberate after an iron fence that courses a half mile down each edge of the tract. Marble sprouts from brilliant grass that sweeps up knolls and drops from sight. It was a fifty degree spring day. The sun beamed early-summer glare; the trees displayed their first buds. The graveyard's vaulting front gates stood open.

I passed through the archway and pursued the road to a solitary building ahead on my left. It looked like the office. I needed to talk to the people there. I had come to find my father, and I was hoping they would tell me the way. I didn't know where my father resided. Two decades had passed since my last call.

A notice was posted on the office door, one saying the building was occupied Monday to Friday, nine to five. It was Sunday and early in the day. Hours remained before darkness. I returned to the car, shielded my eyes against the sun and studied the place I had come from. The twisting road narrowed and diminished in the distance. There were signs pointed at me that said one-way.

I drove slowly toward the eastern perimeter of the grounds. I was searching for a beacon from my past—something that would have made an impression on a boy in Sunday clothes being brought to visit his father, something he would have been sure to notice while he peered from the back seat of his mother's car as it negotiated the winding route to his dad.

I traveled a short way and encountered the chiseled name Hensen. I lifted my foot from the accelerator. I left the car on the shoulder of the road, thinking I might have my signal, and walked into a precinct of graves. The earth was the lighter brown of the season, the dark compactness of winter having yielded to the paler resilience of April.

Mr. Hensen and each of his neighbors had become tenants during the first years of the century. The district had been settled before my father's birth. I walked west and stumbled into a village of immigrants from the 1920s and 1930s. It was Irishtown. The residences of the Murphys', Keenens', Donnelys', Laffertys', Kellys', Sweenys', and Mulhollands' fronted the properties of the McManuses', Strauds', Flannagans', Reardons', Campbells', McAultys', O'Haras' and Meehens'.

The population density was high; the runs of grass between the lines of headstones were merely fourteen feet across. I was forced to trample on graves to read small inscriptions on low marker stones. I tried to step tenderly, to restrain my full weight from coming to bear on the soil, but the earth yielded noticeably under each advancing foot. I moved hastily, not wanting to compound the insult by lingering in one spot too long.

I saw mausoleums by the road, further to the west, and remembered them. They were formidable cubed buildings of rough-cut, gray stone slabs, with columned entrances that border the curving roads near the center of the grounds. We had always passed mausoleums on the way to my father.

"Mom," I had asked then, "why are those little houses here?"

"People are buried in them, Billy," she said.

"Why are some people buried in the ground and other people buried in houses?"

"Rich people are buried in the mausoleums," she said.

"Why do they do that, Mom?"

"I don't know, Billy," she said. "I guess you'll have to ask them."

When we visited my father with his parents, the adults behaved reverently, blessing themselves and murmuring quiet prayers while contemplating the grave. If someone had brought a wreath, it would be placed gently by the stone. Then the adults would gaze off and talk in quiet voices, observing the flora on nearby plots or the freshly turned earth that proclaimed a new death. "Someone in the Bennett family died," my mother would say and read aloud the name that had been hammered into the stone. No one ever talked to my father while we stood at his grave.

I would mimic the adults, crossing myself and mumbling a hurried Our Father, but my recitations were rote. My eyes seemed to be lowered in veneration; actually they were slanting toward the side. I was observing the road, waiting for a family in an expensive car to roll to a stop before one of those little houses. When they did, I was going to tear over as they opened the door. I had an excuse at the ready. My mother had instructed me to ask the owners why they had buried their dead in a building. I was waiting expectantly for my chance.

I knew a kid could get away with posing a question like that, and it would create the dodge I needed to carry out my plan. I wanted to have a look inside one of those houses while the door was pulled back. I wanted to know where the caskets were stored, if they were sitting out in the open or what.

I'd pretend to leave disappointedly when the rich people shooed me away, but then I'd sneak back. I'd creep along the house with my back pressed to the wall until I was positioned for a clearer glimpse inside. I wanted to study what the family did while they were hidden from view. I was certain these families didn't stand around mumbling silent prayers like mine. They didn't buy a fancy stone house just for that.

I had a hunch about what those people did. At least I knew what I'd be doing if my family had one of those places. If my father was buried in a gray stone house, I'd get my hands on the key and hitchhike to the cemetery when I was supposed to be somewhere else. I'd hop the fence, steal to our house and let myself in. I'd lock the door behind me, so no one could order me to leave. Then, when we were alone, I'd have a long private talk with my dad.

I would come and tell my father what was going on with me and forget about the stupid prayers. I didn't want to talk to God when I came to visit my father. God took my father away from me. God could go to hell. I wanted to talk to my dad. I wanted to rest my hand on my father's coffin while we had a chat. Then I would know he could hear me—that he was listening, that he knew I was out here trying to get ahold of him. My father couldn't hear me in a grave under all of that dirt. How could I even be sure he was there?

If we had one of those houses, I'd be able to visit my dad and talk to him whenever I chose. If we had one of those houses, I'd be able to touch my father's coffin and know where he had gone. If we had one of those houses, it wouldn't hurt so much that my dad was dead, because he would still be there for me. I could come and talk to him. Then I wouldn't always feel so alone.

There were tattered but colorful American flags, miniature ones, sprinkled on the graves near the mausoleums, as if a veterans' parade had once marched through behind the flourish of muffled drums. It was the zone of the war dead, men who had come to Holy Sepulcher in the 1940s, right before my dad.

I had been wandering the cemetery aimlessly, and I was uncertain where I had arrived. I searched for the car to establish my position, but it evaded my eye. I quickly rifled my pockets for the keys in vain. I had come to find my father and had drifted off, leaving my car prey to thieves. Someone had discovered the vulnerability and made off with the machine. Now I was marooned in a labyrinth of solitude.

The road climbed to higher ground before me. I raced up the hill, fearfully combing the left side of the horizon with my eyes. My chest humped because my breath quickened and sweat pumped from my pores. Cramps were biting at my calves. I pulled up at the crest.

I was confused and had lost my orientation. I didn't know where I had come from. I surveyed the place behind me. I was encompassed by grass, marble and the dead. All was silent, save the chirping of a bird. My eyes locked on copper-brown in the distance. I squinted at it against the sun. It was my car, safely over Mr. Hensen's way.

I turned to persist in my search and found a long low building a hundred yards off to the north. I received it in a two-step way—the alarm of recognition shook me before the familiarity of the sight propped me up. I knew the building and its location. It was the shed where the groundkeepers stored their equipment. It was situated over there at my right, where it had always been when my family cleared the mausoleums and closed in on my dad.

I remembered the last time I had stood here. I had arrived by limousine rather than my mother's car. It was Pop Pop's funeral in 1962. Pop Pop had died and was about to be put into the ground over my dad. The earthen barrier that separated me from my father had been excavated for the first time in a dozen years.

I had rushed from the limousine and over to the grave before the family, wanting to look down the hole. I wanted to find out if my father's casket was there, to get a glance of it before my grandfather blocked the view. I tried to be nonchalant about my urgency, so the others couldn't detect what I was about to do. I couldn't let them discover me. They would have worried about me and talked among themselves. I'd try to explain that I just wanted to see if my dad was still there, but they wouldn't comprehend. They couldn't know what I had never told them—that I needed to know where my dad was, that I missed him so.

The hump of dirt that had been taken from the grave was stationed off to the side and restrained by a tarp, lest the wind scatter it away. The device that would lower Pop Pop's casket rose above and framed the yawn in the earth. I looked back to the road. Men in black suits were approaching behind sprays of flowers. The coffin was free of the hearse.

I go down on one knee and lean over like I'm inspecting the sturdiness of the fabric belts on the machine that will deposit Pop Pop in the ground. The peat fragrance of earth fills my head. The sides of the hole are slick from the polishing of the scoop on the backhoe. Winter sun illuminates the void that is the hole. I look down, anxious to see my father—but the new grave ends before him. There is only earth. Dirt paves the bottom of the hollow.

I stepped back as the others approached. The pall-bearers came first, their arms straining against the mass of the coffin, as they rested Pop Pop over the hole that would swallow him. The mourners pulled into a knot around the priest who pontificated in Latin and anointed the perched casket with holy water and incense. I shoved my hands into my pockets and ambled behind them, showing boredom in my apartness. Funerals were moronic anyway.

My eighth-grade nun expressed her condolences when I returned to school the next day, but it hadn't been a big deal. Old people in my family had been dying regularly. It had started five or six years before with my great-grandmother. She had been feeble and helpless when we visited her in a nursing home, but, as she was the first person I knew who had died, her death surprised me nonetheless.

When my mother took us to Great-Grandmom's viewing, I watched my Grandfather Glatts. It was his mother who had passed away, and I wanted to see what you were supposed to do when one of your parents died. Grandpop's mother rested there in a white satin bed, a rosary in her hands, flowers by her side. My grandfather said a prayer before the coffin, then moved to a semicircle of folding chairs, where he greeted those who came to pay their respects. My grandfather acted as he did every day. He talked to people and smoked his cigar. My grandfather didn't cry at his mother's viewing. His eyes didn't shine with water once all night.

I grabbed my mother's arm the moment we left. "Mom," I said in horror, "why didn't Grandpop cry tonight? His mother died."

"Great-Grandmom was a very old woman," she said. "She lived for a long time, and she has been real sick for the last few years. I guess your grandpop has been expecting her to die."

I didn't understand how expecting someone to die stopped you from crying when she actually did, but then it might have been me.

I stepped carefully onto the lawn at the brink of my father's neighborhood. I walked slowly, my eyes scanning headstones that were away and to the left. I limited my vision to the distance, acknowledging only stones three or four rows from my path. I didn't want to be close to my father without forewarning. I still craved a final forty paces of reserve.

I walked and searched, knowing only my vision, sensing only what I saw. WARTMAN blipped at me from the periphery. My head bounced back to the right. I judged the name had come at me from four rows south. I took a final breath and eased my head back to the source. WARTMAN—twenty yards away.

I turn to face my father. I don't try to think or talk. I stand there and cry for a very long time. When it feels okay, I walk over to meet my dad.

"Hi, Dad," I say. "I've come to visit you. It's been a long time since I've been to see you. You were hard to find.

"I've been thinking about you a lot, Dad, over the last couple of years. I really missed you after you died.

"You want to hear something stupid? I used to think I killed you.

"I have a son. His name is Joe. He's terrific. I love him so much. I know you would too.

"I'm a writer, Dad, and I teach in college. I bet you'd be happy about that. My son is in college now. He is going to be an engineer—a civil engineer. Mom said that you used to be a draftsman. Joe took drafting in high school and he liked it a lot.

"Everybody is fine. Helen Marie has three boys. Anne has a daughter who is as cute as can be. We all turned out to be great kids. Mom did an incredible job of raising us on her own. You picked a good woman to be your wife.

"But it was hard for Mom after you died. She was sad and it made us sad because she was sad.

"I'm sorry I'm crying so much, Dad. I don't want you to see me crying and start feeling bad because you died. It wasn't anyone's fault. It just happened.

"I told my friend Mike I was going to come to see you today, but I slipped and said I was coming to your funeral rather than your grave. That's why I'm crying so much. This is your funeral for me. I was too little to come when they had the official one, so this is a belated one for me. Let me get these tears out, then I'll be okay.

"I'm doing fine now, Dad, but that wasn't always the way. I screwed up a lot before I got here. It would have been simpler if you had been there, or even if I had known how to reach you. But I've arrived here now, and that's the important part.

"Hi, Pop Pop. I didn't remember you were seventy-two when you died. You lived for a long time, 1890 to 1962. We haven't all died young.

"I found a postcard you had sent me when I was kid, Pop Pop. You mailed it from a retreat house in Malvern, and you said the altar in the picture had candles that were dedicated to my dad. I don't know if you tried to talk to me about my dad other times or not. Even if you did, I was probably too scared to hear you.

"Pop Pop, I used to love it when you took me out on the porch and when we went to the park to play catch. I never told you this, but I was glad you had such lousy aim with a slingshot. I don't mean to be disrespectful, but I don't think you ever hit a pigeon once.

"Hey, you guys, I went to Beechwood Street a while ago. You wouldn't believe how run down the neighborhood is. The playground is a wreck. Dad, our house was boarded up. It's really a shame.

"Joe and I play golf now. Wouldn't it have been great if all four of us had been able to play golf together once? Pop Pop may have been too old, but the three of us could have played and Pop Pop could have ridden in a cart. We could have gone out on the course in the summer and hit some balls around. Then we could have gotten something to eat and had a couple of beers.

"The courses are always crowded now, so it would probably be late when we got back. Mom Mom, you'd probably say to my mother, 'Well, Helen, the boys have finally come home.' Then you'd probably laugh that loud laugh of your's, Mom Mom, and say you didn't understand why we would spend all day in the hot sun hitting a little white ball and walking after it. My dad would hug you and say it was something you had to do to understand."

I talked to my father, pacing back and forth at the foot of his grave, crying when I needed to cry, but needing to less often as an afternoon wind passed and the sun warmed the grounds. As I visited with my father, I knew he was there and that he could hear me, and I smiled through the lifting sorrow. I wasn't lost or confused or lonely anymore. I knew precisely where I was and why I couldn't help smiling. I had found my dad. He was back home. We were together again.

I walked out to the highway, identifying landmarks on the cemetery roads that would make my return visits to my dad more direct. Cheltenham Avenue, a four-lane thoroughfare that fronts Holy Sepulcher was busy and noisy. Across the way was a quiet collection of middle-class homes. German, Irish, Italian and Jewish families had once resided there, now black and Asian families made this their community. It was a neighborhood of continuity and change, where young families started with hopes and plans that were sometimes realized and other times not. Fates—at times unexpected and seeming capricious—unfolded, while people moved forward, working for the future, while growing from the past.

I felt I was a different person from the one who had driven through the gates when I returned to say so long to my dad. I wasn't just Bill Wartman anymore; I was my father's son. There was no hesitancy in my gait as I walked to his grave. I stood at his feet and told him I would be back again soon.

I turned to leave and halted, remembering there was one step left undone. I walked to my father's headstone and placed my hand upon it. The surface was cool and rough, but my palm mated to it instantly. Strength and solidity swirled up my arm and into the recesses of my soul. I stood locked to my father, receiving a transfusion of antiquity and forever.

"It was great to see you, Dad," I said. "I'll be back with my son. You're going to love him."